Welcome to

THE
EVERYTHING
HEALTH GUIDES ®

W **hen you're faced** with a pressing health issue, your first instinct is to find out as much about it as you can. With so much conflicting information out there, where can you turn for professional, supportive advice?

Packed with the most recent, up-to-date data, THE EVERYTHING® HEALTH GUIDES help ensure that you get a good diagnosis, choose the best doctor, and find the right medical treatment. With this one comprehensive resource, you and your family members have all the information you could possibly need—at your fingertips.

THE EVERYTHING® HEALTH GUIDES are an extension of the bestselling *Everything®* series in the health category, which also includes *The Everything® Health Guide to Postpartum Care* and *The Everything® Health Guide to Menopause, 2nd Edition*. Accessible and easy to read, THE EVERYTHING® HEALTH GUIDES provide specific details and clear examples that relate to your given medical situation. If you're looking for one-stop, all-inclusive guides that allow you to understand and become more in tune with your body, this groundbreaking series is the perfect tool for you.

Visit the entire Everything® series at *www.everything.com*

THE
EVERYTHING®

HEALTH GUIDE TO

OCD

Dear Reader,

When it comes to Obsessive-Compulsive Disorder (OCD), you might say I wrote the book! My symptoms began when I was twenty, but it wasn't until I was well into my thirties that I discovered I had OCD. OCD? Didn't that mean you couldn't stop counting ceiling tiles or cleaning your house? That wasn't me. I worried about things that could really happen. (And, I was pretty sure, would!) And I suffered from anxiety and isolation.

We know so much more now. If you have OCD, chances are it'll be recognized and treated much faster than mine was. The more you learn about OCD, the weaker it becomes (especially when you also have effective weapons).

I can't say that fighting OCD is easy. Or even that I've utterly vanquished it. It's a process. But knowledge really is power.

The online community I found truly lit up the darkness. I did cognitive behavior therapy; I read. It may sound syrupy, but almost every book I read about OCD made me feel as if its author was extending a hand to pull me from the well. I hope to do that for you. If you have OCD, you'll need help, information and, ideally, support and luck. I wish you all of those.

Chelsea Lowe

THE

EVERYTHING®

HEALTH GUIDE TO

OCD

Professional advice on handling anxiety,
understanding treatment options,
and finding the support you need

Chelsea Lowe

Technical Review by Judith Lytel, Psy.D.

Avon, Massachusetts

For David—In all the best ways, my enabler.

• • •

Innovation Director: Paula Munier
Editorial Director: Laura M. Daly
Associate Copy Chief: Sheila Zwiebel
Acquisitions Editor: Kerry Smith
Development Editor: Katie McDonough
Production Editor: Casey Ebert
Technical Reviewer: Judith Lytel, Psy.D.

Director of Manufacturing: Susan Beale
Production Project Manager: Michelle Roy Kelly
Prepress: Erick DaCosta, Matt LeBlanc
Interior Layout: Heather Barrett,
Brewster Brownville, Colleen Cunningham,
Jennifer Oliveira

An Everything® Series Book.
Everything® and everything.com® are registered trademarks of F+W Publications, Inc.

Published by Adams Media, an F+W Publications Company
57 Littlefield Street, Avon, MA 02322 U.S.A.
www.adamsmedia.com

ISBN 10: 1-59869-435-9
ISBN: 13: 978-1-59869-435-2

Printed in Canada.

J I H G F E D C B A

Library of Congress Cataloging-in-Publication Data
is available from the publisher.

This publication is designed to provide accurate and authoritative information with regard to the subject matter covered. It is sold with the understanding that the publisher is not engaged in rendering legal, accounting, or other professional advice. If legal advice or other expert assistance is required, the services of a competent professional person should be sought.
    —From a *Declaration of Principles* jointly adopted by a Committee of the American Bar Association and a Committee of Publishers and Associations

Many of the designations used by manufacturers and sellers to distinguish their products are claimed as trademarks. Where those designations appear in this book and Adams Media was aware of a trademark claim, the designations have been printed with initial capital letters.

This book is available at quantity discounts for bulk purchases.
For information, please call 1-800-289-0963.

All the examples and dialogues used in this book are fictional and have been created by the author to illustrate medical situations.

Acknowledgments

Sincere and grateful acknowledgment is made to the following:

Dr. Michael Jenike, Massachusetts General Hospital, Harvard Medical School, McLean Hospital; Brette Sember; Sharon Rennert, Equal Employment Opportunity Commission, Washington, DC; Andrea Lindsay, LICSW; Diane Davey, R.N., M.B.A., and Adriana Bobinchock, McLean Hospital; Dr. Daniel A. Geller, director, pediatric OCD program, Massachusetts General Hospital; The OCD Centre, New York, New York and Belgravia, London, UK; Jonathan Sheff, MSW, MPH; Maj. Anne Edgecomb, United States Army Reserve; Gail Steketee, Ph.D., dean ad interim, professor, Boston University School of Social Work; Colin Riley, Boston University; Westwood Institute for Anxiety Disorders, Los Angeles, California; the Police Department of the City of Boston, Massachusetts; the Arthur W. Melton Library and APA Archives, Washington, DC; Bette Hartley at the Madison Institute of Medicine, Madison, Wisconsin; Erik Sherman, Anita Bartholomew, Edwin Black, Kim Patch, Sue Russell, Fawn Fitter, Mary Foppiani, Emily Norman, Joel Schonfeld, Andrea Weinstein, Lauraine and Ronald Hutchinson; Alice Buckner, principal, Alice Buckner Consulting; Dave G., Mark Maynard, Patricia Perkins and The OC Foundation, Dr. Judith Lytel; Nancy Clark, sports dietician, HealthWorks Fitness Center, Chestnut Hill, Massachusetts; Paula Fuoco Davis, Richard Lowe, Gabrielle Lichterman, Nancy Hall, Susan McCullough, Bill Dyszel, Brenda Hulin, Russell Wild, Sarah Wernick, Randy Burgess, Abigail Esman, David Leonard, Sharron Luttrell, and Pat Olsen. A personal thanks, also, to my family and to my "team:" Ellen Katz, Diane Todd, Stephen Kiser, and Maria Longo.

Contents

Introduction

SO MUCH MORE is known now about obsessive-compulsive disorder than was known even twenty-five years ago. We're familiar with what causes it, how to treat it, and—more important, perhaps—what *doesn't* cause it and how *not* to treat it.

Although OCD can be frustrating to live with (or around), the news is mostly good: It is infinitely treatable. The hardest part might just be getting started.

If you have OCD, or suspect that you do, take heart: you're much better off than your grandmother would have been under the same circumstances. (In fact, if you have OCD, it's likely that others in your family did or do, too, as it's largely hereditary.)

There's truth in the adage that knowledge is power. Hold a little information up to the OCD monster and watch it shrink.

OCD can be unpleasant, but it is not fatal and it is far from hopeless.

If you learn one thing about the disorder, let it be this: It is a neurological condition, most probably genetic. Whether you have it has little to do with your upbringing, experiences or anything other than the workings of your brain. A person who has OCD may act a little "crazy," but absolutely isn't.

OCD can be horrible, but it is also fascinating. And you may be pleased to know that it often affects bright, creative people.

Forget the stereotypes: OCD isn't necessarily about cleaning your kitchen counters endlessly or counting the number of steps you take on the way from your house to the supermarket (although it *can* be). OCD can mean the agony of uncertainty—or of *near* certainty: that you've run over a pedestrian, spread germs, or failed, in some other way, to live responsibly. It can mean constant worry about your health. Or horrifying thoughts that just won't go away, about disgusting or upsetting things (things that you would never even actually do). It can mean living in filth or clutter extreme enough to threaten your life. Showers that last a near eternity. And anxiety. Always, anxiety.

If any of that describes you, welcome home. (There can be many other symptoms, as well.) Your obsessive thoughts and compulsive behaviors might seem a little "out there" to you or to others, but rest assured: they may be commonplace within the OC community. In fact, they probably are.

You might also be surprised to receive more understanding from strangers than from family or friends (although this is not always the case). People often find themselves feeling frustrated when someone they care about begins to make strange demands, or stops doing things he once enjoyed and didn't seem to consider twice.

OCD symptoms can begin gradually or seem to come on "all of a sudden." Young adulthood is a common time for onset, although children and elderly persons can develop the disorder, too. (Especially in the latter case, this is often the result of an illness.)

The happy news about OCD is that it tends to respond remarkably well to treatment, both cognitive and medical (assuming you get the right kinds of both, or either). While it doesn't go away completely, it can definitely recede enough to allow you to live a productive and happy life. It is, in short, nothing to worry about.

CHAPTER 1

Is It OCD?

OCD—SOMETIMES CALLED THE DOUBTING or "What If" Disease—stands for obsessive-compulsive disorder, a condition that torments the sufferer with unwanted thoughts (obsessions). Sometimes, these thoughts become so upsetting or overwhelming that the victim does whatever he can to relieve them. That's where compulsions come in. Here's an example: You can't shake the idea that you've been exposed to dangerous germs (obsession). So you wash repeatedly (compulsion). This chapter serves as an introduction to OCD and offers information about getting a diagnosis and pursuing treatment.

What Is OCD?

Generally speaking, OCD involves worry, often excessive and unrelenting. Usually, the anxiety is about the kinds of things most other people wouldn't fret about that much: fear that you've been exposed to a horrible disease, or a gnawing apprehension that you have not done something you should have (such as locking the front door) or done it well enough (such as writing a paper). If you or someone you care about has experienced something like this, take heart: Your problem has a name and many possible solutions.

You may have different worries: constant fear of personal attack or electricity, or a vague belief that your thoughts or actions can influence events. You may be tormented by bizarre unwanted sexual thoughts, or have a secret fear of harming someone—even a child or spouse you care about very much. You might feel a need to save or collect garbage, or to wash your groceries when you come home from the store. The thoughts and behaviors that can signal OCD really do run the gamut.

Obsessions

People who have OCD tend to obsess about certain things. These obsessions almost always stem from anxiety. The number of objects, situations, and places that people have been known to fear are nearly without limit. If you're terrified of electricity (or, conversely, of electrical appliances not working), cities, tall buildings, certain numbers or colors, vomiting, choking, blood, teeth, various animals, car accidents, or contracting AIDS, hantavirus, rabies, botulism, Ebola, avian flu, cancer, or any number of other serious diseases, you're not alone.

 Fact

The United Nations World Health Organization lists OCD as one of the ten most debilitating illnesses when looked at in terms of loss of income and diminished quality of life—to say nothing of the problems it can cause in the sufferer's interpersonal relationships.

If you sometimes go so far as to do yourself harm trying to escape from the situations that frighten you (if, for instance, you sometimes wash or even gargle with chemical solutions), you're not alone. If your fears sometimes seem to "cancel one another out," (that is, if you fear for example, both diseases and the vaccinations that can prevent them—or the needles that deliver those vaccines); if you secretly worry that you'll shout out a curse word at an inappropriate time (or that perhaps you already have); if you often agonize because you think you might have accidentally hit a pedestrian while driving, even though you don't see an apparent victim; if your head is frequently filled with visions of terrible events; even if you worry about poison or other unwholesome substances in your food or water . . . you're not alone.

Compulsions

To compensate for these obsessive fears and worries, people who have OCD often perform compulsions—certain "rituals" they feel the need to carry out. For example, if you constantly worry about your car being stolen you might spend an hour each day just checking all the doors and windows to make sure all locks are completely secure. The amount of time you take performing your ritual can help a doctor evaluate whether you have OCD and, if so, how severe it may be. Some OCD sufferers end up checking their stoves or door locks, washing themselves or their belongings, or praying against harm for hours at a time. Even fifteen minutes spent making sure your front door is locked are about fourteen and a half more than you need. The amount of time you give each day (or week or year) to obsessions and compulsions may provide a clue about whether you have OCD. Here are a few more examples of compulsive behaviors:

- Washing your hands so often that the skin routinely cracks and bleeds
- Feeling the need to shower after someone touches you—even after a simple handshake or pat on the back
- Avoiding communal objects that are touched by many people, such as elevator buttons, public computers, and library books
- Worrying that you might deliberately or accidentally hurt someone
- Habitually spitting things out
- Checking your clothing for insects before getting dressed

This is only a fraction of the possibilities out there. No matter what your obsessions and compulsions, chances are you're not the only person who experiences them.

Other Components of OCD

But OCD isn't just as simple as obsession and compulsion. There are other feelings, experiences, and behaviors that people who have OCD commonly exhibit:

- **A feeling of powerlessness.** You can't seem to gain control over your behaviors, however hard you try. The need to "ward off" unhappy consequences—or save stacks of magazines or empty boxes, or whatever your compulsion is—overwhelms the desire to relax and enjoy life as others seem to.
- **The knowledge that, on some level, these behaviors are irrational.** While it may seem as if avoiding the feared situation or object has "worked" so far (that is, no harm has come to you yet), you know that other people do not employ these tactics but don't seem to suffer terrible fates as a result.
- **A degree of irrational thinking.** While a person who fears needles might avoid hospitals and people known to use intravenous medicines or drugs, a person with an *obsessive* fear of needles might imagine them everywhere, or go to extreme lengths to avoid all needles, even foregoing lab testing and ignoring medical advice.
- **Heightened anxiety.** When you can't avoid your feared thing or situation, or at least practice the behavior that makes you feel somewhat safe around it, you suffer emotionally. You might also find yourself tormented by visions of disastrous consequences arising from your actions or lack of same.
- **The frequent need for reassurance that your worries are unfounded.** (Often, these so-called "reassurances" fail—and can create conflict in close relationships, besides.)
- **Disruption of your daily life.** For instance, when you make plans, do you always factor in time so you can avoid public bathrooms and run home to use your own? If so, you may have OCD. If you often end up not making plans altogether for fear that you would not be able to practice your avoidance or ritual behavior, again OCD is the likely culprit.

A Historical Overview

According to the Book of Proverbs, there is no new thing under the sun. OCD—although not known by that name before recent times—has been with us pretty much forever. It was documented as far back as the 1400s. In the 1600s, some people were known to have had what was called "religious melancholy." While engaged in prayer or meditation, these individuals found their minds invaded by base or blasphemous thoughts, or they were tormented with doubt that they had said, perhaps, a "dirty" word in church.

Doctors and Scholars

One of the earliest famous persons to suffer from OCD was Dr. Samuel Johnson, a scholar, writer and Renaissance man of his day (the early to late 1700s). Johnson had what would today probably be known as a severe case (stories are told that he drank tea almost obsessively; various reports mention as many as sixteen or even twenty-five cups at a sitting, or as many as forty in a single day), and was subject to movement compulsions, among other kinds of unusual behaviors. On rare occasions when he was asked about them, he blamed "bad habits." He also apparently suffered most of his life from depression, another affliction common to people who have OCD. (In addition, he likely had Tourette's syndrome, which is now believed to be related to OCD.)

In the early 1800s, OCD was understood as a kind of partial insanity. (And you think *you're* afraid to tell anyone about your obsessions, compulsions, and phobias.) By mid-century, the condition received a lot more notice among psychologists, especially in France.

When Freudian theory came into general prominence in the nineteenth and early twentieth centuries, "neurosis" and other now-rather-quaint-sounding terms became the watchwords of their day. Virtually every personality quirk and "abnormal" behavior, it was believed, originated in the home, and was caused by the subject's parents (as well as sexual repression). In fact, truth be told, it was almost always the mother who was blamed for virtually any condition believed to have been psychologically based.

Sigmund Freud studied OCD, too. Although, much later, it would become plain that his "neurosis" theory of the condition was off the mark, he did help to bring OCD to greater prominence. "Obsessional neurosis" patients must have felt at least somewhat grateful to know that they weren't alone, even if the psychologists of their time blamed the condition on all kinds of things that really had nothing to do with it.

Freud wrote that he found the disorder to be among the most interesting he had studied, but he believed that it could not be cured. (In a manner of speaking, he was right. As of this writing, OCD does not have a "cure" per se—and, if it did, it would not be a psychologically but a physiologically based one. However, it can be managed very successfully, to the point that it no longer dominates one's life.)

 Alert

Once you understand OCD as a brain disease or neurological condition, you'll realize—and can help others to realize—that your symptoms aren't just you "acting crazy." OCD originates in the brain. Although types vary, its symptoms overall show remarkable consistency from one victim to the next!

Even after OCD became identified as such, it was believed, well into the twentieth century, to be a psychological illness. As recently as the 1980s, some texts still referred to it as "obsessive-compulsive neurosis."

It wasn't until the mid-1980s that OCD began to be understood as a neurological disorder, and that CBT, the OC Foundation, and most OCD support organizations came into being. (You'll read about all of these.)

Modern Times—The Pioneers

Many doctors impressed the psychological community with their early work with OCD patients. Dr. Michael Jenike founded the first residential OCD treatment center in the United States, which he continues to run today, at McLean Hospital in Belmont, Massachusetts. Dr. Wayne Goodman founded Yale University School of Medicine's obsessive-compulsive disorders unit and was a principal creator of the Yale-Brown Obsessive-Compulsive Scale, or "Y-BOCS" as it is known, a tool that is still widely used to evaluate whether a person's symptoms fulfill the diagnostic criteria for OCD.

Question

Did Lady Macbeth have OCD?
It would appear so. If the fictional character from Shakespeare's Macbeth (written and first performed in the early 1600s) had been a real woman and had lived in modern times, her need to wash her hands repeatedly for long periods, hoping to remove long-faded blood stains, certainly would have suggested OCD.

Dr. Edna Foa was among the first in this country to use a technique you will hear more about, called "exposure and response prevention" (exposing the patient to his feared thing or situation, then preventing him from performing his typical compulsion to relieve anxiety and keep his feared outcome from occurring). In some cases, the treatments appeared rather radical. But apparently, even the more extreme treatments enjoyed more success than had been expected, and the basic techniques are still used with success today.

Dr. Judith Rapoport did groundbreaking research into OCD. In the early 1990s, her bestselling book, *The Boy Who Couldn't Stop Washing*, finally made OCD known and understandable to the general public. The publicity surrounding the book was also responsible for countless numbers of children and adults finally being directed toward an accurate diagnosis and effective treatment.

In 1984, Lucinda Bassett, who had once suffered from a host of panic and anxiety problems, co-founded the Midwest Center for Stress and Anxiety. She later became a popular lecturer and wrote a brisk-selling book called *From Panic to Power* to help others over-come their fears. Her techniques are still being used and taught.

There have been many other excellent and dedicated research-ers and doctors who've paved the way for OCD treatment, as well as a far greater understanding of the condition. (Some of the titles of their published works can be found in Appendix A.)

Conditions that Resemble OCD

OCD is a term that gets tossed around a bit too often these days. If you simply exhibit some OCD-like tendencies, this does not necessarily mean that you have the disorder. Superstitions are a good example of this. While these beliefs have no basis in fact, it's also true that many actors and sports figures, for instance, regularly observe ritu-als that they hope or believe will bring them luck. A baseball player might keep a "lucky coin" in his pocket while playing. Or a "regular person" might toss salt over his shoulder after accidentally spilling some. Is this OCD? Probably not. What matters is how much distress you feel, and for how long, when prevented from observing your par-ticular "protective" behavior.

 Question

If I have OCD, does that mean I'm crazy?
Before you read any further, relax. OCD can be highly troubling, even immobilizing. It can make you feel alienated and alone. But it abso-lutely does not mean you're insane. In fact, if you're questioning it at all, that means you're rational enough to know, on some level, that your behavior doesn't make sense.

Similarly, religious ritual can sometimes behave like OCD. (In fact, there is also a type of OCD called scrupulosity, which causes preoccupation with religious observance. You'll read more about this later.)

Conditions often mistaken for OCD include:

- **Generalized anxiety disorder.** Some people worry a lot—not about specific situations, as people with OCD tend to, but about many things, or "everything" in general. (Hence, the name.)
- **Phobias.** Because OCD usually involves both irrational fears and avoiding things that frighten the sufferer, obsessive-compulsive behavior is often misdiagnosed as phobia. But fear is only part of OCD. A person who has a fear of flying may not necessarily have OCD. He may simply have a fear of flying.
- **Panic disorder.** While OCD is an anxiety disorder, it differs from panic disorder, a condition in which the sufferer finds herself suddenly overwhelmed with dread and unpleasant physical symptoms. OCD can also involve physical symptoms, but a person who has a panic disorder usually does not know *why* she feels frightened.
- **Depression.** Depression is common to many mental and physical conditions. OCD sufferers often are at greater risk than the general population for depression. At least part of the reason probably has to do with brain chemistry.

In order to receive appropriate treatment, you need to be sure you get an accurate diagnosis. Different anxiety disorders require different treatments, such as therapy or medication, and you have the best chances of taking control of your situation if you see a therapist and get diagnosed.

Getting a Diagnosis

If you suspect you have OCD, or that someone you care about does, the first thing to do is find out for sure so you can decide on and begin treatment. The best way to do this is to see a qualified therapist, preferably one who specializes in OCD or anxiety disorders. You can also get in touch with the OC Foundation (*www.ocfoundation*

.org) or other organizations that help people who have OCD. In addition, there are self-assessments you can try (you'll learn about these in the next section).

 ## Fact

Some studies find that women more often start to experience OCD symptoms in their early twenties, while for men, it's usually their teens. Although OCD is a brain disorder, many researchers believe traumatic events often set off the first episode. Some also believe that growing up with rigid rules for behavior may influence whether a predisposed person will develop OCD.

Your therapist may ask you to discuss your worries, and may give you a test (or several), asking you to rate your discomfort level in certain situations. However, there are a few indicators you can use in the meantime. One is the amount of discomfort you feel when prevented from practicing your obsessive behavior (sometimes called a "ritual"). For instance, if you were being interviewed for a desirable job and had to shake the prospective boss's hand, would you become so preoccupied thinking about when you might get to wash that you wouldn't be able to focus on the conversation? If so, it's possible that you have OCD.

Being honest with your therapist will help her determine whether you have OCD and, if so, to what degree. There's no need to feel afraid or embarrassed. "Yes" answers about obsessive thoughts or "ritual" behaviors do not mean you're "crazy." Nor, believe it or not, will the answers be anything the therapist hasn't heard before.

Your OCD Self-Assessment

Your therapist may also give you a test (either to take home, fill out, and bring back to your next session, or to complete in her office, verbally). There are also several OCD self-assessment quizzes available in books, online, and through therapists. Additionally, there are tests (one of which is available through the OCD Centre's Web site, *www.ocdcentre.com*) that family members and others close to the individual in question may take. While these tests may help you determine whether or not you have OCD, it's still best to get a diagnosis from a professional.

The following is the OC Centre's test:

Score questions as follows:
> *Frequency*:
> Never – 1
> Sometimes – 2
> Often – 3
> Very Often – 4
> All the Time – 5

(If you're not sure of an answer, just give your best guess.)

How often does the following happen to you?
1. Repeat tasks because they don't "feel right" the first time, e.g. switching off lights, putting things down, locking or closing doors
2. Collect items that have no value, e.g. magazines, newspapers, etc.
3. Repeat tasks according to a "lucky number"
4. Get anxious about certain words, phrases, or numbers
5. Have rituals for leaving the house, e.g. locking door, touching door, checking bag, windows, etc.
6. Find difficulty reading due to having to frequently re-read sections
7. Find yourself retracing your steps when walking in public
8. Find it difficult to stop doing tasks which are naturally repetitive, e.g. cleaning teeth, flicking through TV remote, pushing buttons, typing on keyboard
9. Regularly feel the need to arrange objects according to a certain pattern, e.g. color code, alphabetical order or symmetry

10. Have to think of a "good thought" to counteract a "bad thought"
11. Distressing images popping into your head for no reason, e.g. harm coming to others, unwanted sexual or violent images
12. Start most of your reasoning with "what if...."
13. Spend long periods of time researching matters that worry you on the Internet
14. Mentally go over and over situations that have already occurred or might occur
15. Clean personal objects such as keys, remote controls, purses, wallets, bags, credit cards
16. Pull your sleeves over your hands before touching handles
17. Spend an unreasonably long time in the bathroom (say, more than 20 minutes or so)
18. Avoid putting dirty washing in with the rest of your immediate household's
19. Worry that you are attracted to the same sex (if you're basically heterosexual)
20. Have sore, chapped, red hands from washing them too much
21. Have difficulty eating food or drink served in public places for fear of germs, disease, or other contamination
22. Outside, walk with head down, scanning for danger
23. Ask others for reassurance about things which only seem to matter to you
24. Worry about loved ones when they leave the house to do everyday tasks
25. Avoid driving because you are fearful of causing an accident
26. Avoid vulnerable groups of people, e.g. children, the elderly, the disabled, etc.
27. Overly check that electrical/gas appliances and taps are turned off
28. Become anxious around knives or other potentially harmful objects

29. Check e-mails to ensure you haven't said something inappropriate
30. Do you have difficulty throwing items away because you may need them in the future?

Please add up your total scores.*

0 – 50: Unlikely to have OCD; if so it is probably mild and not currently intruding upon your life.

51 – 100: It is possible you have OCD and that it is affecting your life. We recommend that you carry out a full assessment (you could try our full version) or seek diagnosis from a mental health professional.

101 – 150: It is highly likely that you have OCD and it is causing you considerable discomfort (possibly to those around you). Please don't suffer further and seek help as soon as possible.

*Please note that this assessment is a useful guideline only and should not replace a full assessment with a licensed professional, either employed by the OCD Centre or elsewhere.

*Reprinted with the permission of the OCD Centre, Belgravia, London and New York, NY; OCDCentre.com.

Listening to Others

Whether or not you have OCD, if friends, family members, and others who care about you tell you that something's wrong, it's probably best to take their remarks seriously.

You may feel as if your behaviors are perfectly reasonable and that those folks don't understand. Okay. But as a wise person once said, "If three people tell you you're drunk, lie down."

Seeking Professional Help

Once you decide to look into getting help for your OCD, you have many options. Of course, choice is not always the best thing for people who have difficulty making decisions, and those who have anxiety disorders often do have a hard time when it comes to choosing between even a small number of things! However, dealing with OCD is not necessarily as hard as it may seem.

Reasons to Seek Professional Help

OCD can wax and wane: Your symptoms may get stronger when you're under stress, and give you more peace at other times. They may even seem to "go away" entirely for long periods, sometimes years, for no particular reason. But, without treatment, OCD is unlikely to disappear. Even with treatment (at least, as of this writing), symptoms should become manageable, but probably won't vanish altogether.

 Fact

> One of the best-known diagnostic tools for OCD is the Y-BOCS, or Yale-Brown Obsessive-Compulsive Scale, written by Dr. Wayne Goodman and others in 1989. It appears in many books and on several Web sites. The Y-BOCS has come in for a little bit of criticism recently because it asks about same-sex obsessions, suggesting to some a heterosexual bias. However, the intention is to evaluate *unwanted*, intrusive thoughts about sexuality, whether homo- or heterosexual.

There are self-help options, too. If you don't have access to a mental health professional schooled and skilled in the treatment of anxiety disorders, or if, for whatever reasons, the other options mentioned elsewhere in this book don't work for you, self-help can be a viable alternative.

What Can You Expect from Treatment?

Treatment can reduce your symptoms to the point that they no longer seem to run your life. While OCD is not "cured" per se, behavior therapy, medication, or both can make a big difference. You may feel only mild anxiety where you once felt wholesale panic, or find that you're simply no longer afraid of, or bothered by, things that used to torment you.

It doesn't even matter if your case is especially "bad." Cognitive therapy and medication (or one or the other) have just as good a chance of working against serious OCD as mild (although, in the former case, it may take longer). You might be thinking, *That's well and good for some, but that stuff will never work for me.* If so, you might just find yourself happily surprised.

The Next Step

Once you know you have OCD, you can get started on reducing it. Chances are, this heretofore-unnamed thing has long overstayed its welcome (such as it was). Although you may not be happy to learn that you have OCD (if you do), at least you know what you're dealing with; that it can be successfully treated; that it isn't fatal; and that there are many worse things (although it might not always feel that way). Just reading this book represents a step on the road to feeling better and increasing your quality of life.

CHAPTER 2

Types of OCD

THERE ARE SO MANY variations within OCD that it sometimes seems as if each is an entirely separate disorder. However, all OCD sufferers exhibit certain distinct characteristics: chiefly, persistent unwanted thoughts and an overwhelming need to perform actions in order to gain relief from them. Most OC behaviors involve a lot of worry, along with the belief that if you engage in certain behaviors, you might be able to influence how things turn out. This chapter focuses on some of the types of OCD, classified in no special order. (Different experts will them in different ways, but there are only so many basic kinds.)

Organizational OCD

A person who has organizational OCD will feel a great deal of distress if things are not put away where and how he believes they ought to be. Some people who have organizational OCD may also insist on "symmetry." For instance, if the sofa has two pillows on its left side, it must also have two pillows on its right side. Or perhaps all of the items on a desk will have to be precisely lined up at right angles to one another.

People who have this kind of OCD feel as if they cannot function when things are "out of order," and will spend a lot of time arranging objects, putting things away, or asking others to be neater. Some might even go so far as to discard objects of an uneven number. (There are people, however, who are merely particular about their homes, appearances, or surroundings; it should not be assumed that these folks necessarily have OCD.)

Fact

> An abnormal fear of filth or contamination is known in psychiatry as mysophobia. This kind of OCD is believed to be the most common. Some experts theorize that the rise of such products as hand sanitizer is partly to blame for increased germ preoccupation on the part of the public. (Conversely, the marketing of such products may be a *response to* greater germ awareness in general.)

Fear of Illness or Contamination

Persons who have this type of OCD, as you can probably guess, worry excessively about their health. Often, they make certain to steer clear of any situation that might present the smallest hint of danger. For instance, they might try to avoid germs by staying away from homeless people (perceived by some to carry diseases), or by staying far away from hospitals where contagion might lurk; avoiding sharp objects that might cut (and thereby infect) them; and so on. A person with an obsessive fear of illness might also frequently check his body for signs of injury or symptoms of disease, especially after any perceived exposure. He might also engage in the kinds of lengthy hand washing and showering behaviors often associated with OCD.

Ironically, persons with excessive fear of illness sometimes do themselves harm in the effort to avoid it. People who have this type of OCD have been known to wash until they bleed; soak their hands in alcohol, or even harsher solutions, for long stretches; or hold alcohol-containing mouthwash in their mouths for as long as ten minutes at a time, going so far as to allow it to burn their gums in their efforts to combat or prevent perceived illness transmission or contamination.

Another problem (though not a dangerous one) frequently faced by people with OCD is wasted time, often a lot of it. Some people are so morbidly afraid of dirt that brushing up against the tile wall or curtain while showering creates a perceived need for extra showering. Those who have washing compulsions tend to spend an awful lot of time in water. So-called "checkers" may take hours before they feel ready to leave the house, as they check and recheck the stove, iron, door locks, coffee maker, etc. Similar delays will plague those who must tap doorframes or open and close drawers a prescribed number of times. Most kinds of OCD, in fact, demand a lot of time.

Ⅼ. Essential

Sometimes, especially in families or other close groups, persons with one kind of OCD will feel superior to, or have a hard time understanding, those with other types. The reasoning typically goes something like this: "Why don't you worry, as I do, about life-and-death matters, instead of whether the window curtains are straight?" or, "At least my organizational behaviors serve a purpose."

Fear of Causing Harm

Some people worry excessively about causing harm to *others*. A person who has this kind of OCD might find himself tortured by the idea that perhaps he ran over a pedestrian and is being pursued by the law. (This is actually a more common anxiety than you might realize.) Or he might fear that he will *deliberately* cause harm to another. A surprising number of parents harbor terrifying secret fears that they will become overwhelmed by the impulse to purposely harm their children, even though they know, on some level, that they would never do this. While some parents and caretakers do harm children, it rarely, if ever, happens that a person who has this particular kind of OCD gives in to the kinds of dark impulses he fears.

Other Responsibility Concerns

Some people who have this type of OCD fear that they will be accused of crimes they did not commit—shoplifting, for example—and will find themselves unable to prove their innocence. Or they may worry excessively about spreading germs to others, causing serious illness.

A person who suffers from so-called "responsibility obsessions" might feel the need to check that nobody has in fact been harmed by his actions. He might repeatedly return to a stretch of road, or carefully look over his car for new dents or traces of blood in an attempt to make sure that he did not hit a pedestrian while driving in the dark. He might even call the police to find out whether any hit-and-run accidents were reported during the time he was on the road. Like people with many other types of OCD, he might ask for reassurance almost constantly from a partner or friends.

 ## Fact

> People who have OCD often have a hard time making decisions, even relatively simple ones, such as what to eat for lunch or what shirt to wear to work, fearing that a wrong choice could end up having disastrous consequences for them or others.

Checking

As you probably know (or have, perhaps, experienced), some people who have OCD check *things*, rather than their own bodies. This is the very well known kind that involves frequent scrutiny of stove burners, door locks, ovens and appliances, etc. As seen in other kinds of OCD, irrational doubt and worry are to blame. ("Is the stove truly off? Can I be absolutely sure? Because if it isn't, it could cause a fire in my absence.") And, as in other cases, the victim (and, often, her family) suffers a great deal of anxiety, and loses a great deal of time as she goes back again and again to make sure she hasn't left the stove on or the door unlocked. In some cases, door locks and stove knobs are actually broken or seriously worn from such repeated use.

Perfectionism

Some people have perfection compulsions that go far beyond the admirable quest for self-improvement. People who have this kind of OCD can often be found checking and rechecking their work or handwriting, among other things. They might also become "fanatical" about matters of diet, personal appearance, or other aspects of their lives. Common perfection obsessions include worrying about not writing or speaking well enough. Some people who have this kind of OCD often try to do virtually everything perfectly, suffering a great deal of anxiety when that perfection is not achieved. Or the sufferer might, for instance, cut her own hair almost daily, forever seeking to perfect her look. (A sub-group of these seemingly "perfectionist" individuals actually has body dysmorphic disorder [BDD], an obsession with their own perceived bodily imperfection. BDD can cause sufferers to avoid social situations or to pursue frequent, unwarranted plastic surgery. In any case, it usually gives rise to a lot of distress.) In some instances, people who have perfection compulsions do things extremely—even pathologically—slowly, to avoid making any mistakes.

Repetition

Some people who have OCD feel a need to count things compulsively or to repeat routine actions a certain number of times in order to feel "okay." A person who has this kind of OCD might turn the mailbox key a specific number of times whenever he retrieves the mail, walk up and down the front steps a set number of times whenever he leaves the house, or sit and then stand a ritualized number of times before being comfortably seated.

Fear of Objects, Places, or Situations

While some people who have OCD try as hard as possible to avoid illness, others stay away from certain things or situations altogether. These may include cemeteries, bridges, or heights, to name a few. Gephyrophobia, the fear of crossing a bridge, is surprisingly common. There are many others. Some people fear dogs (cynophobia) or other animals vomiting (emetophobia), blood (hemato- or hemophobia), or rabies (hydrophobophobia). The number of objects or situations people fear is almost infinite. Again, just being afraid of, say, needles (belonephobia) would not necessarily mean that you have OCD. It is the degree to which your fear bothers you (and, indirectly, the people around you), directs your actions, and takes time away from other activities that may, or may not, indicate the presence of OCD.

Magical Thinking

Perhaps when you were a child, you would hold your breath when passing a cemetery so that the "bad spirits" couldn't get inside your body. (If you were riding in a car at the time, you might also have simultaneously touched the vehicle's ceiling and raised your feet off the floor.) Or maybe you tried hard not to step on cracks in the side-walk out of fear that the old saying about breaking your mother's back might somehow prove true. Some people continue (or resume) such behaviors in adulthood and become convinced that their actions, though unrelated, might sway the fates one way or the other. So-called "magical thinking" might include the recitation of prayers (sometimes, quite elaborate) or flicking a light switch on and off a certain number of times in the belief that a specific person or persons might be guaranteed safety from harm.

Some people who have this type of OCD believe, even though they know it can't be true, that they can prevent harm to others if they try hard: saying prayers, for instance, or engaging in behaviors that they have decided, for whatever reason, will spare their loved ones death or suffering. In an age of so many technological wonders, it may be hard for a highly imaginative person not to believe, to some degree, in "magic." Again, it is the degree to which said thinking, and the behaviors it engenders, interferes with daily functioning that indicates, at least in part, whether you have OCD.

Depending, among other factors, on the culture in which you grew up, you might engage in various superstitious rites such as throwing salt over your left shoulder should you accidentally spill salt, going out of your way to avoid having a black cat cross your path, "making a wish" on your stray eyelashes, or refraining from placing hats on the bed. In most cases, these are not to be confused with OCD. Again, it is a matter of degree.

Essential

It's hard for many people, both those who have OCD and those who do not, not to engage in some degree of "magical thinking." That is, if you hear a certain song on the radio, you believe it will mean a high mark on a test, or a safe flight. Or perhaps you think a "lucky" garment will ensure your success in an endeavor. Many people take comfort in these thoughts and rituals. The idea that we have absolutely no control over events, large and small, in the universe is not always a pleasant one!

For the majority of people who practice superstitious behaviors, these acts are relatively harmless and simply uphold certain cultural traditions. However, if you spent, say, more than an hour obsessing about the harm that would surely come to you (or someone important to you) because of a broken mirror, or an umbrella accidentally opened indoors—or because you inadvertently violated one of your own "rules"—and you feel compelled to try to "undo" your action with a specific ritual, then you could be dealing with something more than ordinary superstition.

Movement Compulsions

Movement compulsions may fall into the categories of magical thinking or perfectionism. A person who has movement compulsions may feel as if he must repeat the same action—crossing a threshold, for instance—over and over until he feels he has gotten it "right."

Such compulsions will sometimes "generalize": it won't be enough to worry about thresholds; soon, the sufferer adds stairs, pathways, and so on.

Touching

Just as some people feel compelled to avoid certain objects or situations, others feel compelled to touch things. A person who has a touching compulsion might feel as if she absolutely had to touch the same fire hydrant on the way to work each morning for "luck," or to feel "okay." Sometimes, a person with a touching compulsion can't remember why she began the behavior in the first place. She only knows that she would find it very uncomfortable to try to stop.

Hoarding

People who are obsessed with order often have to throw things away with regularity to consider their environments free of clutter. Others wouldn't think of discarding anything that might one day prove valuable. People who hoard valueless things such as empty cereal boxes, soap wrappers, or even "collections" of ordinary objects believe they will one day need them, or that these items may become valuable over time. (Witnessing the astronomical growth of the "collectibles" market, one might have to conclude that this is, indeed, possible!) Discarding things is painful to such persons and, frequently, their homes become dangerously full. Threatening the person with eviction or tossing out his possessions usually won't work (apart from the legal and moral questions such activities would raise): The behavior will only start again in a new situation, driven as it is by the compulsion to hoard.

Often, people who hoard not only refrain from throwing things away, but also actively go out in search of new objects to add to their collections. Sometimes, they intend to restore these things for future use or to render them helpful to others. In a great majority of cases, the objects they take home would be considered "junk" by most people.

It Can Even Be Hazardous

From time to time, you will probably see a news story about an unfortunate person who died when his house went up in flames, and firefighters couldn't reach him for all the mountainous piles of newspapers or other clutter. Or maybe there's a house in your neighborhood that's considered a hazard because of all the junk (or even bona fide garbage) in and around it. Perhaps that describes your own home. Obsessive hoarding may be the cause. (Turn to Chapter 8 if you would like to read more about hoarding behaviors.)

Fear of Embarrassment

More like an extreme social phobia, this kind of OCD plagues the sufferer with unreasonable fears about unwittingly embarrassing herself or being humiliated in public. She may also worry about shouting out inappropriate words or ideas. While people who have coprolalia (a rare form of Tourette's syndrome) actually do involuntarily shout obscenities or inappropriate remarks, some people with OCD *fear* that they will do so, or that they unknowingly have.

 Fact

> Some peoples' OC fears conflict with others' OC fears. For instance, some OCD sufferers feel as if they must touch the same outdoor objects every time they pass them, or they will feel uneasy. Others—those who are germ phobic, for instance—fear nothing more than *having* to touch outdoor objects.

There is another kind of recently identified OCD, perhaps related to fear of embarrassment, possibly more closely connected to body dysmorphic disorder, in which the patient believes he (or, more commonly, a part of his body) smells bad and is offensive to others. Persons who have this disorder typically try all kinds of external and medicinal remedies and, as in other types of OCD, seek reassurance; however, they do not usually benefit from it, as they tend to disbelieve whatever reassurance they receive.

Scrupulosity

Scrupulosity is defined as intrusive, unwanted, offensive thoughts with reference to one's faith or belief system. It involves constant vigilance and fear of not "doing the right thing" according to one's God or religious hierarchy. A person who has scrupulosity might obsess about blaspheming, or regularly suffer the torment of perverted thoughts. While most religion involves ritual, as well as both proscribed and expected behaviors, individuals who have scrupulosity take their religious rituals too far, and become preoccupied with whether they and others are observing "correctly," according to their own rigid standards.

They might pray for hours on end—even forgoing food and water—while obsessively examining their evil thoughts or "impure" impulses. The person may continually fear having committed a sin that he's forgotten or insufficiently atoned for. Scrupulosity often leads to tremendous guilt and shame.

 Fact

> Some people suffer only from obsessions, but not attendant compulsions. Obsessions may cover a wide range, including intrusive sexual or violent thoughts, worries about contamination or illness, or fears about causing harm to others. In many cases, the sufferer will fear that he might one day act on his violent or inappropriate impulses. This almost never actually happens, but a person with these kinds of obsessive thoughts rarely feels assured that it never *will*.

To entertain the possibility that one's apparently devout behavior is really reflective of a deep anxiety disorder is to risk feeling inadequate and insufficiently religious—in one's own eyes or in God's. The attendant guilt can be extremely hard to tolerate. Because these thoughts border so closely on the individual's religious belief system, they often involve "overvalued ideation"—that is, they tend to be rigidly held and firmly believed. Hence, scrupulosity may also prove more resistant to treatment than might other kinds of OCD.

 Alert

> Obsessive-compulsive behavior generally begins slowly and, over time, grows more and more extreme. The change may be so gradual that your behavior will continue to feel "normal" to you (or to people who are close to you and used to your ways of doing things), even if it looks mighty odd to other people.

Interestingly, while this type of OCD frequently plagues religious persons, it sometimes affects those who haven't been particularly observant. Often, a person who has this kind of disorder will fear that in displeasing the Almighty, she will bring untold harm to herself or her family. In response to this fear, she'll redouble her efforts to pray, atone, fast, spiritually cleanse, and more.

Non-Religious Scrupulosity

Scrupulosity may also refer to a preoccupation with (or, more accurately, persistent doubt when it comes to) business dealings, or rigidity in adhering to a more general code of good and appropriate conduct. A person with scrupulosity may incessantly fear that he may have unknowingly cheated his customers or broken the law.

Neutral Obsessions

Some people suffer from so-called "neutral" obsessions. That is, they can't seem to stop thinking about, and fixating on, insignificant details, such as song lyrics or sports scores. Some sufferers torment themselves with complicated, "mind boggling," or largely insignificant questions. While most of us at times find a tune, name, or other sound going around in our heads for a seemingly endless time, or are bedeviled by a tip-of-the-tongue question ("Oh, what was the name of that actor?"), those who have neutral obsessions find themselves bothered by such things with far greater frequency, often to the point of not being able to give their full attention to school, work or family.

Lesser-Known Kinds of OCD

People who have *hypergraphia* (also romantically, if not entirely correctly, termed "the midnight disease") feel an overwhelming need to write. This condition is also often associated with temporal lobe epilepsy or with the "manic" phase of bipolar disorder. Alcohol and drug use can also give rise to temporary hypergraphia. Several famous authors, including Dostoyevsky, are believed to have had it. Interestingly, quite a few well-known persons who were *not* professional writers are believed to have had hypergraphia as well. These include Van Gogh, who wrote two or three long letters a day to his brother, Theo. He also painted just as energetically. (Compulsive reading, by the way, is known as *hyperlexia*.)

Sound Sensitivity

Some people who have OCD are especially sensitive when it comes to noises, particularly sudden ones. That does not, however, mean that they themselves are incapable of shouting or making other loud sounds. Other people with OCD may be extra sensitive when it comes to textures and fabrics.

Multi-Symptom OCD

It is not uncommon for people who have OCD to have more than one kind. Sometimes, a second type becomes more noticeable over time, or may increase as the symptoms of the first kind diminish. Untreated, OCD can generalize, or "spread." That is, a person who has one type may find herself so overwhelmed with anxieties that she may become fearful of still other things or situations.

 Fact

> Many people who have OCD keep supplies of things they believe they need to have on hand at all times, or for dealing with their feared situations. Just as a person who does not have OCD might carry extra cash in case he should need it, a person with OCD might carry all kinds of cleaning, decontaminating, or antibacterial-type supplies "just in case."

Don't See Yours Listed Here?

Even if you haven't read anything in this chapter that really resonates with your experience, you may still have some type of OCD. The types listed here make up the majority of OC behaviors, but the truth is that obsessions and compulsions can be almost limitless in type. (That said, even the most unusual OC worries will most likely fall into one of the categories covered in this chapter.)

From a fear of eating certain foods to being afraid to fall asleep, any kind of excessive and persistent worry could indicate OCD. It's in your best interest to consult with a professional to know for sure.

CHAPTER 3

The Science of OCD

IN YEARS PAST, OCD was believed to be psychological in origin. Now, it's a virtual certainty that it's a neurological condition. For one thing, OCD often runs in families, and it's less than likely that family members, including cousins, grandchildren, and others not living in the same household, would share a single neurosis. Also, the demonstrated worsening of OCD symptoms in some children following strep infections (and in older adults following other illnesses) suggests that the condition has a physical cause. Finally, modern brain-imaging techniques have revealed vastly different brain activity in patients who have OCD than in those who do not.

Your Brain

The primary parts of the brain are: the frontal lobe (located exactly where its name suggests; it includes the prefrontal and orbital cortex); the temporal lobe (beneath it, and extending back); the occipital lobe (the small section at the back); the parietal lobe (between frontal and occipital); the cerebellum (at the bottom); and the brain stem (beneath and beside it).

Deep inside the brain, the basal ganglia—containing the caudate nucleus, the putamen, and the amygdala—seem to be where much of the OCD activity happens in people who have the disorder. The orbital cortex (located directly behind the eyes) also plays a role; imaging studies have shown increased activity not only in the orbitofrontal cortex but in the cingulate gyrus as well. The increased metabolic activity in these regions—the orbital frontal cortex, the cingulate gyrus, and the caudate nucleus—has been shown to modulate after successful treatment for OCD.

 Fact

Brain scans have shown that, over time, medication or cognitive behavior therapy (or both) can actually physically alter the brain's chemistry. OCD is also sometimes known to be associated with seizures (usually more than one) or brain injury.

There are also neurotransmitters (specific brain chemicals that help neurons or nerve cells to communicate), one of which is serotonin—the one you'll hear so much about, particularly in the phrase "selective serotonin reuptake inhibitors," or SSRIs.

Serotonin (also known by its scientific name, 5-hydroxytryptamine) regulates sleep, mood, appetite, and other things. It is essential for well-being and general functioning. It is believed that a deficiency of this crucial chemical contributes tremendously to the presence of OCD (as well as to depression). It is also believed that a lack of serotonin is an inherited condition, which could help explain the apparent genetic link.

Some brains do not have enough serotonin. In people who have OCD, the neural pathways have been shown to be much more active than in persons who don't. Many good books are available that can explain the exact science in detail. The upshot, however, is that OCD is initiated in the brain, not in the mind. (Although it is common for those who have OCD to intellectualize, or rationalize, their unusual behaviors with complex, after-the-fact explanations, these retrospective thoughts are not the *source* of the OCD. The mind seeks to explain activity generated in the brain.) Also, calming actions can actually be seen to slow down all that repetitive, negative activity.

⌐ Essential

Research suggests that OCD symptoms can arise in some people following traumatic brain injury. Studies already show a connection between head injury and the development of psychiatric disorders, although OCD tends to develop less often than other behaviors (such as poor impulse control). There can be a lag between the time of the injury and the time symptoms develop, so it's not always clear that the injury caused the behaviors.

Mental or Physical Illness?

Today, OCD is understood as a physical illness (although some experts in the field say that it also has a psychological component). However, it is still often described as a mental illness—a holdover, perhaps, from times past, when there was no way for doctors to "see" OCD. If you look on any mental health organization's Web site—for instance, the sites of the National Alliance for the Mentally Ill (NAMI), the National Institute of Mental Health (NIMH), and others—you will see OCD listed and discussed there. (Of course, taken logically, many illnesses currently understood as mental, including such "dramatic" ones as schizophrenia and bipolar disorder, are also believed to originate in the brain and have little, if anything, to do with their victims' upbringing and experiences.) Perhaps someday very soon, nearly all of the conditions we now understand as mental illnesses will be reclassified as physical ones.

Physical illness generally can be observed. A broken bone, for instance, will of course be obvious once an X-ray is taken. Not so a "broken heart." Or OCD...until recently. However, in the late 1990s, Dr. Susan Swedo, Dr. Judith Rapoport, and others at the NIMH were finally able to see evidence of OCD in children who developed symptoms after having had rheumatic fever (which results from an acute complication of untreated "strep throat"). These children may develop a disease called Sydenham's chorea, an illness marked by strange movements, such as tics, as well as obsessions, compulsions, and other unusual behaviors. It is estimated that about 70 percent of Sydenham's chorea patients have OCD symptoms. A diagnostic category was created to identify such children; it is known by the acronym PANDAS, for pediatric autoimmune neuropsychiatric disorders associated with streptococcal infections. The researchers discovered a protein in the blood of these patients that was missing from other patients. They compared those samples with blood samples from children whose OCD or Tourette's syndrome had worsened or become apparent after strep infections and discovered that a high percentage of the children with OCD and Tourette's also had this protein in their blood. Other illnesses may also cause OCD to develop or worsen.

Essential

Is brain surgery an option for OCD patients?
Some researchers have experimented with implanting "a pacemaker for the brain" (actually a surgically implanted chip) to reduce symptoms in people whose OCD has not responded to more conventional treatments. The device has also been used to treat patients who have Parkinson's disease, and may be used for other conditions, as well.

The Genetic Connection

OCD seems, in large part, to be a hereditary illness. However, it is not fully understood why different family members frequently have different types of OCD. It seems unfair that one family member could have organizational obsessions and another, health preoccupations, but that neither one could really understand the other. Yet that's what often happens. On the other hand, it may be that if all family members had the same kind of OCD, no one would ever get help for it. The behavior might become "normalized" within the family—that is, it would seem perfectly natural, at least in that household, for people to stay in the bathroom for hours, say, or routinely go over homework again and again before considering turning it in. Still, it is often useful for therapists, when attempting to arrive at a proper diagnosis, to inquire about other extended family members' "unusual behaviors."

Can OCD be "Helped Along?"

It does appear possible, and perhaps even probable, that certain environmental factors do (or, at least, *can*) contribute to the development of OCD in those who are already predisposed toward it. Some of these are abuse, problems in relationships, and constricting childhoods marked by demands for order or adherence to rules.

 Alert

> Despite possible psychological influences, OCD, it is not "caused" by bad parenting or abuse. A therapist who blames your early home life entirely may lack understanding or education when it comes to OCD, and will probably not be right for you.

Some researchers also believe that a single traumatic event can set off the first major episode in a person already genetically predisposed toward OCD. However, it is no longer believed that these events and conditions alone are responsible for causing it.

An Ounce of Prevention?

Unfortunately, it is not possible, at least as of this writing, to prevent OCD from developing in a predisposed person, or to make sure that any children you have will not also have it. (In fact, this is true whether or not you, your partner, or both of you, have OCD. That said, the disorder *is* usually seen more often in people whose family members have it, or have had it, than in others.) There are also medical treatments, discussed in Chapter 17, that may reverse some of the damage certain strep infections can create in children. However, although OCD is not preventable, it is quite treatable and, unlike a relatively short time ago, can now be considered manageable. And it is infinitely possible, now that so much is known about the disorder and its treatment, to prevent it from getting worse once it's recognized.

Option One: Therapy

As you've read, OCD is now understood to be a neurological condition. It's believed that in OCD patients, the brain sends the wrong messages time and again. It can be compared to a phonograph needle getting "stuck in the groove" of a record. For this reason, the more traditional "talk" therapies are generally not recommended for OCD. Analysis and older therapies may be useful, however, in addressing the loneliness, depression, or isolation that many people with OCD feel. In fact, depression is extremely common in OCD sufferers (more on depression in Chapter 10).

Essential

There are many support options (also discussed elsewhere in these pages), and it is highly recommended that you check them out. Like most problems, the burden of OCD tends to lighten when it's shared. Plus, from a practical standpoint, support group members can help keep one another up-to-date on the latest treatments, and share experiences about what works, what doesn't, and why. (Of course, keep in mind that what doesn't work for some will work for others, and vice versa.)

Cognitive Behavioral Therapy (CBT)

As you'll read in detail later, one type of therapy has proven very successful against OCD. It's called cognitive behavioral therapy, or CBT. (You may also hear the terms "behavior" or just "behavioral therapy.") CBT uses a couple of techniques to battle OCD. The most prominent is called exposure and response prevention. You'll read about this in detail, too, in Chapter 4.

 Fact

One cognitive strategy uses tapes that the patient records, detailing her fearful thoughts. The patient is then instructed to listen to them for a few hours a day. Although the thoughts can be extremely distressing at first, in time they generally become boring and lose their ability to torment the sufferer.

Cognitive therapy can also help you examine the ways in which you automatically perceive such things as the risk of danger. For instance, it's common for people who have OCD and other anxiety disorders to engage in negative and skewed thinking. Example: "I heard about a horrible plane crash. All 310 passengers onboard were killed. Therefore, all air travel is obviously unsafe. Therefore, my next flight will crash."

While you may know that a particular belief is untrue, it almost certainly feels true when you say or think it. A cognitive behavioral therapist can work with you on challenging your assumptions. (Oh, and don't worry that CBT will make you lose all inhibitions and put yourself in dangerous situations. This is so unlikely that it's probably not worth thinking about.)

There are other kinds of therapy, as well, and you'll read about many of these.

Finding a Therapist

There are many good ways to find therapists in your area who are familiar with OCD and other anxiety disorders; you'll read more about this in Chapter 6. In the meantime, here are a few suggestions, succinctly stated, to start you on your way:

- Search the OC Foundation Web site's database of therapists, listed by geographic area.
- Call your local university or teaching hospital and ask for the psychiatry or neurology department, or a related department.
- Look in your local phone directory under "mental health services" or similar listings.
- Ask for recommendations from your physician, current therapist, or friends.

Option Two: Medication

Medication and cognitive therapy have proven particularly effective when used together. If this is an option for you, we urge you to explore it. Some people, however, for any number of reasons, will choose medication alone. Medication can help reduce anxiety (and, often, depression) tremendously, and has helped many, many people who have OCD to live calmer, happier, and more productive lives.

 Fact

Increasingly, hypochondria—a morbid fear of, or intense worry about, having or contracting diseases or a specific disease—is seen as a type of OCD. Like many OCD symptoms, it can be treated successfully with medication, CBT, or both. It's believed that as many as 60 percent of doctor visits may be unwarranted.

You might choose a psychiatrist, psycho-pharmacologist, or your family physician, among others. Your decision will probably depend on your health plan (if you have one), your geographical location, the number and kind of doctors available in your area, and so on. The important thing is to get started.

Option Three: Intensive Therapy

For especially resistant cases (and for other reasons detailed else-where in this book), you might want to look into intensive therapy. Intensive programs are generally residential and of short duration (usually a few weeks, depending on the severity of the case). In-patient programs provide CBT (and medication, if appropriate), just as out-patient treatment would, but it is done in a controlled environ-ment where the therapist is available to see you do the exercises.

For many, if not most, patients, CBT can be scary. But it has dem-onstrated a high rate of success. Getting started is usually the hardest part. Think about how much better your life can be after you com-plete your treatment. In other words, "Keep your eyes on the prize."

Essential

McLean Hospital in Belmont, Massachusetts, runs the country's old-est in-patient program. You can search the OC Foundation's Web site (key word: "intensive"), or go to *www.ocfoundation.org/ocd-intensive-treatment-programs.html* to find others. There's also a list of some in-patient programs in Appendix B at the back of this book.

To ascertain whether your treatment in the program is working, you'll have to give it a chance. This does not mean that you should keep taking a medication that makes you sick. (In fact, if this should happen, talk with your prescribing doctor right away.) However, if you want to know whether a therapy or medication is working, you'll need to do it or take it long enough to draw a reasoned conclusion.

If you don't have a therapist or health insurance, a self-directed program, such as the one in *The OCD Workbook* by Bruce Hyman and Cherry Pedrick, might be helpful. However, because support is such an important component of CBT, working with a therapist is still your best bet. If you begin treatment, particularly CBT, early, it may take less time to reduce your symptoms than if you wait for things to get worse. (Plus, you'll spend less time feeling anxious and miserable!) Even the worst cases often improve significantly with treatment.

CHAPTER 4

Non-Medical Treatment Options

A LOT OF PROGRESS has been made in the world of OCD. More knowledge and treatment options exist than ever have before, and there is a far greater awareness on the part of the public. If your grandmother had OCD, she might have been considered an oddball, or silly. People probably would have called her "nervous." She would have felt very much alone outside the confines of her home and family (and probably even there). Happily, much more is known today about OCD, and you have many more options.

Managing OCD with CBT

OCD cannot yet be cured, but it can be managed. This means that, while your symptoms probably won't go away entirely, they may diminish to the point that they are no longer a big problem. No one really knows why OCD doesn't go away completely; we just know that, at least for now, that's the way it is. However, a significant decrease in your OCD symptoms can make a big difference in your quality of life!

Medication and CBT (especially in concert) have so far demonstrated the best results. Neurofeedback (brain-based biofeedback) is becoming increasingly well known and more widely used in treating OCD, as well. Other symptom-management choices include meditation, visualization, alternative therapies such as acupuncture, and herbal preparations. These don't necessarily diminish OCD per se, but they can help reduce the anxiety that is such a large part of it.

Why Cognitive Behavioral Therapy (CBT)?

A journey of a thousand miles must begin, according to ancient wisdom, with a single step. That is exactly the way treatment for OCD begins. Let's take a look at cognitive behavioral therapy, or CBT. Cognitive therapy differs from traditional or "talk" therapy in that it is an "action-oriented" therapy that employs suggestions for specific changes in behavior. That is, the patient is encouraged to look at the entrenched, illogical aspects of her thinking and to work to correct them.

 Fact

It may surprise you to know that, prior to the 1970s and even the 1980s, before the advent of CBT and the widespread use of medication for OC symptoms, OCD was considered largely incurable.

A good example of illogical or irrational thinking is the classic OC idea that danger lies in wait virtually everywhere. While a traditional therapist might help the patient to arrive at a useful insight, a cognitive therapist will strive to help her see the fallacies in her idea. Generally, cognitive behavioral therapists place far less emphasis on discovering the origins of problematic behaviors, focusing instead on how to change them. This structured type of therapy is used to treat many conditions, including the spectrum of anxiety disorders (OCD, trauma, body dysmorphic disorder, simple phobias) as well as depression.

The chief component of CBT, when used to treat OCD, is a technique called exposure and response prevention (ERP) sometimes called "exposure and ritual prevention." This technique, which involves gradually exposing the patient to the thing or things he fears, can be practiced on one's own or with a therapist.

(Working with a qualified therapist is strongly recommended, however. As you might imagine, ERP can be difficult to practice alone. It is often difficult even with a therapist, but having specific techniques and supportive help as you confront your fears can make all the difference.)

What to Expect from CBT

You might initially work with your therapist on creating a "hierarchy," or ordered list, of feared things or situations. You will probably also spend time working together on learning and practicing techniques for anxiety reduction so that you can put these skills into practice as you confront your fears. Only after your anxiety has significantly abated will you be encouraged to move on to the next step.

L. Essential

If you suffer from agoraphobia or another condition that prevents you from going to see a therapist, you may find a therapist who will be willing to come to you, at least for the first several sessions. Together, you will work on overcoming your highway, driving, or leaving-home fears.

Although CBT techniques will not expose you to actual danger, of course, they will help acclimate you to relatively harmless but anxiety-inducing situations (anxiety inducing for you, that is). The idea is gradually to reduce your level of discomfort in situations that now cause you a lot of stress and may even, in some instances, impede your ability to function. Therapists sometimes use a technique called "habit reversal training" (HRT) for people who have specific behavioral disorders, such as trichotillomania, or compulsive hair pulling. (Trichotillomania was once considered rare. It is now believed to affect slightly more people that OCD itself. More women than men—perhaps almost a three-to-one ratio—suffer from this condition.)

Let's say you have a fear of driving over bridges. Perhaps it's not so bad now, but you find yourself taking other routes, when possible, so that you won't have to travel over water. Or maybe you make excuses, declining invitations that would require you to drive over any bridges. A cognitive behavioral therapist might encourage you first to imagine driving over a bridge, and then to try actually driving over one very low, or short, bridge. You would then progress to longer or higher ones, until the situation gave you virtually no discomfort. Or you might have to start by just driving *near* a bridge or walking to the edge of one, until you were able to tolerate the anxiety this provoked.

In time, you should become acclimated enough that driving over even high or long bridges gives you no real difficulty. Remember: Your symptoms probably developed gradually. Gradual increments are the key to overcoming them, as well.

⌐ Essential

Confronting a feared object or situation produces anxiety, but that discomfort *can* be tolerated. In fact, CBT is based partly on the knowledge that anxiety will not increase without end; eventually, it will subside. "Habituation" will occur, albeit at the cost of some uneasiness.

One benefit of CBT is that it carries no risk of side effects. Another is that its gains are believed to be lasting. That is, once you finish treatment, you should not have a recurrence of OC symptoms. Not true of medication, which, once discontinued, may stop working. The occasional flare-up, or return of symptoms under stress, is not unexpected, however, and can be managed by once again implementing the CBT strategies you've learned and incorporated. A therapy "tune-up" session or two is sometimes not a bad idea, either.

Prevention as a Cure

The *exposure* part of "exposure and response prevention," as described in the previous section, is easy to understand: The patient is gradually *exposed* to the thing or situation that she fears. The "response prevention" part makes it interesting: She is then encouraged to refrain from the usual things she does to make her worrisome situation tolerable. Simply put, with ERP you get exposed to your obsession and prevented from performing your compulsion.

Along the way, of course, you also learn techniques to help you tolerate the anxiety. This is the paradox on which ERP is based: People who have OCD often go to extreme lengths to *avoid* their feared object or situation in an effort to prevent the anxiety associated with it. The idea of exposure and response prevention is that it's necessary to experience anxiety in order to eventually get rid of it. Anxiety cannot accelerate forever. (Although you may at times doubt that!)

Alert

CBT can rarely be accomplished without some initial discomfort. Work through it! If you can stand up to your anxiety with the support of a therapist, a great reward may await you: freedom from your OC fears and the limitations they impose.

An Example

Let's say you feel terrible dread whenever you find yourself in the vicinity of a cemetery. Every time you pass one, you feel your whole body tense up and you become overwhelmed with a desperate longing to flee. You hold your breath for fear that evil spirits might enter your body, or, worse, that some terrible thing will happen to you or to someone you care about. A cognitive behavioral therapist might encourage you and help you prepare to take a brisk walk just inside a cemetery gate. She might even accompany you. Instead of holding your breath and running past the area, as you usually do, you would be encouraged to try standing in place and breathing deeply for several long moments, then calmly walking away. You might be encouraged to repeat an affirmation to yourself, something like, "I am perfectly calm. I feel comfortable wherever I am." Later on, you'd try again, this time venturing farther inside and staying for a longer period of time. (Again, you might have to start by just standing outside, and then make your way past the gate on subsequent visits.)

After getting enough practice, you would ideally be able to take on the task without undue anxiety.

An Exercise in Restraint

A clearer example of response prevention can be seen in patients who have contamination phobias. After contact with the feared object or situation (shaking hands, say, or touching a doorknob), the subject is asked to refrain for a period of time from washing his hands. At first, this usually causes significant distress, but with time, the amount of discomfort diminishes, perhaps even entirely. The patient has the experience, usually repeated, of seeing his anxiety peak—but then subside! Soon enough, he often finds, he is able to shake hands or use doorknobs without fear, perhaps without even a second thought.

⌐ Essential

In most cases, your cognitive behavioral therapist will assign "home-work exercises" for you to do on your own, and you'll report back about your progress or challenges. In addition, you might also learn relaxation techniques to help you tolerate the feelings your feared situation may elicit.

Whether ERP sounds doable or difficult will depend on your particular fear, how long you've had it, and how much you believe your compulsive "response" helps you to avoid danger to yourself or the people you care about. (This is where cognitive therapy comes in, helping you learn to assess the degree of real, versus perceived, danger.)

Changing the Way You Think

One big reason you might find it difficult to begin practicing your particular exposure and response prevention treatment is that people who have OCD typically fear risks, even small ones. After all, for the great majority of sufferers, anxiety is what OCD is all about! However, it is important to keep in mind that ERP will almost certainly not expose you to genuine harm, and it has a very high rate of success.

 Fact

> One of the earliest practitioners of ERP was Dr. Edna Foa of the University of Pennsylvania, who instructed germ-phobic patients to pass their hands over a toilet seat, then, without washing, pick up and eat a sandwich! In most cases, the crude technique worked: Patients got over their fears. Most ERP exercises, however, are not nearly that drastic.

Over time, you can get used to any situation, bad or good. That's exactly how ERP works (although the hope is that you'll ultimately find it good rather than bad). If you are practicing ERP as part of therapy, make sure to discuss your progress frequently with your therapist. And be honest. The old saying is true: If you report more improvement than you've actually made, you will, indeed, only be cheating yourself. Plus, you'll be depriving yourself of your therapist's support.

Getting Started

In some cases, your cognitive behavioral therapist may accompany you while you take on your feared task. She might, for instance, go into a hospital with you if you're afraid of hospitals and germs, walking closely by those whose white coats might signal danger to you. Perhaps she will calmly "model" certain other desired behaviors, such as petting a dog or discarding a newspaper, before encouraging you to follow suit.

You may well have more than one fear; for example, you might be afraid of germs and saying blasphemous things. Perhaps *several* things cause you excessive worry. (The longer your OCD has gone on, the more likely you are to have multiple fears, as anxiety is known to "generalize.") The good news is that as CBT begins to work, *all* fears tend to diminish. Just as the circle of anxiety gradually widened, so, with treatment, will it shrink over time.

Your Belief System

Another part of cognitive behavioral therapy for OCD is examining your belief system. Believe it or not, a big part of what's wrong is your thinking! Cognitive therapy is based on the notion that your thoughts drive your emotions. A psychologist would say that your "core beliefs" create your automatic (habitual) thinking, leading to a certain reflexive emotional response.

It may not seem so right away, but when you stop to consider this, you'll probably realize that your long- and firmly held beliefs have a lot to do with the way you feel. It's as if, over time, you've developed a "negative filter" that refracts the information you take in about the world around you in an anxious, worried direction.

Put a little more simply: You may worry, for example, that you are spreading germs to others, endangering their health or even their lives. A cognitive therapist can help you re-evaluate your thoughts and beliefs.

 Alert

Maybe you avoid difficult situations on days when you feel especially stressed or fragile. Generally speaking, this is not a good idea. Avoidance is a hallmark of anxiety disorders (and OCD specifically). In all probability, if you give in to your impulses, you'll end up avoiding your feared situations more and more often. Don't let down your guard. Treating OCD requires daily vigilance.

For instance, your therapist may ask you how it is that other relatively healthy individuals seem to pass through their social and professional circles without spreading wholesale infection to the people they encounter. Depending on your answer, another question, or series of them, may follow as the therapist helps you to arrive at a more realistic evaluation of your risk to others. You may eventually concede, after all this Socratic interaction, that you do not, in fact, pose a serious danger.

Do You Believe in Magic?

People who have OCD sometimes engage in "magical thinking," believing they can influence events that are actually beyond their control. Everyone probably does a little of this from time to time. You might pray that the people you care about do not come to harm. That is perfectly normal (even if several people who were close to you died in spite of your entreaties). But let us say you've discovered another seeming correlation: If you refrain from eating before phoning your mother, she will be well. Otherwise, you believe, she'll get sick. You probably know, on the face of it, that that's untrue, that no real correlation exists, yet you persist in this belief. Why? Well, that's simple, really: You've drawn an illogical conclusion. Your technique seems to have worked well in the past—that is, your mother has come to no harm yet—so, you reason, you must be doing something right. Of course, sadly, you are wrong. If life were that easy, so many more people would be alive and well that the planet would be overrun!

Thinking It Through

Your therapist can help you to redirect your thinking in a number of ways. Some of these might be painful, but only temporarily. For example, if you fear doing harm to your child, you might be encouraged to explore verbally and in depth exactly what you're afraid you might find yourself doing. In the huge majority of cases, a patient will realize after verbalizing her fears that she would not, in reality, act on any of them. Getting from Point A to Point B in such a case might cause the patient a great deal of distress. However, the expected reward would be a tremendous reduction in anxiety and OC symptoms. Well worth it, you'd have to agree! Very often, people who have OCD overestimate risk to a huge degree. Cognitive behavioral therapists are trained to gently confront these false, if tightly held, beliefs and estimations of risk. It is said that people thrive on the familiar, so confronting even a positive change may be hard. That means you have to work at it.

L. Essential

Unlike medication, behavioral therapy requires effort on your part. You must be committed, at least to a degree, to change, and you have to be willing to work at it. Achieving any change, even good change, can be difficult.

Beyond Therapy

Therapy may not have helped you in the past, but that in itself is not a reason to believe that it can do you no good now. Traditional or "talk" therapy, while helpful in that it gives anxious persons someone with whom to talk through their fears, has not been shown to be very effective against OCD in particular.

Or you may have chosen a cognitive behavioral therapist, but found that she was simply not the right match for you. Therapy is a lot like employment: There are many potential jobs and many possible candidates to fill them; some matches will be almost perfect, others not so good.

One important thing to keep in mind about CBT is that, with the help of your therapist (and later, ideally, on your own), you will need to maintain your gains. Don't neglect to continue to practice your newly learned beneficial behaviors—every day, if possible.

An Intensive Cure?

Some therapists offer "intensive" programs that work on the same principle as language immersion classes, promising quick results in very short amounts of time. However, unlike learning a language, the idea is to try to *un*learn undesirable behavior.

Will an intensive program work for you? Here is a question to consider: How much of your behavior are you willing to let go, and how soon? If you're determined to vanquish the problem, and soon, you may be able to get through the discomfort (which will probably be more intense than what you would experience in a weekly, or twice-weekly, therapy session). Also, see if you can speak with former clients, preferably those who completed the program a while ago. You want to make sure that, if you try this method, you will be able to maintain the progress you make.

Staying Power

Sometimes "intensive cures" are done on an in-patient basis. That is, you stay on the premises, usually a psychiatric hospital. This can be a plus if you want to conquer your symptoms quickly in a controlled environment, or a minus, as it will take you away from work, school, or your other usual activities, for the duration of the program (usually no more than a few weeks, sometimes much less; the length of your stay will likely depend on the severity of your symptoms and the dictates of your health insurance, if any).

Only you, of course, can tell whether an accelerated program might be right for you. If your symptoms are very bad, to the point that they're seriously impeding your work and home lives, or if you're ready to work intensively on the OCD immediately, this option may be worth serious consideration.

OCD Remedies

While some herbal preparations such as omega oils or St. John's wort (generally used against depression) are believed to be helpful in reducing anxiety, no over-the-counter or herbal remedy is currently approved for use on OCD, or believed to treat its symptoms. In 2002, the FDA issued a warning about kava kava, a Pacific island root believed to contain calming properties, reporting that use or overuse of the popular herb had been linked to reports of serious liver damage.

Neurofeedback—Retraining the Brain

Neurofeedback, a type of biofeedback also known as "brain biofeedback" or "EEG (electroencephalogram) biofeedback," is an alternative therapy that began in the 1920s but gained popularity in the late 1960s and early 1970s. It offers another option for treatment of OCD. Neurofeedback is a painless method whereby, after an evaluation by a trained clinician, one or two sensors (electrodes) are attached to the scalp (usually by a special paste) and the patient is seated in front of a computer. These electrodes are connected to an amplifier, which relays the patient's brainwave activity to the monitor. On the screen is a program that resembles a video game. The brainwave activity alone drives the game.

There are many kinds of games from which to choose; sometimes the patient selects which one he would like to use. Typical images include scenes that resemble driving down a placid highway or watching the scenery on a tranquil tropical island. However, the game is played solely with one's brain! The patient is not expected to do anything other than calmly focus on the screen, and is not connected to the computer except by the sensors on the head.

 # Question

Does neurofeedback hurt?
No. The electrodes or sensors only *measure* brainwave activity; they do not *apply* any electrical impulse. And they certainly don't read thoughts, as some anxious patients have wondered.

The computer measures the patient's brainwave activity, and some kind of reward—a pleasing image, game points, or a sound—usually accompanies any increase in calm, focused brainwaves. As the session progresses, the clinician observes the patient's brainwave activity and adjusts the reinforcement as necessary. Practitioners say this process reduces the repetitive, obsessional quality of thought known as "brain lock."

Over time—perhaps twenty to thirty half-hour sessions, sometimes more—the patient's brainwave activity should show a significant reduction in anxiety. (Repetition is necessary, as this form of "brain exercise" needs consistent reinforcement, just like physical exercise at the gym.) Gradually, the patient should be able to attain that state of calm on his own whenever needed.

Neurofeedback has not been definitively proven to reduce anxiety and OCD symptoms, but has so far shown promise, and there is anecdotal and case report evidence to support its use. Many therapists are enthusiastic about this option, which is also used to treat attention deficit hyperactivity disorder (ADHD), epilepsy, and other neurological and behavioral conditions. At least one recent study showed benefits retained at ten years post-treatment for ADHD, and many other patients have seen lasting gains.

Essential

In rare cases, neurosurgery might be considered for OCD. This option is almost always reserved for severe cases that do not respond to medication, CBT, or anything else. New techniques have made it possible to reduce the incidence of infection and other post-surgical complications, and are said to be painless. However, surgery can carry a risk of undesirable side effects.

As of this writing, most health plans do not cover neurofeedback alone, as the process is considered experimental. However, many will agree to cover it under the general procedure code for biofeedback. Some will pay for the treatment when it is done in conjunction with more traditional psychotherapy. This option may be a good one for people who are phobic about medications or unable to take them because of medical or physical conditions, including pregnancy or breastfeeding. Neurofeedback has no known lasting side effects, although some patients may feel a little "spacey" or experience other mild symptoms, such as fatigue, for perhaps an hour after the session.

Self-Help

A guided self-directed program might be useful if you cannot find a qualified behavioral therapist in your area or if you or your insurance cannot pay for one. (Or, indeed, if you do not have health insurance.) However, be aware that self-directed therapy comes with potential pitfalls, especially where a condition like OCD is concerned. Why? Unlike in the case of, say, smoking, you probably hold onto a small belief that your OC behaviors are serving you in some way by keeping you safe from harm and anxiety. While a habit like smoking presents the obstacle of physical dependence, you may find that you are *emotionally* attached to your obsessive ideas.

 Fact

Researchers at the University of Pisa in Italy believe that they have discovered a biological similarity between OCD and infatuation! Preliminary research found repetitive thoughts and lower-than-normal serotonin levels in both people with OCD and those in the early stages of romantic love.

If you choose the self-help route, you can find books and other programs, such as DVD or video courses. A DVD or video program may prove easier to follow than a written course. However, workbooks may provide a better way to record your progress.

Regardless of the treatment method you choose, make sure to enlist the help of your "community"—friends, significant others, and so on.

Other Therapy and Treatment Options

There are a few other possibilities you may want to consider. While CBT or medication (or both) probably offer your best hope, other therapies and treatments can be useful, especially if, because of financial, geographic, or emotional circumstance, you may want to try an alternative. For example, you could consider anxiety therapy or hypnosis. Other possible treatments for OCD include Eye Movement Desensitization and Reprocessing (EMDR), Thought-Field Therapy (TFT), and Electro-Convulsive Therapy (ECT). There are undoubtedly others. None of these, so far, has been proven to work against OCD, although most are probably harmless, and the modern form of ECT has shown some effectiveness against depression.

Anxiety Therapy

A growing number of therapists specialize in the treatment of anxiety alone. You might try a computer search including your geographical area, or ask a friend or another therapist for a referral.

As in any situation that involves engaging a professional, do your best to check the person's qualifications, either by asking, going online or speaking with one or two of the therapist's other patients, if possible.

Hypnotherapy

Occasionally, OCD is treated with hypnotherapy (hypnosis). Although we know of no specific studies about hypnosis for treating OCD, we do know that it can be used effectively against anxieties as well as habitual behaviors such as smoking. Given that OCD involves both anxiety and habitual behaviors, it stands to reason that any therapy that works on either of those would also work against OCD; certainly, as an adjunctive treatment, hypnosis may have much to offer. Contrary to widespread belief, hypnosis does not involve "going under." It is merely focused attention, very much like visualization.

Self-hypnosis or visualization might also offer some benefit, especially in reducing anxiety. There are several good books available on both subjects. Visualizations can help you to change disaster images into positive ones. Affirmations may help change your negative thinking and reassure you that you're relatively safe in the world.

Acupuncture

Acupuncture enjoys a loyal following, and some of its adherents find it beneficial in treating anxiety. As in any medical endeavor, choose qualified, licensed professionals. Seek a personal recommendation, if possible, and make sure you know you're getting unused needles. (Virtually all acupuncture practitioners today use disposable ones, so the risk of transferred infection is unlikely.)

CHAPTER 5

Medication

CERTAIN MEDICATIONS CAN BE enormously helpful in the treatment of OCD. Because OCD is primarily a neurochemical disorder, it only makes sense that working with the brain's chemistry would be a logical way to treat it. For more than twenty years, medication has been shown to be successful against the condition's more troubling symptoms. This chapter covers how OCD medications work, what results you can expect, potential side effects, and other important information.

Medical Advantages

Medication offers several advantages over other OCD therapies and treatments. In some cases, depending on your health plan (if you have one), it may be a less expensive option than weekly or twice-weekly therapy sessions, especially if you choose a therapist outside your plan (or, again, if you do not have a plan that covers mental health services). It may also be a good choice if you're unable to find a cognitive behavioral therapist in your area or on your plan.

Another advantage is time. You may not be willing, or able, to spend the time you need to diminish your symptoms step by step with CBT. You might find that you don't have sufficient motivation or patience to stick with a CBT regime. Contemplating CBT, specifically exposure and response prevention, may also frighten you to a degree that would make it impossible to begin. Your therapist might suggest that you try medication to help you tolerate beginning ERP, should you choose that type of therapy.

Different Kinds of Medication

Anafranil (generically known as clomipramine) has perhaps the longest history among drugs used to treat OCD. It is a tricyclic drug, meaning that it affects not only serotonin (the brain's so-called "feel good" chemical, the neurotransmitter responsible for boosting soothing feelings) but also dopamine and other brain chemicals. Anafranil may hold advantages for patients who want to go with the "tried and true." Some doctors, however, prefer to use newer medications, largely because they are believed to carry less risk of side effects. Most of these are antidepressants in the selective serotonin reuptake inhibitor (SSRI) class.

How Do SSRIs Work?

SSRI medications do not produce serotonin, but they can make more of it available in your brain. They do this by (selectively) inhibiting the reuptake of serotonin at the synapse, thereby allowing more of it to remain available to produce its calming effects. Any psychiatrist or psychopharmacologist should be able to explain the exact mechanics, if you're interested. SSRIs don't work for everyone, however; you may enjoy better results with another kind of medication.

Medications Used to Treat OCD

You will probably recognize many of these SSRI drug names as those of popular antidepressants. They include:

- Prozac (generically called fluoxetine)
- Luvox (fluvoxamine)
- Paxil (paroxetine)
- Zoloft (sertraline)
- Lexapro (escitalopram)
- Celexa (citalopram)
- Cymbalta (duloxetine)

Other medications that are neither quite SSRIs nor tricyclic anti-depressants include Effexor (generically, venlafaxine) and Remeron (mirtazapine). Effexor and Remeron are known as SNRIs, or sero-tonin-norepinephrine reuptake inhibitors; this means they act on both of these neurotransmitters.

 Alert

Effexor recently has been cited as potentially associated with greater-than-average risk of overdose (possibly fatal), particularly when used in combination with alcohol or other drugs. However, it is believed to present a *lower* risk than that seen with tricyclic antidepressants.

There are other medications as well. In some cases, your doctor may want to try a combination of two (or, rarely, more). However, make sure she knows what other medications, even over-the-counter ones, you may also be taking, as some drug interactions can be dangerous.

One newer medication that has shown promise in working against anxiety is BuSpar (buspirone). This can be used in concert with other medications to treat OCD.

Monoamine Oxidase Inhibitors (MAOIs)

A third class of medications called monoamine oxidase inhibitors or MAOIs is used occasionally when other treatments have failed. These drugs have been around much longer than the others mentioned but are much less commonly used now. They carry the risk of more serious side effects, cannot be combined with many other medications, and come with dietary restrictions as well, so they are rarely used for treating OCD.

When Do They Take Effect?

Unfortunately, the full benefits you receive from your medication will not likely "kick in" for a few weeks (perhaps as many as six to twelve). However, if you are going to experience side effects, you will probably feel those right away. Of course, you should discuss any side effects with your doctor so you can decide whether to stick with the prescribed medication or try something else. You might be advised that the side effects may well diminish over time, and if they are tolerable in the short term, this could prove an acceptable course of action. On the other hand, if you experience unpleasant side effects, such as vomiting, you ought to talk with your doctor right away.

Essential

Certain medications, such as Cymbalta, can present a greater-than-average risk for liver problems to patients who already have liver disease or use alcohol regularly, so discuss your general health and lifestyle with your provider. (You can find out whether you have liver problems by taking a blood test for liver function. You may also be advised to have regular monitoring for this, depending on your individual circumstances.)

Always make sure you know how to "go off" your medicine should you wish to do so. Many prescriptions require the user to taper off gradually to avoid serious problems, so don't just stop taking a medication without consulting your doctor.

Common Physical Side Effects

Unfortunately, virtually all medications come with the possibility of side effects. You might not have any, or those you do experience may be temporary or very mild. You will need to talk with your doctor before taking any medication to find out exactly what the potential side effects might be.

Many so-called "nuisance" side effects go away within the first few weeks. Others may diminish over months as your body becomes used to the medication. Side effects are by no means certain to occur. Some people do not experience any. Others experience symptoms that can be managed easily or are mild enough to cause no significant discomfort.

If you do experience side effects, but find that yours are fairly minimal, you may want to "tough it out" to give the medication a chance to work. Otherwise, schedule an appointment with your doctor as soon as possible so that you can plan your next step. Do not allow a brief setback to discourage you from pursuing treatment once you have begun to move forward in dealing with your OCD.

Headaches

Headaches are a fairly common side effect of medication. However, they often diminish, if not disappear entirely, as one's body adjusts to the medication. Most headaches can be treated with standard over-the-counter remedies. There are also relaxation exercises that may help.

Non-Medicinal Headache Cure

One technique that seems to work remarkably well on headaches (as well as other kinds of pain) is this:

Close your eyes and sit or lie in a relaxed position. On a scale of one to ten (one being not-so-bad, ten being worst-ever), rate the severity of your headache. Next, ask yourself the following questions, keeping your eyes closed and your position relaxed. Before going on to the next question, make sure you've fully answered the one before it:

- Where is the headache? (Don't point; figure out in words exactly where the pain is.)
- What size is it? (Again, don't use your hands to illustrate. Give it a size in inches or centimeters, or use an image, such as a tangerine.)
- Describe its shape.
- How far in does it go?
- Describe its color. (Yes, it will have a color.)

Within three repetitions (usually less), the headache should be gone.

There are many other good pain visualizations (and many books in which you can find them, such as *Visualization for Change* by Patrick Fanning). Just closing your eyes and relaxing for a few minutes may also help to assuage headache pain.

Acupressure Headache Cure

Another good, and quick, way to relieve a headache without medication is to grasp the skin between the thumb and forefinger between those same two fingers on your other hand. If the headache is on the left side, grasp the right hand, and vice versa. Choose the part of the hand farther in, toward the wrist, and press hard for several seconds. It will help relax the muscles associated with the headache if you breathe slowly and deeply as you are pressing the "headache spot." A third method is to press firmly just above the wrist, on the thumb side.

Fatigue

Because most of these medications affect serotonin, the "calming" brain chemical (which also has to do with regulating sleep cycles), fatigue is not an uncommon side effect. Usually, your system will get used to the medication within a few weeks, and this will no longer be a problem. In the meantime, you and your doctor might decide it's best for you to take your medication a few hours before bedtime so that you can benefit from any mild sedation by getting a good night's sleep.

You might also find it helpful to have a little coffee or cola during the day, but take care: Caffeine can significantly increase anxiety. Some teas and soy drinks contain low amounts of caffeine and might be preferable. Better still, some exercise during the day—ideally, a brisk walk, at the very least—should bring your energy level up naturally.

Keep a close eye on diet, as well: High-protein, low-fat choices such as eggs, fish, lean chicken breast, or small quantities of nuts can also help keep you more energetic throughout the day. Avoid starchy foods such as potatoes or white bread, as those carb-heavy choices can make you sleepy. You'll also want to avoid high-sugar treats, which will probably just make you feel revved up and possibly anxious at first, and then tired later.

 Alert

Antidepressants, including many of the most popular, have been shown to increase suicidal thoughts and actions sometimes in teens and children. If you are seeking treatment for child or teen OCD or depression, get the facts. Talk with medical professionals and learn as much as you can before deciding on a medication. Make sure to provide appropriate follow-up and monitoring.

Sleep Disturbances

If your new medication is keeping you from getting a good night's sleep, you may simply be able to change the time of day at which you take it. Talk with your doctor. She may also be able to prescribe a temporary mild sleep aid that will not conflict with the OCD medicine.

Simple relaxation exercises or a calming bedtime routine might also help you to enjoy a full night's rest. General sleep advice includes choosing the same bedtime each night so that your body gets used to going to sleep then, and refraining from vigorous exercise (gentle stretches are okay, and may even be beneficial) or reading stimulating books right before bed.

Your bed, most insomnia experts advise, should be used only for sleeping or sex, so that you associate it with rest and tranquility. You might also try to turn off repetitive restless thoughts by replacing them with more benign ones. Thinking of, and perhaps even visualizing, a beautiful, peaceful place, whether real or imagined, in all its calming and restful detail, can often be sleep inducing. Some people find it helpful to play passive types of word games, such as "A, My Name Is Alice": ("A, my name is Alice, and my husband's name is Art. We come from Arkansas and we sell apples. B, my name is Bonnie and my husband's name is Brad . . ."). These kinds of thoughts generally do not unduly tax or overstimulate the brain. If you find that they do, switch to something else.

 Fact

> One rather common side effect is increased dream activity. You may discover that your dreams take on a more vivid or active quality. You may also find that you have been more physically active while asleep than you are used to. This is harmless (although if it causes you distress, you might want to evaluate how well your medication is working for your OCD). However, some antidepressants, though not those primarily used to treat OCD, can cause a greater-than-average incidence of nightmares.

Another tactic often suggested is to avoid staying in bed for more than thirty minutes or so if you find that you can't fall asleep. Rather than toss and turn, it might be more helpful to get up and engage in a boring, repetitive task, such as cleaning out drawers or paying bills. Keep a mindless task or two at hand for those times when you just can't sleep; a short while at one of these, and your bed—and sleep—may become entirely appealing again!

Nausea or Vomiting

Nobody likes to feel queasy—or worse. Taking your medication with a little bit of food or at certain times of day might help offset this problem. Eating or drinking ginger-containing products may help, but read the label, and do not have more than 1000 mg (one gram) of ginger in a day. If the nausea persists, get in touch with your doctor without delay. You should be able to change the dosage or type of medication.

Certain medications seem more likely to cause one side effect than others. One might be more closely associated with appetite changes, for instance, and another with insomnia or fatigue. Although many of the newer drugs pose less risk of side effects than their older counterparts, not all medications work for all patients, which is why the older drugs are still used, as well. Discuss the side effect profile of any proposed medications with your doctor to address these specifics in terms of how they relate to you.

 Alert

If you're having problems with vomiting or excessive diarrhea or nausea, talk with your doctor as soon as you can. Adding physical misery or poor nutrition to your problems will definitely not be therapeutic.

Diarrhea

Drink plenty of liquids to replace the fluid your body has lost. Vitamin or sport drinks can be especially helpful. An over-the-counter preparation might be beneficial, as well. (However, some physicians might advise against this.) As in all cases, consult your doctor or pharmacist before taking any additional medicines. When you're ready to eat, start slowly and gently. Saltines, white rice, dry toast, and tea are soothing foods for a troubled stomach, and unlikely to overtax it. If the situation persists for longer than a day, or if you also have a fever, get medical advice quickly.

Constipation

Your best bet for handling this may just be to employ common folk wisdom: drinking prune juice and eating high-fiber foods such as fruits and vegetables, popcorn, beans, and bran-containing whole grain-breads or muffins. Drink plenty of water. Over-the-counter preparations are not recommended for use over long periods of time.

Excessive Perspiration (Hyperhidrosis)

Obviously, hyper-perspiration is also not much fun. On the plus side, it is a less troubling side effect than some in that it is mostly just a nuisance (although, at its worst, it can be socially disabling).

 Alert

If you tend toward low blood pressure, you might want to take extra care with tricyclics and other medicines known to affect blood pressure, particularly if you are older. Lowered blood pressure or diarrhea, if it has caused too much dehydration, can be responsible for dizziness. Some medications cause dizziness even without those other symptoms. One way to combat this is to stay well hydrated.

Beyond carrying a handkerchief, taking extra showers, and making sure not to neglect the use of a good antiperspirant or deodorant, there are limited choices for dealing with this problem. A dermatologist can prescribe a topical gel to help control it. Only you can know whether this side effect is bad enough to cause a re-evaluation of your meds, or whether it's worth putting up with when you consider the benefits.

Changes in Appetite

One thing you may notice once you begin your medication is an increased craving for sweets. This is not necessarily your imagination. Some medications do increase carbohydrate cravings. A very sensible way to combat this is to choose foods that give some illusion of sweetness without a lot of sugar and calories.

Low-fat yogurt, bananas, strawberries, sweet potatoes, oatmeal with low-fat milk and a handful of raisins, and cold cereal (choose a crispy rice or grain cereal with minimal sweetener) can help you to satisfy sweet-food cravings. Fruit "smoothies"—fresh fruit blended with skim or low-fat milk—can also help take the edge off. Many Web sites offer weight-loss (or maintenance) tips along with healthful and nutritious recipes. Don't neglect exercise, either. It can help reduce appetite and weight gain.

Sexual Side Effects

Like many other kinds of drugs, the medication you use to treat your OCD may present what are known as "sexual side effects": delayed or non-existent orgasm or erection, decreased (or, less commonly, increased) interest in sex, and other concerns. There are several possible solutions.

First of all, you *must* talk with your doctor before stopping or making any changes to your medication. Don't feel uncomfortable discussing these things—your doctor has almost certainly heard them before.

Some patients find that they can "go off" their SSRIs on weekends so that they can at least enjoy sex during that time. Others find a change in medication or dosage works in their favor. Remember, these problems are not uncommon, and they are not impossible to solve.

Less Common Physical Side Effects

There are a few other possible physical side effects; however, please keep in mind that these are pretty rare. They may have happened to some people and hence are reported in the medical literature and on the package insert, but that doesn't mean that they will necessarily happen to you. For example, some medications can cause hand tremors. These can often be treated with the addition of beta-blockers or other medications. The following are some other uncommon side effects.

Urinary Retention

Urinary retention is also possible, though unusual. This condition should be monitored because it can lead to urinary tract infections and other problems. (It's also not much fun on its own.) Urinary retention can be treated with other medicines. Don't neglect grandma's advice about cranberry juice, either. Try to drink a glass each day, and choose a juice that has as little refined sugar as possible. As in any similar case, you and your doctor will need to decide whether the medication's benefits outweigh its side effects when deciding whether to stay on your OCD medication.

Blurred Vision

This side effect is generally temporary. A change in dosage, a prescription eye-drop or a supplemental medication may help to ease the problem. Also, don't neglect to have your eyes examined by your eye-care professional, just in case.

L. Essential

Any reported side effects noted during the time your medication was being tested for use in humans was reported, so if one person complained of headache, for instance, that potential side effect appears on the information that accompanies your prescription from the pharmacy. The higher the incidence of a reported side effect—that is, the more people who complained of it—the higher up in the package information it will appear.

Rashes and Allergies

It is also possible, though unlikely, that you will develop rashes or other allergic reactions to your medication (possibly from the dye in the pills). In most instances, these are not serious, but should be looked into, just in case. (FYI: a *compounding pharmacy* should be able to mix your medication without dye. You may need to go online to find one, or you can ask your regular pharmacy for a recommendation.)

Memory Loss

Some antidepressant users report slight memory deficits during the time that they use certain medications. (Severe depression has been known to cause this, as well.) This symptom seems to be temporary. Most users find that any memory loss is not sufficient to warrant a change in medication (although, you, of course, may feel otherwise). One tip for handling this problem, should it arise, is to make an extra effort at organization, writing down anything you absolutely have to remember. Memory exercises might also prove helpful.

Emotional Side Effects

So far, we've talked about several of the potential *physical* side effects involved in treating OCD with medicines. Some side effects can include *emotional* changes, as well. In other words, sad to say, your anxiety symptoms may get worse! You may feel a greater than normal amount of fear, for instance, or sadness or other mood changes. (And, of course, your anxiety about starting to take medication in the first place may come into play.) It's important to stay in touch with your prescribing doctor and any therapist you may have, so that you can get the support you need, as well as help for the immediate psychological problem.

Nervousness

Some medications, most notably SSRIs, can increase anxiety or cause restlessness or agitation. (Indeed, at first you may not be able to tell whether you're more jittery or just experiencing your usual anxiety.) In some cases, your doctor might try decreasing your dosage for a short time, gradually bringing it back to its original level if necessary. Some people are just more medication-sensitive than others, so trial and error might be the only way to determine how well you tolerate the medication in question.

Fearing the Worst

It's natural to feel some anxiety about taking medication, especially when you're reading about all the potential side effects! However, it's important to realize that you might not experience any of these. Or you may find that you have one or two mildly annoying symptoms, but that the benefits of living a happier, less fearful life far outweigh them.

Over the last twenty to thirty years, many people who have OCD have been helped (in some cases, tremendously) by medication. Also, keep in mind that giving medication a try does not mean that you have to take it for life, or even for very long. Trying medication is by no means an irrevocable decision. If you do decide you'd like to do so, and later find that you have disconcerting side effects or grave misgivings, you can certainly stop taking it—with your doctor's guidance, of course.

How to Use Medications

Taking medication for OCD can greatly improve your quality of life, but it's not a decision to be made lightly. As you now know, some medications are powerful and can have a strong effect on you. Make sure you discuss all possibilities in depth with your doctor. Also, be sure to keep your doctor up to speed on your progress. If you're having trouble with one drug, she can guide you toward another one to try. If you're having success, she can monitor you and make sure you don't backslide or experience other difficulties down the road.

Your Doctor and You

Don't be afraid of looking foolish or taking up your doctor's time. If you don't understand something, ask for clarification. Make sure you understand dosages, potential side effects, and procedures for changing medications should you want or need to. (Your pharmacist is also a potential source of excellent information about your medications; don't hesitate to call and ask questions.)

If you do not feel as if you enjoy good communication or rapport with your doctor, don't be afraid to make a change. You may be concerned about hurting your doctor's feelings, or reluctant to "start all over again" with someone new. Or you might fear that your new doctor will understand you even less. Any of these is possible, of course, but you may also find better compatibility with your new health care provider. (And you should never stay with the wrong doctor out of concern for hurting her feelings. That isn't your responsibility. In any case, a good doctor should know that not all patients respond to the same personal style.)

Occasional-Use Medications

You and your health care professional may decide that you would benefit from a medication that you take "as needed" instead of every day. It's important to keep in mind that these drugs will *not* get rid of your OCD. However, they might be able to help you to calm down when you're particularly stressed, or to sleep when you otherwise could not.

 Fact

> It is possible that at some point your OCD medication may not work as well as it once did. This is rare and can usually be corrected with an increase in dosage, a supplemental medication, or a change in the type of medicine.

Such medications can carry a risk of dependency or even addiction. You might also notice that they become less effective the more often they are used. These drugs include: Xanax (alprazolam), Valium (diazepam), and Ativan (lorazepam). Given the sedative nature of these medications (which are known as benzodiazepines), drowsiness may be expected. Pay serious attention to package information about driving and other physical activities in conjunction with these medications, and remember that alcohol use may increase their effects or even prove harmful.

In some cases, benzodiazepines can make users, especially those unaccustomed to taking them, a little "high." Taking them with food, or lowering the dosage, can help mitigate this effect.

Better Together

Many patients have found that medication or CBT alone are not as effective as both together. Medication can help you to achieve your CBT goals faster, and behavior therapy can enhance the value of your medicine. You will, of course, need to stay in close touch with the doctor who administers your medication, even if you are also working with a cognitive behavioral therapist. Another advantage of working with a therapist is that you should be able to keep better track of your progress. Therapy sessions generally run longer than doctor visits and are held more often (usually at least once a week).

In some cases, patients stay on medication after completing a course of CBT. In others, they are able to stop or to use a lower dosage to maintain their progress. It all depends on your personal desires and needs as the patient.

CHAPTER 6

The Therapy Route

YOU'VE READ IN DETAIL about the medication option. Now it's time to learn more about therapy treatment for OCD. If you decide to look into therapy, you'll need to think about the type of therapy or therapist you want to look for. When you begin work with your therapist, you and she can decide together whether medication might be a good option for you, as well. As you read earlier in the book, there are a few different types of therapies and several good ways to find the right therapist for you. This chapter covers much of what you need to know.

The Decision to Try Therapy

Before you do anything else, make sure you are clear about what you hope to gain from therapy. If you want help for family problems, for instance, you'll probably want to look for a therapist who deals with those kinds of issues. If your primary goal is to get help for your OCD, you will likely want to look for a therapist who specializes in cognitive behavioral therapy for OCD or anxiety disorders. Some therapists look at both the OCD and the patient's day-to-day life and challenges. You might want a therapist who works on both the OCD and the other things that are going on in your life, as personal events and situations can affect OCD (as well as other conditions).

The majority of people who have OCD suffer from depression as well. Another common problem is the strain OC behavior can put on close relationships. Spouses, children, friends, and parents of people who have OCD often have a very hard time with it, as its symptoms can cause disruption in their lives and therefore create considerable stress. If you are also experiencing depression or family problems, discuss these with your therapist, or would-be therapist, as well. You should be able to get help for all three problems.

As discussed in Chapter 4, there are several types of therapy available to treat OCD. Although cognitive behavioral therapy (CBT) is most often recommended, you may decide, for any number of reasons, that you would prefer to give neurofeedback, or hypnotherapy, or another option, a try instead. (Remember, you can always try something else if you don't get what you need the first time.)

 Alert

Don't let a therapist or counselor tell you that your OCD was caused by parental mistakes, abuse, and so on. That old-fashioned idea is no longer credible in educated circles. Look for a cognitive behavioral therapist instead. You'll almost certainly enjoy more success against your OCD.

If you decide on a "talk" therapy, you will probably want to narrow your choice down further into type. For instance, some therapists do CBT. Others psychoanalyze. Still others practice what they call "interpersonal therapy" and work primarily on the patient's relationships. Other therapists will describe themselves according to different disciplines. We recommend a cognitive behavioral therapist—ideally, one who has had lots of experience (and success) in treating patients who have OCD.

How to Start

Often, a good way to find a capable therapist is to ask friends for referrals. If a friend feels his therapist has helped him, he will probably make a recommendation confidently (unless, for some reason, he spends a lot of time at the therapist's talking about you, in which case, it would be better for both of you to see different providers).

However, unless your friend also has OCD, it's not necessarily likely that his therapist will be the right one for you. So what do you do?

Psychiatrist, Psychologist, or What?

If you are considering treating your symptoms with medication, or a combination of medicine and therapy, you might feel a little stuck when it comes to getting started.

First, let's try to clarify: As you may know, a psychiatrist can prescribe medication, while a psychologist cannot. (There are also licensed clinical social workers. They do not prescribe, either.) However, two things a psychiatrist probably will not do are work with you on reducing your OC symptoms (except inasmuch as medication can do that) or spend a lot of time with you. A clinical therapist (one who sees patients)—psychologist, psychiatric nurse, or social worker—will probably do both.

Of course, if you would like to use medication in conjunction with therapy (a very smart idea), you can engage a psychologist for CBT and a psychiatrist or psycho-pharmacologist for your prescription. (Your psychologist can probably recommend a doctor who can prescribe medication for you. In a way, this provides kind of a nice little checks-and-balances system: Both professionals will have to agree on your diagnosis before anything is prescribed.)

╚ Essential

Don't get discouraged. Finding a therapist may take a surprising amount of time and energy, and require that you make a number of calls. Keep in mind the adage, "Present pain for future gain." Once the initial time outlay is past, you might find you've discovered a long-term therapeutic relationship.

You will likely meet with your psychiatrist, psycho-pharmacologist, or doctor on a regular, but not necessarily frequent, basis to assess how well your medication is working. Generally, appointments with your prescribing doctor will take place more frequently at first, then taper off if your medication seems to be doing its job. You will still need to see your prescribing doctor every so often after that, just to make sure that all is working as it should.

Your sessions with the prescribing doctor will probably be short, perhaps as brief as ten minutes all told! You should use your appointment time to discuss any concerns you may have about your medication, in addition to how well it seems to be working (or not). Of course, if you should have any problems with it before your next scheduled appointment, by all means, make another appointment for a sooner time—or, at the very least, get in touch with your provider over the phone. That's what he's there for.

Getting to the Bottom of It

There are many kinds of therapy. However, many traditional psychological therapies rely on insights to help bring resolutions to problems. In the case of OCD, all the insights in the world will not necessarily suffice. An OC patient may know what triggered his OCD, but that usually has little, or nothing, to do with treating it.

(As discussed in Chapter 3, the condition is not believed to be "caused" by events, but rather by brain chemistry, usually hereditary. Often, a traumatic event *can* set off the first major episode in predisposed persons, but that does not mean the disorder itself is brought about by that one thing, or even by several things. Similarly, some researchers say that a childhood marked by strict rules can foster the development of OCD. Even so, it is now understood as a neurological disorder, and not the result of early trauma.)

Finding a Cognitive Behavioral Therapist

It is recommended that you get started by looking for a therapist who is familiar with, and practiced in, CBT. How do you find a cognitive behavioral therapist? There are several good possibilities. The following sections present a few.

Speak with Your Insurance Company or Employee Assistance Program (EAP)

If you have health insurance and it covers mental health services, you can call the help number and explain that you are looking for a cognitive behavioral therapist who can treat OCD. Don't take "no" for an answer, by the way. Depending on your state of residence, your health maintenance organization (HMO) or insurance company may be obligated to provide you with appropriate care for your condition. Explain calmly, clearly, and patiently that you are looking for a therapist who treats OCD or anxiety disorders. If you work for a company that has an employee assistance program (EAP), you can also call their help line with the same request. Or, your company EAP may send you to a counselor, who can then recommend a cognitive therapist.

Search the OC Foundation

By logging on to the OC Foundation's Web site (OCFoundation. org) and doing some minimal searching, you can find and browse a list of providers in your area. You'll be prompted for the city or county and state in which you're searching. You will be asked to register, but it is free, safe, and confidential to do so. If you're not comfortable providing your name, a nickname should be fine. You will have to give an e-mail address, however. Doing so did not cause a problem for us when we tried it. (The site does offer opt in/out for e-newsletters, but the organization is a non-profit and pledges not to share your information with anyone else.)

 Fact

The OC Foundation's list consists of providers who have given their names. The Foundation does not evaluate these therapists; it only lists them. That said, the roster contains the names of several well-known professionals in the field of OCD and related disorders.

Armed with a list of providers, you'll have to start making calls. You will likely need to use some patience. Some of the therapists you call will probably not be seeing new patients, or they won't accept your particular health insurance. Do not despair. One therapist may be able to recommend another. After a few calls, you should enjoy more luck.

School Services

If you're in school, confidential mental health services should be offered. If you're not sure how to avail yourself of them, check your student handbook or ask your adviser. In most, if not all, cases, full-time students are required to have health insurance, whether through their parents or purchased through the college or university, so you should be able to go off campus, as well, should you choose to. (That said, if your school offers a more convenient program, you might want to check it out, assuming it meets your needs in terms of providers, hours, and location.) Even if you're not yet in college, you may be able to obtain confidential help for OCD, although we do hope you're able to discuss your situation with your parents or guardian.

Your Other Providers

You can also get referrals from your regular doctor, your clergyperson, or even your local hospital (depending on its the size and location, many hospitals, mental hospitals, and other health facilities in larger cities have OCD centers). You can also check your local phone book. It should provide listings under "mental health services."

Another great resource is your local university or teaching hospital. Most of the larger schools will have a department of psychology, psychiatry, or related disciplines. Some of these will have clinics or offer sliding scale payment options. (That is, the patient pays according to income level.)

If you don't have an EAP, school counseling service, health insurance, or a plan that covers mental health, another possible resource is the U.S. Department of Health and Human Services' Bureau of Primary Care. Visit the Department's Web page at *www.ask.hrsa.gov/pc* and click on "mental health and substance abuse." You will be asked for your geographical area. Once you type in your state and county or city, you should see a list of free or low-cost providers and facilities in your area. You can get more information at *www.ask.hrsa.gov*. Please note, however, that these listings pertain to mental health in general and not to OCD in particular, so not all of the information will apply (or necessarily be up-to-date).

Making Your Choice

Once you have a name or have made an appointment, it might not be a bad idea to search the Web for information about your would-be provider, as you would for any professional you were planning to hire. You probably don't want to make a lifetime study out of this; you just want to make sure that the person's name doesn't come up repeatedly in connection with more than one questionable incident.

Why This Is Important

When you stop to think about it, choosing a therapist is an important decision, one that has the potential to greatly affect your health and well-being. Therapy may become, for a time (probably a matter of months, if not years) a very important part of your life.

You will likely spend a lot of time talking with your therapist and, when not actually in her office, doing the exercises she gives you and thinking about the work you do together. You can always make a change down the road if you need to (and you should, if your therapeutic relationship is not working out) but it's better, of course, if you can choose wisely the first time.

A Question of Style

Once you've narrowed your list (ideally) to a provider (or to one or two), you'd be well advised to talk with him to get an idea about whether and how well you might work together. You can talk on the phone before making an appointment, or make the appointment and bring a list of questions. It's usually a good idea to schedule an initial "trial" session to get a sense of whether you and the therapist will be "compatible"—that is, whether your communication styles mesh, whether you are on the same "wavelength," and what kind of impression you get about the therapist's approach, conversational style, and ability to help you. A therapist who has the best professional reputation in the world will only be helpful to you if the both of you can work and communicate effectively together.

 Alert

One impediment to your treatment might be a friend, roommate, or spouse who has unwittingly become your "enabler," providing you with ready reassurance. This, as you might imagine, can slow your progress in learning to confront your fears actively, potentially causing your therapy to stall.

Getting It Right the First Time

Many therapists consider the first few sessions a mutual evaluation period: In addition to assessing your symptoms, the therapist will probably devote some time to addressing the question of whether you will be able to work well and comfortably together. Between your first meeting and the next, you might want to give some thought to your interactions and comfort level so that you can discuss any concerns you might have. In the case of an obviously poor fit, the therapist might be able to refer you to a colleague.

Asking the Right Questions

You are perfectly within your rights—and, in fact, would be well advised—to talk with your potential therapist before starting your work together. Here are some questions you might want to ask (keep in mind that there aren't necessarily any "right" answers):

- **What is your professional orientation?** Does the therapist practice CBT? Is she holistic—that is, does she consider the whole patient: physical health conditions, family and work situations, and so forth, or does she look almost exclusively at the OCD?
- **Are you state licensed?** You might want to hear a "yes." This designation should give you extra reassurance; it's a requirement for clinical practice in most states.
- **Are you board certified?** Keep in mind that many highly trained, competent psychologists are not. Board certified psychologists have applied for certification (verification) of their rigorous training by the American Board of Professional Psychology (ABPP), though their training is generally no different from that of their non-certified counterparts.
- **How much experience do you have in treating OCD?** Also, what kinds of OCD does he usually see? (The second question will matter less, as success in treating one type of OCD will likely indicate ability to treat other types.)
- **How do you feel about medication?** (You don't necessarily have to agree on this, but it will probably be better for you if your therapist is at least open to the possibility.)
- **How long do you think my treatment would take?** You might not want to ask this until you meet, as it may be a difficult question to answer before you have discussed your symptoms in detail. Any number of factors will probably determine the response: How entrenched is your OC behavior? How long have you had it? Do you have other problems in addition to the OCD? If so, how serious are they in nature? And so on.

How to Tell If Your Treatment is Working

In most cases, CBT (and, for that matter, medication, or both together) will work gradually. It may take a while for you to notice any progress.

One way for you to measure your improvement is to write down your symptoms. Rating their severity on a one-to-ten scale can be helpful, and may enable you to see small changes as they occur. You might do this with your therapist or on your own.

 Question

Will I ever be able to stop taking my medication?
Quite possibly. If you've been making progress with CBT, it may be fine for you to stop taking your OCD medication. Ask your prescribing doctor and therapist, who will help you slowly discontinue any medications that require you to decrease dosages gradually before stopping altogether.

Checking Your Own Progress

Start by writing down a list of the things and situations you fear, or (for example, in the case of cleaning rituals) those that cause you discomfort. If you can, use the psychologist method of "rating" the anxiety you feel about each one on a scale of one to ten (ten being strongest, one being not so bad). Check back weekly to measure your current level of discomfort with those objects or circumstances, and expect to see it subsiding. This should give you a good idea of how well your treatment is working (or not). If you feel as if you are enjoying a good rapport with your therapist and are making progress, of course you will want to continue. If you definitely feel the opposite, you will undoubtedly want to explore other options. However, if you're not certain whether your therapy is working, you may simply want to give it some more time (and possibly extra effort), and evaluate it again a little later.

Simultaneously, you may want to talk with your therapist specifically about what you feel isn't working well enough, or what areas, if any, you would rather focus on. Therapy, especially one-on-one, should be flexible enough to allow for changes and adjustments.

Alert

> If you feel "stuck" in your therapy, do discuss your feelings with your therapist. Also, ask yourself honestly whether it's a bad professional match or whether you're resistant to treatment for some other reason, such as fear of doing the prescribed CBT.

Will It Ever Go Away?

Although OCD can be managed very effectively, it's unlikely that it will ever actually "go away" completely. However, it's more than likely that your OCD can "go away enough" so that it won't continue to make problems for you. That is, you might, for example, be able to pick up objects that have fallen on the floor, but still not feel comfortable taking off your shoes and running around barefoot on the carpet. You may in time be able to discard a greater number of useless things, but not become exactly monastic in your living style. It's a matter of degrees.

Most likely, your OCD can be managed to the point at which it's no longer a big problem for you. OCD is considered a chronic condition, but it does not have to remain debilitating. (And who knows? Not that long ago, OCD was considered absolutely hopeless.) Treating OCD successfully is kind of like turning a lion into a housecat: It will still be there; it just won't be dangerous or disruptive, at least to the same degree that it once was.

A Few Alternatives to CBT

Unfortunately, there are still not as many therapists who specifically treat OCD as there ought to be. However, if you are unable to find a cognitive behavioral therapist, there are still some things you can try. You could see a "regular" psychologist who is willing to study up on CBT techniques. Particularly if you plan to try medication in addition to your therapy, this can be a good choice.

Some therapists specialize in anxiety, but not specifically OCD. An anxiety therapist may be a good starting point and will have many useful skills for addressing your OCD.

Essential

You might also want to consider whether you'll be more comfortable with a male or a female therapist. In some cases, it will make no difference. However, if you feel self-conscious about, say, unwanted sexual thoughts, you may find it easier to talk with a therapist of your own sex.

There are a number of good self-help programs available if you can't find a provider who practices CBT. (A few of these are listed in Appendix A.) However, you might want to undertake such programs with the cooperation of a psychologist because ERP programs can be hard to follow on your own, just as any skill is usually easier to learn in a class than by yourself.

You might even want to consider telephone sessions with a cognitive behavioral therapist, especially if you can find one who practices just outside of the distance you are willing or able to travel. This way, you might be able to meet in person, say, once a month, and work by phone once a week, besides. Good long-distance phone plans are easier to come by these days than low-cost gasoline!

You might also want to consider an intensive in-patient program. Although such a program might not be available in your immediate area, a one-time trip may make more sense for you, from a geographic standpoint, than a long-term arrangement. If you have vacation time coming to you from work or school, or some time between jobs, this might be a good way to use it. The other advantage, of course, is that intensive treatments can work much more quickly than traditional ones.

CHAPTER 7

The World Around You

WHETHER YOU'VE THOUGHT ABOUT it or not, if you have OCD, chances are your ritual or avoidance behaviors are affecting the people in your life. Some of your friends may have expressed concern. Coworkers may have acted curious or puzzled. Your symptoms might have caused problems for you at work or at school, or in one or more of your friendships or family relationships. Or perhaps the strain of hiding your behaviors, or the anticipation of more stressful situations, may be causing you undue anxiety. It might be time to decide whether to share, and with whom, and when to take other people's opinions to heart.

Time to Take Action

The old saying goes, "If three people say you're drunk, you should lie down," meaning that if enough people tell you the same thing, you might want to listen. The people around you may serve a more valuable purpose than you know. If important people in your life are telling you that they're worried about you or that your behavior alarms them in some way, you might want to give their words some weight. It may be time to seek help.

You probably know that, in today's world, there's no stigma attached to therapy, medication, or other treatments, and that everyone needs help at some time or another. Life is hard. Life with OCD can be especially so.

If you need a little (or more than a little) help, there is nothing wrong with getting it. In fact, you could be letting yourself in for many problems if you don't. As you probably know from having read this far, OCD grows. Without treatment, it generally gets worse. As with most disorders, the quicker you catch it and arrest it, the quicker you can get it to retreat, and the better your chances of success at conquering it. If friends, family, and others close to you are making the suggestion that you do something about your symptoms, it's probably time to listen. (Oh, and chances are that, with treatment, you'll end up feeling much better and far less anxious than you would otherwise. And that will improve not only your life in general, but also your interpersonal relationships in particular.)

L. Essential

Keep a close eye on your own behavior. Whenever you find yourself considering doing something that might be fun, or at least harmless, ask yourself the following question, and make sure to respond with absolute honesty: "Would I be able to do this activity without anyone helping me?" If the answer is yes, or even maybe, go for it, unassisted. It's always better to fly on your own if you can.

Your OC anxieties may get in the way. You might find that you're fearful, for any number of reasons, about getting treatment. That's okay. You can give it a try. If you make a decision to visit a therapist even once, that's one more time than none at all.

Using Modifications

Modification for dealing with OCD is a controversial concept. Some folks will argue—and they have a point—that making modifications allows you to hold onto your same old OC behaviors comfortably, giving you little motivation for change. Others will tell you that anything that gets you out and doing things that feel a bit outside of your "comfort zone" or participating in activities you used to enjoy, are all to the good. Here's the main caution: Don't allow yourself to get too comfortable if you do decide to use one or more modifications.

Alert

> Modifications should be regarded as steppingstones—transitional moves—and not as ends in themselves. Once you can do without your particular modification, try to go back to your pre-OC way of doing things.

Modification simply means adapting yourself to your situation in any reasonable way you can. Examples of modifications might include things like:

- Having someone come to your home to cut your hair *if* you're afraid to go out and have it done and are therefore *not getting your hair cut at all.*
- Traveling with a stadium chair *if* that's the only way you'll get out to concerts, plays, and other performances. (Remember, you should do this only if *not* doing so would prevent you from participating in the activity in question.)
- Choosing a coupe when renting a car to reduce your door-checking time by half.

Modification may mean doing something like buying your own dental tools so you can have your teeth cleaned, rather than staying away from the dentist's office for years, if not longer. If you're seeing a therapist, modifications would be a good thing to bring up with her. Keep in mind, however, that your therapist may disagree with them in principle.

You Decide

Let's assume, for just this moment, that you would like to try modifications with an eye toward making overall progress. Only you will know what types to choose for yourself—although you may not know, right away, exactly what modifications to use. You might have to give your particular fears a lot of thought before coming up with solutions. Strange as it may sound, you may even need to ask a close friend, your therapist, or another OCD sufferer for advice.

An Example of Modification

One OC woman wanted to vote, but couldn't bear the idea of using her community's touch-screen voting machines, which are heat sensitive and therefore won't work if the user is wearing gloves. She put this dilemma to her online support group and was delighted to receive the suggestion that she simply wear an adhesive bandage on her index finger. After voting, she could peel off and discard the disposable bandage and be on her way. (She will now use touch screens when absolutely necessary, but still does not like them. This is very much in keeping with what you can reasonably expect from treatment. While some former OCD sufferers become virtually fearless, most become much less anxious than before, but not exactly daredevils.)

Again, some will argue that such adaptive behaviors may simply "enable" you and your OC behaviors, and that is certainly a point worth making. Modification works like many other things: It carries a potential for great benefit or great misuse (sort of like cell phones, TV, and the Internet).

Talking with Acquaintances and Strangers

When it comes to whether, what, and how much to share with others about your OC behaviors, you have an almost unlimited number of choices. Certain people (a partner, close friends, family members) may have to know about your condition, but other people in your life will present you with a decision to make. Here are some options for those relationships:

- **Don't say anything.** Other people will not notice, figure you're a little weird, or recognize that you probably have OCD (not the worst thing in the world).

- **Simply say, "I have a thing about that."** Whatever "that" happens to be—shaking hands, taking off your shoes, trying on clothing in a store dressing room, and so forth—we are all allowed some kind of "thing" that bothers us or that we cannot do. In all probability, no one would think twice about it after hearing this.

- **Refer to your situation in a slightly euphemistic (but entirely truthful) way.** For example: "I have an anxiety disorder." One plus is, it's vague. While people may automatically associate OCD with excessive hand washing, compulsive cleaning, sidewalk crack counting, or other stereotypical behaviors, it's less likely that the words "anxiety disorder" will conjure such images. Anxiety disorders are also by far the largest class of mental disorder, so many people can relate.

- **Be direct and say, "I have OCD."** This may not be the way to go with utter strangers (on the other hand, why not!) but you can use it as a jumping-off point to educate your friends, family members, or acquaintances. They may have questions, which you can use to help dispel the myths surrounding OCD and let others know what it is really like to live with the condition.

How you handle these situations is up to you. Just remember: once you tell someone, you can't "untell" that person, or keep him from mentioning your news to other people. Be sure this information is something you are ready and willing to share. As in many situations, there are several possible paths.

For instance, you might decide to share with only your closest friends or a partner. Way over on the other end of the spectrum, you may feel as if it's not a secret worth keeping. OCD, after all, is no big deal. Maybe you would prefer to tell your boss, your coworkers, your kids, your parents, your gardener, and the 200 regular readers of your blog. The right answer, of course, is, whatever you think will work for you.

If You're in School

If your schoolwork is suffering because of your OC symptoms, it would make sense in most cases to let your teachers or academic advisers know that you have OCD. You may also want to talk with your parents about what's going on (particularly if they're helping to pay for your education).

You might want to tell your roommates, if your relationship is generally good and you think your behavior needs explanation, or if you simply need some support. Take into account, however, whether your roommate or roommates are likely to gossip and, if so, whether this would bother you.

Health Care Providers

When it comes to health care providers, depending on your particular obsessions and compulsions, it may be necessary to speak up. (You'll read more about this later in the book.) Of course, if you are on medication for your OC symptoms, you will need to let your regular physician know, if she doesn't already. That information should absolutely not be kept a secret. If you have cleanliness or contamination concerns, you will probably need to explain to your doctor and dentist not to take personally your requests that they wash their hands, and so on.

Others in Your World

There may be other people worth discussing your situation with briefly. These may include any of the service professionals with whom you interact in the course of a year: your barber, for instance, or your mechanic, letter carrier, librarian. But this applies only if your symptoms affect your interactions with them, or if your relationship is particularly friendly.

If you have "issues" related to your dealings with any of these people, chances are they're already obvious. It may (or may not) be helpful to offer a few words of explanation. There's probably no need to go into a lot of detail, unless you want to. A brief mention may be just fine.

Talking with Family

If you're close with your family members, many of them probably already know, or at least have an inkling, about your condition. Since OCD tends to run in families, you may have a parent, sibling, or other relative who also exhibits OC behaviors. If this is the case, you—and your OC family member—may find in each other a ready source of support and information.

One thing to keep in mind is that family members will be more likely than others to worry about your health and show concern for your well-being—perhaps even exhibiting some protective tendencies. Try not to take offense; this behavior is undoubtedly driven by love and care for you. Still, you may need to establish some boundaries. If your mom calls every day to see how your treatment is going, for instance, that will probably only contribute to your anxiety. Set guidelines for yourself and your family.

Essential

One reason to consider telling your family that you have OCD is that it runs in families. Other family members may have it and not realize this. While you can't diagnose others based on your experiences, you can, perhaps, set them on a helpful path.

Also keep in mind that some family members will have the opposite reaction and either start treating you in a negative way or avoid interaction with you. OC behaviors may make people uncomfortable. More likely, relatives may wonder why you've only recently started behaving in ways they don't understand. They might think you're trying to be difficult or different, or get attention for the sake of it. The best thing to do in this situation is to try to educate the person in small doses. (You'll read more later about some ways to do this.)

Talking with Your Spouse or Significant Other

If you're in a relationship, chances are your spouse or significant other already knows either that you have OCD or that you have strange, distressing habits. Your significant other also knows by now that your OC behaviors are affecting the relationship in negative ways: She has to wait while you check the stove—again—or reassure you that the spot on your back is probably not cancer—again. How you talk with your spouse or significant other about your OCD will probably depend on a few factors, as well:

- Does she already know you have OCD?
- Are you planning to stay in the relationship?
- Is your partner generally supportive?

If your partner does not know that your behavior is caused by OCD, you might think of your conversation about it as an opportunity. One way to discuss the subject might be something like this: "I know that many of my behaviors have caused you frustration and created tension between us. I didn't know then that I have OCD. The good news is that I know what I'm dealing with now, it can be treated, and I've made an appointment to talk with a doctor" (assuming, of course, that all of those things are true).

Another useful thing to add would be that your partner can help with your recovery—a lot. (In Chapter 11, you'll read in more specific detail about how your significant other can support you without enabling your OC behaviors.)

Depending on the circumstances, your significant other might want to accompany you on your visit to the psychotherapist or psychiatrist. Your therapist may be able to provide education, reassurance, and support for both of you.

If your partner is less supportive, it may be because he is frustrated with your behavior and how it affects him and his life. (He might, for instance, feel tired of always checking for you, or weary of your constant health worries, or other anxieties.) In such a case, you would also be well advised to explain that you now know what's causing your behaviors and that you are committed to getting treatment. A reasonable partner should understand. There are many books, and other sources of information and support that can help as well.

 ## Question

What if a friend or family member doesn't understand or support me?

This is unlikely, but not impossible. Often, people with OCD can't tolerate uncertainty. Unfortunately, the only way to know for sure is to give it a try. Keep in mind that friends and family will generally want to be supportive. Remember, a *pleasant* surprise is just as likely. Good luck!

It might also be useful to know that you have OCD if you, or others in your family, are considering having children. Often, parents with OCD have children with OCD. That said, OCD is not the worst thing one can pass on, nor is it untreatable. It just might be good, for a variety of reasons, to know about. (For one thing, a child who has OCD can get help much faster if his symptoms are recognized than if they aren't.)

What to Expect

Humans are naturally curious creatures. Some people you tell about your OCD may want to know more about it. Others may think they know all about OCD from things they've read or seen, or from other people they've known. Some of this information may be stereotypical, or offer only extreme examples. You will probably want to show patience in such cases and explain that while those examples represent one end of the spectrum, OCD is like any other condition: some cases will be mild, others severe, and many variations will exist within those boundaries.

L. Essential

Telling someone close to you that you have OCD doesn't have to be a big "moment." You don't need to announce that you have something important to discuss. It can be a short, perfectly matter-of-fact conversation that happens naturally and with virtually no planning.

You may be asked about, or simply feel like sharing, examples from your own life and struggle with OCD. Share as much, or as little, as you feel comfortable discussing. While OCD is nothing to be ashamed of, it is for you decide how much you want to tell others about the disorder and about yourself. If you find yourself on the receiving end of questions you'd rather not answer, it's perfectly all right to say, "I'm very pleased that you're interested, but that's not something I'm really comfortable talking about just yet. Thanks for understanding." Then, simply go on to another topic.

A Lingering Stigma

It's possible that a few acquaintances, or even friends, might avoid you, believing that you're mentally ill and therefore dangerous. (Few people with mental illnesses actually are dangerous to others, but stereotypes persist.) Try not to take such reactions too personally. In these cases, your best bet could be to offer correct information to replace the misinformation your friends or acquaintances have picked up. Anyone who's sincerely interested in learning about OCD has a huge number and variety of resources to choose from. There are organizations, books, Web sites, and other resources. (Several are listed in Appendix A at the back of this book.)

Extra Support

Keeping a secret can be tantamount to carrying a heavy burden. You may have tired of making up excuses for your behavior. It might be helpful for you to have at least one person (other than a therapist or spouse, who pretty much has to know) in whom you can confide for emotional support.

Other places to find support include in-person and online support groups. We *have* to interact with all kinds of people. We can also *choose* to interact with others with whom we share something like OCD. Having a support system is important when dealing with any major problem. Do not neglect this valuable resource.

The More You Know

You may find that the more you learn about OCD, the more help you get for your symptoms, and the more comfortable you become with the subject in general, the more comfortable you'll feel discussing it with others. You might even be able to help other people by sharing your own experience and knowledge.

Essential

> Don't worry if you don't have all the answers to friends' questions. It's absolutely fine to say, "I don't know. I'm still learning about this disorder myself." Anyone who is truly interested in learning more about OCD can find numerous resources to help her do so.

How you choose to approach the subject (if you do) is also up to you. Others may take their cues from you and joke with you about your OCD if you do so yourself, or feel concerned for you if you present it as something that causes you a lot of distress. As always, strike whatever tone makes you feel most comfortable. (That said, a little humor, if you can bring yourself to see any in your situation, might help to put others at ease.)

The Right Time?

How other people will react will depend on them, and the circumstances of your conversation, and not just you. A friend who snickers might feel uncomfortable or uncertain, for instance. Except in the case of parents or children, you may want to talk with people one-on-one, so that no one feels as if he has to act a certain way for the benefit of others in the conversation.

If you decide to share, try to pick a time when your confidante-to-be is not especially stressed. For instance, if you decide to tell your roommate, you might not want to wait until just before the final exam, parents' weekend, or a big date. On the other hand, when it comes to disclosing sensitive information, don't wait for the *exact* right time, either. Chances are, there isn't one. And putting off a difficult task will only make it scarier and harder and just postpone the relief you will probably feel once it's done.

CHAPTER 8

Things You Might Not Know

YOU NOW HAVE A pretty good idea of how OCD can affect your life—personally, professionally, and otherwise. But there is still a lot that you probably don't know about OCD. For example, do you know how many people have it? And that there are other conditions related to OCD? Do you know which kind of OCD is hardest to treat? These and other details are covered in this chapter.

OCD by the Numbers

Just how many people have OCD? You're certainly not alone if you do. According to the OC Foundation, approximately one in 40 adults and one in 200 children suffers from OCD at some point in their lives. That's more than 5 million people (some estimates say as many as 7 million) with OCD in the United States right now. Chances are, each of us knows at least one person who has OCD. (The numbers may even increase as more people reveal their symptoms and get diagnoses, and diagnoses become more accurate.) Of course, OCD can be found in populations all over the world.

OCD is an *anxiety disorder*. This classification also includes post-traumatic stress disorder (PTSD), agoraphobia and other panic disorders, social phobia, and generalized anxiety disorder. Two to three times as many people suffer from OCD as from bipolar disorder. There are many more people who have OCD than there are schizophrenics. Anxiety disorders are considered the most common of all mental illnesses. That said, the majority of experts now consider OCD a neurological condition rather than a mental illness.

 # Question

Does past illegal drug use contribute to OCD symptoms?
Many people who have OCD have wondered about this. One study of cocaine and marijuana users suggests a correlation, but as yet, that question has no conclusive answer.

OCD is said to be the fourth most frequently diagnosed psychiatric disorder, following phobias, depression, and alcoholism. Many treatment options have been proposed over the years. Some of these have been traditional, others less conventional. (This is covered in more detail later in the chapter.)

Inaccurate Diagnosis

Some experts say the average person with OCD waits ten years or longer before finally receiving an accurate diagnosis. Why? Several reasons:

- Until quite recently, OCD was not all that well understood or prevalent in the popular culture.
- OC behaviors mimic, or are related to, many other kinds of disorders, such as phobias (that is, irrational fears), panic disorder (sudden, overwhelming physical symptoms of anxiety with little or no apparent cause), and others.
- There are many types of OCD. Often, sufferers themselves have literally no clue that they have it. If your idea of OCD is compulsive housecleaning, for example, and your symptoms are centered on fears about catching fatal diseases, you might not put two and two together. Why would you, really?

- Even in today's world, where few secrets are kept, some people feel fearful or ashamed when it comes to talking about their OC symptoms or behaviors, and are reluctant to confide, even in professional therapists. It may sometimes feel as if "everyone else" in the world can accomplish simple tasks such as shaking hands, trying on clothing in a store, or driving from one place to another without experiencing terrifying anxiety.

- People who have OCD (or for that matter, any problem requiring therapy) often worry that they won't be believed or understood, or that they'll be told to just pull themselves together. You might worry that people will think differently about you than they did before, or differently than they think of others. You may even fear, as many anxious persons do, that if you reveal your secret, you'll be told you're "crazy," or that you'll be "locked up." This virtually never happens!

- Some people believe they can manage the symptoms on their own if they just make more of an effort. This, too, is usually not true, unfortunately.

That said, therapists generally now recognize OCD much more often than they used to. It has become much more visible lately than ever before.

Depression and OCD

Another reason for occasional misdiagnoses may be that many people who have OCD also suffer disproportionately from depression. As is the case with other conditions, sometimes, the first thing a therapist notices, and therefore diagnoses, is depression. But often, that's only part of the larger problem of OCD.

Although you'll read much more in Chapter 10 about depression and OCD (which are probably chemically related), there can also be psychological reasons for depression when you have OCD. In a relatively short time, you might find yourself feeling very much alone. Friends and family members, frustrated by your limiting behaviors, might avoid you or even ridicule you (although, of course, we hope that this is not the case).

Alert

> Untreated, OC behaviors generally worsen over time. A person who is afraid of driving on interstate highways, for example, might later find herself afraid of driving anywhere at night, then anywhere at all. In time, she might even avoid getting anywhere near a road.

You might also feel like a prisoner of your compulsions. Rarely, if ever, does an OCD sufferer enjoy these. More often, it will feel as if you're the captive of a crazed dictator. No wonder depression goes hand-in-hand with so many other conditions!

School of Thought

According to the Anxiety Disorders Association of America (ADAA), more and more U.S. college students are using campus mental health services. However, the group says, many college counseling facilities still have insufficient staff to meet students' needs, and do not offer help for anxiety disorders specifically. And treatment for anxiety disorders, the association reports, is the most frequently requested. (However, according to the organization, most colleges do offer many different mental health services.)

OCD-Related Conditions

Some experts consider OCD a "spectrum disorder." That is, there are several conditions closely related to OCD. They share some characteristics, such as compulsion, and may respond to similar types of treatments.

In Chapter 1, you read about conditions often mistaken for OCD. Others are related to OCD. These include:

- **Trichotillomania**, or the compulsion to pull out one's own hair, eyelashes, or eyebrows.
- **Impulse-control disorders** such as pathological gambling, compulsive spending, shoplifting, or sex addiction.
- **Body dysmorphic disorder (BDD)**, an extreme dissatisfaction with one's appearance, or the belief that one, or a specific part of one's body, is ugly, despite reassurances to the contrary.
- **Eating disorders** such as excessive, compulsive dieting (anorexia), and binge eating (bulimia).
- **Tourette's syndrome**, which causes involuntary movements (tics) and sounds. (Coprolalia, the compulsion to shout out "dirty words" or inappropriate remarks, is perhaps the most famous form of this disorder, but it is actually very rare.)
- **Self-mutilation:** most commonly, cutting one's own skin with razors or knives or burning oneself with lighted cigarettes or flame, but not with the intention of suicide.
- **Obsessive-compulsive personality disorder**, a hyperactive focus on order and "rightness," along with other symptoms. OCPD is actually quite distinct from OCD.
- **Free-floating anxiety.** Related to panic attacks (which involve only the physical symptoms of anxiety: shortness of breath, perspiration, heart palpitations, or other sensations), free-floating anxiety causes bouts of nervous feelings or vague senses of foreboding for no readily understandable reason.
- **Social phobia**, also called social anxiety disorder, can include physical symptoms accompanied by a morbid dread of spending time in the company of other people, speaking in public, or performing virtually any action in front of others.
- **Subsyndromal** (also called "sub-clinical") OCD. This is essentially OCD, but the obsessions and compulsions are so minimal that they cause virtually no disruption to the quality of life.

Similarly, obsessive-compulsive behaviors are sometimes part of another condition, such as bipolar disorder. Not everyone who has bipolar disorder has OC symptoms, and certainly not everyone with OCD has bipolar disorder or other illnesses.

OCD is also related to agoraphobia. As you probably have heard by now, that term is derived from the ancient Greek word *agora* or "marketplace," and has to do with fears of open or public spaces. More accurately, for many people who have agoraphobia, the fear lies in the possibility of finding oneself in danger, or perhaps in an embarrassing situation, from which there is no possibility of escape. Agoraphobia is usually classified as a panic disorder, as the sufferer typically experiences an unexplainable feeling of dread when away from home or familiar situations.

 Fact

Some studies suggest that, for women who have OCD, symptoms can worsen during pregnancy. In some cases, each successive pregnancy brings even greater anxiety. It is believed that the hormones associated with menstruation and breastfeeding can also affect OCD. (This is true for other disorders, as well.)

You probably also know that persons who suffer from agoraphobia feel insecure outdoors or away from their homes or certain "safe" places. An agoraphobic, however, may not feel safe only at home. That is an extreme. Persons with agoraphobia often feel safest when they are *close to* home (or in their cars), but many can venture short distances without feeling panicked, depending of course on the degree of the disorder.

Which Kind of OCD is Hardest to Treat?

Hoarding remains among the most intractable (and dangerous) kinds of OCD. It is even possible that it has helped contribute to the astronomical growth of the self-storage market in recent years. The

OC Foundation Web site links to a site devoted only to hoarding, and reports that self-help groups may be the best bet for most people who have this compulsion.

Ɫ Essential

People who have OCD tend to be highly suggestible. You might come to think that anything dangerous that you hear about on the news can also happen to you—and, in all probability, will. Of course, as you may already have found out, avoiding all dangerous things and situations soon proves exhausting, not to mention, impossible.

Particular Dangers

One serious danger for people who have hoarding behaviors is fire. Not only can clutter, particularly paper items, create ideal conditions for fires to spread once they begin, it can also impede or prevent rescue or escape. Extreme clutter has also endangered, and indirectly claimed, the lives of many firefighters attempting to save victims in "Collyer's Mansions." (This term refers to the well-educated Collyer brothers, who, during the first half of the twentieth century, filled their Fifth Avenue, New York City, home from floor to ceiling with junk. When one died, apparently in an accident exacerbated by conditions in the house, the other, who was blind, paralyzed, and had been dependent on his brother, perished of starvation. The Collyers' bodies were discovered by shocked police officers and neighbors. Their possessions were said to have weighed more than 100 tons.)

For fire safety, sanitation, and other serious reasons, hoarding behaviors should be arrested if at all possible. As many people who have hoarding compulsions already know, the behavior can also get you into trouble with neighborhood associations, building management companies, and so on. In extreme cases, the Department of Social Services might become involved if children are living in unsanitary or dangerous conditions.

Other Possible Consequences

Some people who hoard end up making their living spaces unfeasible. Gigantic collections can weaken floorboards. It becomes difficult to clean around piles of "stuff," and the attendant dust or allergens can create respiratory and other physical problems. Vermin can remain undetected. Kitchens may become so full that they can no longer be used, forcing household members to depend on take-out, a costly choice and one that can cause or contribute to serious weight and health problems. Understandably, children of hoarders often feel ashamed to invite friends home.

 Question

> **Do other animals get OCD?**
> It appears that they sometimes do suffer from compulsions. (Obsessions would be much harder to know about.) Repetitive skin- or feather-picking behaviors have been noted in wild animals and in pets, prompting the first veterinary use of Prozac in the 1990s. (Prozac, however, is not the primary drug prescribed for OCD in humans.)

Like people who have other kinds of OCD, hoarders often worry about unwanted consequences of therapy. The most common concern is that a therapist will discard the person's treasured possessions. This does not happen, even in cases in which the therapist visits the home to help the person learn to manage his clutter and the impact it has on him and his household.

OCD's Typical Course

Most people who have OCD report an onset of symptoms in their teens or early twenties. (There is also childhood OCD, which often strikes at around age twelve.) It may start with a seemingly mild fear or idea that, like the eponymous Blob in that 1950s horror movie, grows until it's just about taken over your world. Although symptoms often remit on their own—in some cases, for years—they will generally return unless treated.

Finding out that you have OCD can be difficult. You may feel depressed, upset, or even scared. But that first step—knowing what you're dealing with—is also the most important when it comes to reducing your symptoms.

Essential

OCD worries and compulsions can be constant, or they can come and go. You might find yourself free of anxiety and doubt for months at a time—but chances are that the OCD, like any living enemy, is waiting for you, and will return. Treatment and vigilance are your best bets.

OCD is not fatal. It doesn't even have to be chronic. It responds remarkably well to treatment. Like most bullies, it's not half as frightening as it looks, and it will back down as soon as you begin to fight it!

You may also be pleased to know that you're in excellent company: people who have OCD often are very creative, above average in intelligence, and (as you no doubt know by now) imaginative. In fact, many famous people, past and present, have, or have had, OCD. Unfortunately, as you probably also know, imagination can sometimes get out of hand and, when it doesn't have enough to do, cause lots of trouble.

If you do have OCD, there's plenty of good news: You have lots of options, lots of company, and lots of reason for hope. Obsessive-compulsive disorder (even advanced, multi-symptom OCD) has a high rate of successful treatment.

CHAPTER 9

Coping Strategies: When Anxiety Attacks

AS YOU'VE LEARNED FROM reading this book (and possibly through your own experience), OCD does not technically have a "cure." Medication, CBT, and other treatments can be very helpful in improving quality of life and quelling certain obsessions and compulsions; however, dealing with OCD on a daily basis also means developing coping skills. Luckily, there are several simple things you can do right now, if you need to, to reduce your anxiety. This chapter covers several effective strategies.

Calming and Coping Techniques

Sometimes OCD can work just like quicksand: The harder you struggle against your obsessive thoughts, the deeper you'll sink. By giving them less power—that is, by inviting them to come into your head—you may find that they quickly deflate. Some therapists actually advocate this method. If you're curious, give it a try it and see. The next time you experience anxiety, allow yourself to feel it instead of trying to suppress it.

On the other hand, every person who has OCD is different. Pushing away the anxious feelings through creative distraction could prove a better strategy for you. In that case, find out what works: getting absorbed in a crossword puzzle or book, perhaps, or working, or reaching out and becoming engaged in positive ways with others. This can be as simple as e-mailing a friend, phoning an elderly family member to ask how she's doing, or becoming involved in a volunteer project. And volunteering is a wonderful way to get outside of yourself and your problems, and to do good for others, too. Win-win! Just keeping busy by doing a useful task can go a long way toward reducing anxiety.

Time to Panic?

Other experts recommend employing what they call "worry time," a technique that works in more or less the same way as the "controlled burn" firefighters sometimes use to prevent forest fires when conditions are ideal for them to start. Using worry time means that, when a troubling thought arises, you actually set aside your anxiety until a special time—say, one half-hour every afternoon. The reasoning goes that if you can learn to delay your worries briefly, when you're ready for them, they will have reduced in size and scope.

Worry time also allows you to set aside temporarily those upsetting thoughts that might otherwise keep you awake or interfere with work by arising at inopportune moments. This affords you a measure of control (as in, "I'll worry about that later").

Act As If

Twelve-step programs call this "acting as if," and it essentially means pretending that you feel perfectly calm. If your body doesn't begin to mount that terrible fear response, you may be able to keep worry at bay—or, at least, to a minimum. (Remember the song about whistling a cheerful refrain when you feel scared!)

Simple as this may sound, you might also be able to stop obsessions simply by saying to yourself, "That is not true" or "That is just a silly idea, and I'm not going to pay attention to it." No one's suggesting that it is easy to get rid of OCD obsessions. However, if you can rob them of their power, you can greatly diminish their ability to wreak havoc against you.

Just Say No

You might also want to take a page from the CBT book and vow not to give in to the compulsion part of your OCD. You may not be able to stop worrying, but you can stop checking your body for signs of injuries or disease; you can refuse to recheck your stove or locks or seek assurance from others. You might be surprised to notice a significant reduction in your overall anxiety once you do. It may not be easy, but it definitely is possible. Next time your anxieties rage, give these techniques a try.

 ## Question

Can the way we think affect the way we feel?
Yes! Try putting a big smile on your face and shouting with true appreciation, "I feel wonderful today!" Now, how do you feel? You might be shocked to discover that those four words have indeed changed your mood. Research has shown that a smile can initiate a cascade of positive neuroendocrine events: It can actually cause your brain to orchestrate the release of "feel-good" chemicals into your bloodstream.

Accept What You Cannot Change

There probably will be times when you are just going to have to feel anxious, as virtually everybody does. Unfortunately, no one escapes from life on Earth completely unharmed. When you experience unshakable anxiety, know that, although it is very unpleasant, it will end. Allow yourself to feel some anxiety some of the time.

If it becomes unmanageable and is interfering with your work, sleep, relationships, or functioning, make sure to talk with your therapist or health care provider as soon as possible. It may also help to have a support system of people you can confide in. Connecting with others who have OCD will probably prove helpful, as well.

Preventing Anxiety

A generally healthful lifestyle should help you to reduce your anxiety level overall. Try to limit the stressful influences around you as best you can. Choose a kind of exercise you like at least well enough to do regularly. Eat a variety of nutritious foods, stay hydrated, and strive for a good night's sleep as often as possible. One more thing: Don't neglect to spend time at wholesome activities you enjoy, in the company of people you like.

Other Well-Being Strategies

In addition to those things, it is recommended that you learn one or two generally accepted anxiety-reducing techniques. These include yoga, progressive muscle relaxation, visualization, and breathing exercises. Yoga, an ancient spiritual and physical practice, involves using stretches, poses, and breathing to bring about a feeling of calm naturally. Many adult education programs offer yoga classes, and there are also many instructional books and some television programs that teach it.

Progressive muscle relaxation techniques teach you how to tense and then relax individual muscle groups. This can confer a feeling of comparative calm (and also help you to fall asleep). Deep breathing exercises are another avenue you might want to explore. There are many CDs and tapes you can order online that can guide you through progressive muscle relaxation, breathing exercises, or creative visualization.

Visualization uses the power of the imagination to create feelings of calm and well-being. You can use visualization to hasten healing or lower blood pressure, or to try to create a positive outcome, such as getting a raise at work. Reduced to a simple explanation, visualization techniques can be *guided* (you imagine what you would like to have happen) or *receptive* (take what comes). There are several good books on visualization (two of which are listed in the appendix) that can help you get started, if you wish.

Like yoga, meditation is a long-established Eastern practice that involves focused attention and quiet. There are also many excellent books, CDs, and tapes on this subject that can help you learn it.

Don't Give Up

Don't expect every technique to work every time. Generally, you can count on more success when there is less overall stress in your life. If you are going through a crisis, unfortunately, your OCD or other health problems will probably grow worse (although for some people, having something else to focus on may reduce OC symptoms somewhat). Other factors, such as your surroundings, the time of day, and so on, may also have a bearing on whether a specific strategy will work for you at a given time. If a technique works only passably, why not try it again next time? Different conditions might create a more positive outcome.

The OC Traveler

Travel, whether for necessity or pleasure, can be one of the most stressful situations a person with OCD can face. In travel, so many things are out of your control and beyond your ability to predict. Things that sounded like "no big deal" when you considered them from home, or well in advance, may take on enormous and terrible qualities on the road.

Travel can bring up any number of personal "issues," such as fears about the journey itself—flying, train travel, driving or crossing bridges, for instance—or about dirt, germs, or a host of other things and situations, including just plain uncertainty.

Feelings of Instability

Travel, of course, will interrupt the normal routine that probably lends a degree of comfort and stability to your life. Airlines today allow so little in the way of carry-on luggage that you may have to leave comforting and familiar books or other objects behind. Not to mention that terrorism has given rise to feelings of tremendous unease and to increased security measures that often leave one feeling anything but secure. Travel may also upset your sense of order, and you may find yourself preoccupied with worries about lost luggage, fears about difficulty finding your way around a strange city once you arrive, or any number of other unpleasant possibilities.

Like many things, travel will probably become easier the more you do it. (But, of course, this may not be feasible for you, as travel can also be expensive and time consuming.)

Reasons for Traveling

Coping with travel may depend on whether the reason for your trip is pure pleasure, as in a vacation, or obligatory, as in a business trip. If you have to travel to attend a funeral or a family function, expect your stress level to be that much higher. Stress, unfortunately, will generally make bad things worse. Sometimes, very little can be done to alleviate that; but don't forget to use the skills you've learned: meditation, visualization, and cognitive strategies.

Essential

Sometimes, you may have to travel alone. Other times, you might be traveling with coworkers or family. Both situations can present their own stresses and challenges. If traveling with a coworker, it might be wise to let him know beforehand that you are nervous about flying or other situations.

If you have to travel for business, your main objective may simply be to get through it. Some things you may be able to do to make your journey and your stay more comfortable include bringing reassuring or familiar things. You might want to carry a photo of your child or significant other, for instance, or a favorite plush toy (ideally, one small enough to fit easily into your travel bag), an enjoyable book (always a good idea), your favorite music, crossword or other puzzles to get your mind off the strangeness of the situation, and so on.

If you know you have a business trip coming up and have adequate time to plan, you may want to use that period to take a fearless flying course. Some companies will pay for employees to take such classes, or will reimburse for them. You could be one of the lucky ones.

We don't advocate using alcohol or occasional-use medications to counteract fears about flying. There are many good reasons for this. Generally, staying alert while you travel is a good idea. And if you have to travel often, you will only find yourself needing to take these things more often, too.

A First-Class Idea

Some experts believe that traveling first class may help reduce some of the fear associated with flying. This is especially true if you are also claustrophobic (uncomfortable in tight spaces). If you are lucky enough to work for a compassionate and generous company, by all means, ask about this option. Sometimes, planning your trip far in advance can help you to obtain good deals on flying first- or business-class. Or ask about an upgrade using your travel miles (or someone else's donated ones).

Use Your Coping Strategies

Try to learn relaxation exercises if you can. (There even are a couple of books of yoga exercises you can do on airplanes! One is called *Airplane Yoga* and was written by Rachel Lehmann-Haupt and Bess Abrahams.) Observe the usual advice about reducing stress: Refrain from drinking caffeinated beverages before your flight. Try to get a good night's sleep the night before. Have all of your belongings, as well as tickets, flight information, and your arrangements for transportation to the airport, ready so as to keep stress at an absolute minimum.

At the airport, you may want to read or watch television to distract yourself from your surroundings. Or you might want to call a friend or make light conversation with other travelers (observing, of course, all common-sense behavior, and caution about talking to strangers).

Some fearful fliers find it helpful to start with short flights and work their way up to longer ones. You may also want to choose an airline that you know features in-flight entertainment. Many offer not only movies but also a choice of these (as well as classic TV shows, etc). Keeping your mind involved in something other than the flight itself can serve to keep anxieties under wraps. You might be surprised to find that time passes quickly when you have something pleasant to focus on.

A Healthy Benefit

It may also help if you take some time to consider and focus on any benefits associated with your trip: Will you get to see a part of the country you haven't seen before? (And, if so, can you take a little time out of your trip to enjoy a museum, nature preserve, shopping outlet, restaurant, theater production, or other attraction?) Or might a good performance at an out-of-town meeting translate to a better possibility of promotion? Could this conference contribute to your learning new job skills? Will you get to meet people you frequently speak with over the phone, but have not yet had the chance to get together with in person? The more you think about it, the more "positives" you will probably be able to find. (One certain benefit: You'll gain practice at traveling!)

 Fact

Some people are afraid to fly not because they worry about crashes, but because air travel can involve many other typical anxiety triggers: confined spaces, lack of control, and fear of heights, to name just three.

Working with your cognitive therapist or beginning a course of medication may well make it easier for you to travel. A cognitive behavioral therapist may give you a series of exercises you can do in the weeks or days leading up to your trip.

One fun way to try to get used to travel would be to pick a desirable destination and take off at a moment's notice, leaving behind the over-packing and over-planning you might normally do. At first, you might experience a great deal of anxiety. But anxiety can only go on for so long. Sooner or later, the flame will burn out, and perhaps you will actually enjoy your trip. You might start by bringing along another person or persons you feel comfortable traveling with, and the next time, graduate to a tour or something more independent.

⌶. Essential

OCD isn't called the "What-If disease" for nothing. Chances are, you regard new situations with dread, wondering *what if* this or that goes wrong. Next time, try something new: ask the same "what-if" about fun possibilities: "What if I see new things, meet new people, and have a good time?"

OCD at Work

One of the most stressful situations for many people who have OCD is dealing with symptoms while at work. Work life can present enormous challenges. First of all, there are the normal stresses associated with most job situations. Then, you have an almost infinite number of possible OCD triggers. Your work might require you to shake hands, travel, or drive over a bridge, for instance. You might work around animals, or in food service or health care, and have phobias related to those things. You might have to handle cash. Any of these situations—and many, many others—can be launching pads for anxiety when you have OCD.

Common Work Concerns

While it's unlikely that you would be fired merely because you have OCD, you might find yourself concerned about getting into trouble at work because of your OC behaviors. Perhaps you're frequently late because of the time you spend checking and rechecking your doors or appliances before leaving home in the morning. Or you might take such long showers that this is affecting your arrival time. Or perhaps your worries about having hit a pedestrian on the way to work cause you to go back, again and again, to check and make sure you haven't. You may have a hard time *leaving* the office, worried, perhaps, that you left your computer, or the office coffeemaker, on.

 Fact

Social anxiety is among the most common psychological disorders, and is said to affect as many as 5 million Americans. Social phobias can be "generalized" or specific, as in a fear of eating or writing in front of others, or of public speaking, a fear shared by many.

You may have perfection obsessions and worries about doing your job correctly, going over your work again and again, or asking for an unreasonable amount of reassurance from bosses, coworkers, or customers.

You may fear airplane trips but have to travel frequently for your job. You might have germ phobias, but be expected to shake hands with clients and others. Or perhaps you have social phobias that prevent you from giving presentations, interacting with others, or attending company functions. You may have obsessional slowness, and have a hard time getting started with your work, until you feel conditions are "right."

Laboring Under a Handicap

Depending on various factors, your OCD might be severe enough to qualify legally as a handicap. Cases in which disability compensation is sought usually require the applicant to furnish some kind of proof. However, we hope that your OCD hasn't reached a point at which it would be considered a disability.

In Chapter 12, you'll read more about job situations and OCD, particularly about "reasonable accommodation." If you are otherwise qualified to do your job, your boss may be expected to offer you some kind of alternative if she knows that you have OCD. If you're a salesperson who can't travel by plane, for example, perhaps your territory can be traded with that of another employee. However, most of the time, at least, most people who have OCD do not want to be considered handicapped. Assuming that's the case for you, you have a few choices:

Alert

Some people do become disabled by OCD and spend virtually all of their time at home. If this is the case for you, please consder treatment. With proper care, even very severe OCD can often be managed.

- Get help for your OC symptoms as soon as you can—not only to help you succeed at work, but also to help you enjoy your life more overall. You should be able to schedule your CBT sessions around job.

- Work on CBT techniques, with a therapist or on your own. This should help you to begin to do again many of the things you now consider too frightening. Don't neglect to ask for support from friends or family members, and remind them to praise your progress.

- Let your boss know that there are certain things that give you difficulty. (You'll probably want to limit these to just one or two, if at all possible.) You need not mention OCD specifically, unless you want to. Together, depending on your situation, you and your boss may be able to come up with alternatives—traveling to meetings by train, for instance, instead of by plane.

- Simply tell your boss that you have OCD (or an anxiety disorder) and ask for his help in finding alternatives for you. Once you've disclosed your situation, your boss (depending on the size of the company and a few other factors) will probably be obligated to offer reasonable accommodation, in accordance with the Americans With Disabilities Act. (See

Chapter 12 for exceptions.) Perhaps you can stay later on days when you come in late. You, too, can make reasonable accommodation.

- Many companies offer employee assistance programs, or EAPs. Do not be afraid to check out yours. These programs are confidential and are designed to help you function better at work by helping you with problems in any area of your life. You may be given a referral to a psychiatrist or cognitive behavioral therapist.

OCD at School

If you are away at school, you may be experiencing more stress than you did before. This is not unusual in new situations. Although your family might be used to your OC behaviors, you might find yourself hiding, or trying to hide, them from roommates and new friends, classmates, acquaintances, and teachers. Performing your OC "rituals" and trying to keep friends and others from finding out about them, can be exhausting. (Never mind that, at the same time, you also need to study, read, write papers, and take tests!) In addition, you may feel homesickness or have difficulty getting used to new, strange surroundings and new people. If you have other pressures, such as family problems, for example, or social phobias or roommate difficulties, it should not surprise you if your stress level soars.

Ways to Cope

If you find that your OC symptoms are affecting your schoolwork—let's say, you're turning in papers late because of the amount of time you spend rechecking your work—you might want to employ a couple of strategies.

First, of course, you'll probably want to get treatment for your symptoms so that you can continue your schoolwork and, beyond that, your life, without all of these difficulties. Many, if not most, schools offer psychological counseling services. Do not hesitate to look into these. If your school does not offer a counselor versed in CBT, or if you fear other students finding out that you are seeing a counselor, you may be able to explore other arrangements. (However, we don't think that getting the help you need should be any cause for embarrassment; colleges offer counseling for a reason.) Depending on your family situation, it might not be a bad idea to talk with your parents and perhaps ask for their help in finding a good cognitive behavioral therapist.

L Essential

Reducing your overall anxiety can help you better manage your OCD symptoms. When you're calmer to begin with, you'll be that much farther from extreme anxiety. Think of it as the difference between getting bad news after a relaxing vacation versus during your most stressful day at work.

Depending on your situation, you may be covered by insurance, either under your parents' plan, or by insurance purchased through your school. (Be sure to ask; it's possible that this information "fell through the cracks" while you were applying to and getting ready to attend college.) Medication is another option you may wish to explore; again, see someone at your college counseling center for help with this decision. The folks there will either be able to prescribe for you, or refer you to a local psychiatrist or psycho-pharmacologist.

You might also need to talk with your teachers or administrators to let them know you are doing the work (assuming, of course, that you are). You may decide to work out some kind of arrangement— an understanding, for instance, that the teacher does not expect perfect papers. Some instructors will probably be sympathetic and informed; others undoubtedly won't be. In any case, it will be helpful to reduce your symptoms early, to keep them from holding you back from achieving your life and career goals.

Talking to Friends

If you're living on campus, you may find that friendships often form (and sometimes end) very quickly. When it comes to confiding in your new friends, you might want to keep a few basic things in mind:

- Many people today know a lot—but not quite enough—about OCD. Stereotypes about the disorder persist. Try not to feel hurt if you hear joking remarks about OCD that do not involve you specifically. ("After picking up that filthy stray cat, I washed my hands like I had OCD!") It is natural for people to joke about topics that they don't necessarily understand well.
- If you explain matter-of-factly that you have OCD, a largely neurological condition that sometimes makes you worry too much or do things that can look strange to others, your friends may well understand. They might have questions for you. This is natural, too. At the back of this book is a list of resources you might want to offer those who express interest. (Learning more about the condition yourself may also help you when it comes to managing it.)
- If your OCD symptoms are not a big deal but perhaps were more troubling in the past, you can talk about that. If you find, unfortunately, OCD has become a permanent unwanted misery that seems to rule every aspect of your life, you may want to talk about *that*. Be honest, of course, but share only what you're comfortable sharing.
- Well-meaning people might harangue you about the importance of not letting fear run your life. It might make you angry to hear such things ("Say! There's an idea! Why didn't I think of that?"), but try your best to let it go. Tell the person you appreciate that he cared enough to share his thoughts with you.
- If you should find your friends unsympathetic, you might want to look into forming new friendships. Extracurricular activities are a great way to meet other people outside of class and

dorm situations. Don't neglect to look for nearby or online OCD support groups, either. You could even be lucky enough to find one on campus, or you might want to consider forming your own, perhaps with assistance from the counseling center staff.

OCD at Home

OCD, as you undoubtedly know, can wreak havoc on your home life. This is true whether you live alone or with roommates, parents, children, or a spouse; it is true however old you are. If you live alone, you might find it hard to accomplish seemingly simple tasks, such as taking out the garbage or washing your dishes. If you live with others, you already know how hard it can be to try to hide your behaviors, and you know how impatient others can get. Family members may feel resentful when they find themselves giving in to your compulsions, such as rewashing their clothes, double-checking the stove, or assuring you that you are not immediately dying. They will undoubtedly feel frustrated with you for not being able to do simple things such as picking up a pencil that's fallen onto the floor or leaving the house without checking the stove endlessly (or worrying obsessively about not having an opportunity to do so).

Hard to Live With

Caring for a person with a physical illness is very hard. Caring for a person who has a severe mental illness is also hard. But dealing day-to-day with a person who seems normal except for her "peculiarities"—behaviors that she seems to insist on dragging into every aspect of her life—can be frustrating, indeed. Some family members of people who have OCD feel guilty when they don't give in to the person's compulsions or requests. Others may feel angry or resentful, as if the person who has OCD is trying to "control" them.

Bringing family members along to one or two therapy sessions, if possible, would probably be ideal. Your family may need insight into

OCD, help learning about ways to work with you to banish its symptoms, and support for dealing with a difficult family situation.

Working on Working Together

You will also want to get real help for your symptoms. Once family members see that you are working on the problem, they may become more sympathetic—although out of habit or years of frustration, they might still show signs of impatience with you and your behaviors. Communicating is almost always helpful. Both you and your affected family members should have a chance to tell one another how you feel and what your principal concerns and difficulties are. Such communication can often be facilitated by meeting with an experienced therapist; if family members are resistant to that idea, perhaps they will at least be willing to read more about the disorder. Many books on OCD have sections directed toward family members and how they can begin to understand and to help. (In fact, so does this one—see Chapter 11.) Some even are written exclusively for the family of the person who has OCD (see Appendix A).

CHAPTER 10

OCD and Depression

SOME EXPERTS ESTIMATE THAT as many as 60 to 90 percent of people who have OCD also suffer from depression. Not surprisingly, depression can impede any progress you're trying to make in fighting OCD. When you feel depressed, you may not feel like doing much of anything. Worse, when a person is depressed, he tends to lose his ability to believe in himself or his capacity to change and improve his situation. Being depressed often means being stuck. In this case, it would most likely also mean being stuck with OCD!

Why You Might Be Depressed, Too

There is a growing belief that the same imbalances in brain chemistry that are responsible for depression also cause OCD. The good news is that many of the same medications used for OCD often show tremendous success in treating depression, as well. Certain other therapies can also help to alleviate both depression and OCD.

Feeling Alone

It may also be that OCD can cause depression for the very same reasons *any* illness does: It can be isolating, frustrating, debilitating (even disabling), and very unpleasant. Few of those who are not affected by it may be able to understand its symptoms and the torment it causes. OCD, while it afflicts a great many people, still does not affect the majority of the population. Therefore, sufferers often feel very much alone. OCD can also make one feel like a prisoner of its demands.

It is not uncommon for people who feel overwhelmed by frequent or constant anxiety to feel hopeless, even to the point of experiencing active or passive suicidal thoughts. You might find yourself thinking, *So what if I die? Anything has got to be better than this.* Luckily, depression—whether biochemical or circumstantial—can be treated. (If your depression feels serious or overwhelming, please skip ahead to the section "Depression, Large, and Small.")

Getting Help

Medication is one way to go, and it has proven very helpful against depression, as well as OCD. However, if you can't tolerate medication, or if you fear it, there are other options, also. Cognitive behavioral therapy, either alone or in conjunction with medication, can be quite helpful.

You may remember that CBT helps patients to change compulsive actions gradually while at the same time helping them to examine their negative thinking patterns (such as, "There's danger everywhere you look"). Cognitive therapy techniques can also be used against depression.

 Alert

The way we think has a definite bearing on the way we feel. If you keep thinking, *I'm a failure, I'm nothing, my life is worthless,* you'll come to believe it. People who are generally happy tend to have as many external problems as those who are miserable. The difference is outlook. You can actually learn to respond differently to life's challenges.

Just as cognitive therapy helps you to look at and understand how your thoughts influence your beliefs, so can it help you to realize the ways in which they can influence your feelings. (For example, if your thoughts, from morning till night, run along the lines of, *I'm a loser; I haven't gotten anywhere and I never will,* you will almost certainly feel worse overall than the person whose thoughts generally lean toward such sentiments as, *I feel so lucky to have a supportive family and a job I enjoy for the most part.*) A cognitive therapist can help you to recognize your entrenched, negative thought patterns and encourage you to find positive ideas where you couldn't before.

Question

What's the best way to treat depression?
There's no one answer for everyone, of course, but therapy in conjunction with regular medication seems to be quite successful in a large number of cases. Several medications and therapies work well against both OCD and depression.

In addition to CBT, there's interpersonal therapy (generally a short-term treatment that focuses on the patient's interactions with others). There are other types of "talk" therapy, as well. Medication along with, or before beginning, any type of psychotherapy, is believed to increase its chances of success.

An Older Therapy, Re-Examined

In some cases, electroconvulsive therapy (ECT)—formerly known as "electroshock therapy" or by the less formal name, "shock treatment"—may be an option. ECT uses electrodes to deliver a brief (approximately thirty-second) burst of electricity into strategic centers of the brain and is generally done over several sessions for a relatively short period. ECT has shown some promise in the treatment of depression, particularly serious or dangerous depression, or in cases in which medication is not a good choice.

ECT, once used widely for the treatment of an array of mental illnesses, fell out of popular favor in the later part of the twentieth century, as it was considered dangerous and unpleasant, or even barbaric. Then, as now, it was known to cause memory damage. Significant improvements over time have made ECT far less traumatic than it once was. However, while sometimes useful for intractable depression, ECT is not believed to have much, if any, effect on OCD.

 Fact

> In 2006, Kitty Dukakis, wife of former Massachusetts governor and one-time Democratic presidential candidate Michael Dukakis, co-wrote a book with medical author Larry Tye about electroconvulsive therapy. Tye wrote about it from a historical perspective, and Dukakis, from a personal one. Dukakis said her treatment-resistant depression responded positively to ECT.

Depression, Large and Small

As you probably know, most people experience some form of depression—that is, sadness, feelings of apathy, a "down" mood—at some time in their lives. What we commonly call depression can range from mild "blahs" or "blues" to full-scale despair.

Clinical depression (a syndrome that meets certain diagnostic criteria) involves persistent despondency, a sense of hopelessness and helplessness, feelings of guilt, inadequacy, and possibly suicidal thoughts. If what you are feeling is a case of occasional blues, meaning that you feel "down" and it lasts for a short time, you may be able to ride it out using some of the techniques below.

If you are dangerously or seriously depressed—for example, you have little appetite, sleep for much longer than eight hours a day as a means of escape, find yourself unable to get out of bed or to function in your daily routine, cry easily, or have constant or near-constant thoughts about harming yourself or others—you need to get help right away.

Other signs of depression include lethargy, problems with concentration or memory (or both), lack of interest in activities or things you used to enjoy, and feelings of worthlessness, helplessness, and hopelessness.

Help for Serious Depression

There are several good options for treating serious depression. All of them begin with communication (which may feel difficult when you're depressed but is essential nonetheless). You will want to talk with someone you trust, ideally a professional. Your therapist, doctor, or clergyperson would be a good place to start. One good treatment choice is medication. A great many depression problems arise from chemical imbalances in the brain. If the problem is biochemical, then it's logical that the treatment would be biochemical, as well. Many current antidepressants are said to specifically target those areas of the brain that are responsible for depression.

 Alert

While it's not uncommon for people to think occasionally about suicide, formulating a plan to kill yourself (or others) is a giant danger sign. If you feel hopeless or desperate, call the National Suicide Prevention Hotline (1-800-SUICIDE), or your therapist, clergyperson, 9-1-1, or the nearest hospital emergency room immediately. There's help for even serious depression.

Of course, if your depression is circumstantial, it will probably help to talk about it, to keep busy if you can, and to try to do good for others. If your depression is situational but serious—that is, if it has caused you to lose interest in the things you used to enjoy, and you have felt this way for more than a week or two, or you find you are thinking often about suicide or other dangerous behaviors—get help right away.

If you feel suicidal, call 1-800-SUICIDE (the National Suicide Prevention Hotline) or 1-800-273-TALK (the National Strategy for Suicide Prevention hotline). Most communities also offer local suicide-prevention services. You can find them easily in the phone book, online or by calling the Samaritans 1-877-870-HOPE (4673) in the U.S. (The

Samaritans and other suicide-prevention groups are available in other countries, as well.) You really do not have to suffer alone.

Therapists usually have emergency numbers for patients. Keep your therapist's emergency number on hand. (Don't worry that you might be "imposing." If your therapist believes you are crossing any boundaries, she will tell you so. In the meantime, she's there to help you.) If your therapist is unavailable for any reason, you need to get to the nearest hospital emergency room; there will be a trained clinician there to help you.

 # Fact

> There is evidence to suggest that more people are affected by depression today than at any other time in history. According to the National Alliance on Mental Illness (NAMI), depression is the biggest contributor to disability in the country (and in other developed countries, as well).

The In-Patient Option

For serious or suicidal depression, you may also want to consider (or your clinician may strongly advise) hospitalization. Aside from actual hospitals, there are many mental health facilities that offer therapy and medication in tranquil, pleasant settings. Your therapist might help you decide on one, or you may be able to find listings in the telephone directory or online. (Try such key words as "in-patient," "mental health," and "depression," or look under "Mental Health Services." Add the name of your state for Internet searches.) Just be sure to check out the facility before deciding on a stay there, as you would any professional service, or ask the referring clinician why this particular facility is recommended. You might want to involve a family member or friend in this decision if you're not feeling up to the task.

Help for Mild or Middle-Sized Depression

For most people, depression will probably lie in the middle ground: not disabling, but not light enough to shake off, either. If this is you, you might be surprised to learn that the same options—and more—are available.

Medication is still one avenue to explore. If you are already on medication for your OCD, it makes sense to talk with your prescribing doctor about changing your prescription or dosage, or perhaps adding another medication. Often, a small dose of a second medicine will act with the first to help you feel much better, so do not dismiss this option.

Sometimes, the body becomes accustomed to a medication and the same prescription no longer works as well as it once did. Or perhaps your medicine was prescribed primarily (or exclusively) for OCD and doesn't necessarily treat depression. Many medications work well for both depression *and* OCD, so a switch might be in order.

If you're not currently on medication, now might be the time to consider it. Treating the depression first will likely help you to treat the OCD more successfully.

⌊. Essential

In some cases, the reason for depression might be medical. Certain viral infections, for instance, can cause many of the same symptoms as depression. A medical exam would not be a bad place to start. Make sure to let your doctor know about any medications (over-the-counter and prescription) that you may be taking, and don't neglect to mention your OCD if your doctor is unaware of it.

Depression can be insidious, as well as dangerous. Just because you're not actively suicidal or homicidal doesn't mean you shouldn't get help for this serious problem. Don't let anyone tell you, "Oh, everyone gets depressed. Just buck up!" If you need help, you should absolutely get it. In addition to following the general advice given throughout this book, there are several small but significant things you can do to help brighten your way of thinking. Again, if you feel as if your depression has gotten to the point at which it might be dangerous to you or others, seek help from a qualified therapist right away. Otherwise, here are a few more ideas for beating the blues:

- Even though you might not feel sociable (and, in fact, probably don't), do not give in to your inclination to isolate yourself. Try to get out, even for a short time, among people whose company you enjoy. A "change of scenery" can also help; try taking a short walk, preferably in the morning sunshine, as exposure to sunlight can positively affect your mood.

- Share your troubles. You may want to confide in a close friend or family member. Sometimes, it really does help to talk. (This is not, of course, meant to substitute for a therapist or other qualified professional.)

- Join (or become active again in) a spiritual community. Find a local church or synagogue and start attending regularly; religious involvement has been shown to have long-term benefits for those who participate. And you just might find yourself becoming part of a community with similar values.

- Get a pet. Assuming you're not allergic and you like and can care for (and are able to keep) a dog, cat or other animal, you may want to explore this option. It's well documented that animals have a therapeutic value for humans. Even watching a tank of fish swimming, it's said, can help generate a feeling of calm.

- Although you may feel bleak, remember the saying that "laughter is good for the soul." Watch a movie that makes you laugh. (The Marx Brothers? *Tootsie*? A romantic comedy?) Listening to music you enjoy may also help lighten your mood. Don't forget to sing along. Singing can be a great blues buster, too.

- Write. Keeping a journal has been shown to have a healing effect. Or work on writing something even more creative: a book, a play, a song or poem, or what-have-you.
- Any kind of creative activity, such as painting, writing, or dancing, can help you to feel good. (Dance or other physical activities carry the added benefit of being good exercise. Exercise helps people to feel good, too.) Creativity is thought to release endorphins, the brain's so-called "feel good" chemicals.
- Do something nice for someone else. Seek out volunteer opportunities; get ideas and local referrals through charitable organizations, your place of worship, the newspaper, or online. Whether it's dropping in to visit a lonely older neighbor or spending the afternoon preparing bags at your local food bank, if you feel as you're contributing to the world around you (and you are!), you will likely begin to feel more a part of it.
- Remember to eat well. Giving in to sugar cravings will almost certainly make you feel worse ultimately, as will *not* eating very much. Eating balanced meals and drinking plenty of water will probably help to stabilize your mood.
- Dress up. Sometimes it can feel cozy just to laze around (especially when the weather outside is bad) in soft, worn, not-very-presentable clothing. However, like just about anything else, too much of it probably won't be good for you. Even if you're only going to the corner store for a quart of milk, make an effort to look nice. You may just find that you feel better, too.
- Act as if you feel better than you do. Sigh contentedly. Smile. Say out loud, "What a gorgeous day!" (Or maybe, "I *like* rain.") "I feel great!" Think about one thing, or more, that you feel truly happy (or at least pretty good) about.

If you suffer from seasonal depression or "winter blues," (also known as "seasonal affective disorder" or SAD) you might want to consider adding light therapy to your routine. (Some people use it for non-seasonal depression, as well.) SAD is common in residents of northern climates where there is insufficient sunlight throughout the winter months. Generally, light therapy involves sitting in front of a specially designed lamp or light box for a specified period each morning, often thirty to sixty minutes. Many types of light boxes are available.

Formerly at the fringes, light therapy seems to be gaining mainstream acceptance. If you'd like to give a light box a try, make sure to look for established guidelines for making this purchase.

Time for a Change?

If you have been on the same medication for a while and have felt depressed for longer than two weeks, you might want to talk with your prescribing doctor about changing your prescription. Why? Over time, some medications stop working as well as they once did. Your body gets used to them. Changes in weight and hormone balance can also affect the way some medications work.

Therapy Isn't Therapeutic Unless It's Helping

You may also feel "stuck" in your therapy. If you have been seeing the same therapist for a while and don't feel as if you're getting significantly better, you might want to discuss this with the therapist. It may be that you have made as much progress as you can with that particular person. He may even be able to help you find a new therapist.

Don't feel guilty for needing a change. You might simply "click" better with someone else. Or you may want to try a type of therapy, such as cognitive or interpersonal, that your current therapist does not provide. (That said, do make sure you're giving your current therapy enough time and enough of a chance to work. Though difficult at first, a frank conversation with your current therapist may open up the treatment to new and more effective avenues.)

Change Can Be Hard

Any kind of change, whether in medication (or giving medication a try for the first time), or a therapist (or giving therapy a try for the first time), can be a little scary. But making a big change in your life while you're in the midst of a horrible depression can be very difficult, indeed. You may feel stuck in more ways than one, and find it hard to get started. Many people have strong opinions about pharmaceutical companies, for instance. (True, they are large and profit driven. But their products also have been known to offer great benefit to large numbers of people.) However, when it comes to treating your depression, you'll want to make the best choices for *you*, rather than focus a great deal of your attention outward.

 Alert

> When changing medications, you may need to wait a week or two in between the old and the new, to allow the first medication to leave your system completely. Another option your doctor might suggest is to reduce the dosage of one gradually while steadily increasing the new medication to proper therapeutic levels. Also, tell your dentist or any other doctor about all prescriptions and over-the-counter medications you use; this can prevent dangerous drug interactions.

Ask for help from a trusted friend or family member; such a person will likely have noticed your predicament and will want what's best for you. Having support can make all the difference in taking those first steps toward getting the help you need and deserve.

Beware of Self-Medicating

Many people who suffer from anxiety disorders end up turning to a behavior known in psychology circles as "self-medicating"—that is, using alcohol or illicit or misused drugs to assuage their feelings of sadness, anxiety, or shyness. You probably know that this is not a good idea. Self-medicating has often been shown to lead to serious drug or alcohol problems, even full-blown addiction.

Fact

Depression usually lifts gradually, not all at once, which definitely belies the cliché, "snapping out of it." Don't expect too much of your-self too quickly—but know that depression can improve, especially with treatment. One day soon, you may realize that it isn't there anymore.

Alcohol and other drugs often cause dependency so that you need to keep using the substance to achieve the same feeling of well-being. It also leads to tolerance: Your body gets used to the alcohol or drug and then needs more (and more) to get to the same level of calm, high, or diminished inhibition. While medication specifically prescribed for OCD or depression can help to regulate your mood, alcohol or illegal drugs cannot. In other words, just because you felt great the last time you drank, that doesn't mean you'll feel just as good every time you drink. In fact, most probably, you won't. Alcohol and many illicit drugs act as central nervous system depressants—just what you were trying to avoid.

Other Reasons to Exercise Caution

There are other good reasons not to self-medicate. For one thing, alcohol and illegal drugs will impair your physical coordi-nation and reaction time, meaning that you definitely should not drive under their influences. Doing so could be very dangerous for you or others.

These substances can also alter your judgment. That is, under their effects, you might find yourself doing or saying things you'll wish you hadn't. These can range from embarrassing to downright unsafe. When it comes to self-medicating, remember the ancient say-ing: "He who is his own doctor has a fool for a patient."

Common-Sense Remedies

The best ways to control depression are also the best ways to handle OCD: Choose medication or CBT, or both. Have a good support system, if possible. Limit the stresses in your life as much as you can. Take care to maintain a balanced diet—go easy on the sugar and caffeine, get at least a moderate amount of exercise, and get enough sleep each night. Have some fun activities in your life, as well: a class you can look forward to attending every week, or a night out with your friends. Volunteer for something you believe in. And again, don't neglect to seek professional help whenever depression or any other symptom becomes noticeable or threatens to overwhelm you.

Evaluating Your Depression

The following is a test you can take yourself to find out whether what you're feeling is depression, and, if so, how serious it might be. It's not meant to substitute for a visit to your doctor or therapist; it's intended only as a guideline.

This test was created by Pfizer, Inc., and is reprinted with that company's permission. The best way to use it is to fill it out and bring it to your therapist's office to discuss it.

Over the last two weeks, how often have you been bothered by the following problems:

1. Little interest or pleasure in doing things
   - ❑ Not at all
   - ❑ Several days
   - ❑ More than half the days
   - ❑ Nearly every day

2. Feeling down, depressed or hopeless
   - ❑ Not at all
   - ❑ Several days
   - ❑ More than half the days
   - ❑ Nearly every day

3. Trouble falling or staying asleep, or sleeping too much
   ❑ Not at all
   ❑ Several days
   ❑ More than half the days
   ❑ Nearly every day

4. Feeling tired or having little energy
   ❑ Not at all
   ❑ Several days
   ❑ More than half the days
   ❑ Nearly every day

5. Poor appetite or overeating
   ❑ Not at all
   ❑ Several days
   ❑ More than half the days
   ❑ Nearly every day

6. Feeling bad about yourself—or that you are a failure or have let yourself or your family down
   ❑ Not at all
   ❑ Several days
   ❑ More than half the days
   ❑ Nearly every day

7. Trouble concentrating on things, such as reading the newspaper or watching television
   ❑ Not at all
   ❑ Several days
   ❑ More than half the days
   ❑ Nearly every day

8. Moving or speaking so slowly that other people could have noticed, or the opposite—being so fidgety or restless that you have been moving around a lot more than usual
   - ❑ Not at all
   - ❑ Several days
   - ❑ More than half the days
   - ❑ Nearly every day

9. Thoughts that you would be better off dead, or of hurting yourself in some way
   - ❑ Not at all
   - ❑ Several days
   - ❑ More than half the days
   - ❑ Nearly every day

You can also take this test online at *www.mayoclinic.com/health/depression/MH00103_D* and get your depression score and some suggestions for what you can do about it. A similar screening test is available at *www.depressionscreening.org/screeningtest/screeningtest.htm*.

There are other diagnostic tools for depression, as well. One of the best known is the Beck Depression Inventory (BDI), a questionnaire widely used by doctors and therapists to evaluate depression and follow treatment response. There are many others. In Appendix A, you'll find a number of books, Web sites, and other resources. But your best bet is still to get a physical exam from your doctor and, if the cause of your depression is not physical, to look into treatment, either with therapy, medication, or both.

Help for Special Problems

If you'd rather not use medication, or if allergies or other problems prevent its use, cognitive therapy is an effective and safe option. As you now know, there are many kinds of depression treatments available. Keep in mind that you do not have to stick with anything that isn't working for you, whether it's medication, therapy, or, for that matter, depression itself.

If You Can't Stomach Meds

If stomach or other problems prevent you from taking pills, you might enjoy more success with a transdermal medicine patch. (That is, one that delivers the medication through the skin.) The patch is placed on the back, upper arm, stomach, or other part of the body where there is a lot of skin and where it will be out of the way. One caveat: Nausea can still occur with the use of transdermal patches, so use with care.

Many medicines are also available in liquid or syrup versions. If your pharmacy cannot accommodate you, seek out a *compounding pharmacy*, which can formulate its own medicines. You might start by asking your doctor or pharmacist for recommendations.

For Treatment-Resistant Depression

New possibilities are emerging for depression that has not responded well to conventional treatment. We've already mentioned neurofeedback as one of the newer, drug-free possibilities.

Researchers have also begun experimenting with other techniques such as magnetic seizure therapy, deep brain stimulation, and transcranial magnetic stimulation (TMS), all of which work directly on the brain. Magnetic seizure therapy and deep brain stimulation require hospitalization and general anesthesia; transcranial magnetic stimulation does not. Deep brain stimulation has the longest history, as it is currently used in the treatment of Parkinson's symptoms. It does carry a risk of side effects, however. Transcranial magnetic stimulation, though not always effective, seems to pose few risks and have few side effects, but it is prohibitively expensive for most, and only available currently in a very limited number of clinical and research settings. As of this writing, only small numbers of people have tried any of these depression treatments in clinical trials. More research is needed to determine their safety and effectiveness.

CHAPTER 11

Your Personal Life

OCD, LIKE ANY HEALTH condition, can affect virtually every aspect of your life. Many people who have OCD manage relatively well at work or school—suffering tremendously, perhaps, but keeping their worries and compulsions hidden, at least to a degree. The same cannot often be said about home life. Sooner or later, in most cases, it becomes impossible to hide compulsions and fears from people you live with or see very often (assuming you have made an effort to hide your behaviors from other members of your household in the first place). Family members and significant others often come to feel ruled by the other person's OCD.

Stress and OCD

OCD is no different from just about any other kind of disorder, in that stress just makes it worse. You almost certainly have seen this for yourself already. Obviously, the two most important things you can do for yourself, then, are to keep your general stress level down and, at the same time, work on treating your OCD. Keep in mind that both of these things require effort, and that neither will ever be "finished," in all likelihood.

Just as you couldn't do yoga or floor exercises or swimming practice for a few months and expect that you were now in shape and would stay that way for the rest of your life, neither can you reduce stress or get OCD under control just once for all time.

You have to work at it, and you have to keep it up.

Maintain the Gains

While it may be possible for you to reduce or even stop taking your medication (however, you should not do this without discussing it with your doctor), keeping stress and OC symptoms at bay should be things you work at all the time.

The good news is that, as you work on the stress, the OCD should follow. The two, more often than not, go hand in hand. By minimizing stress through exercise, good nutrition, adequate rest, wholesome and enjoyable activities, as strong an emotional support system as you can put together, and perhaps a calm-inducing discipline such as yoga or meditation, you will most likely put stress on the run. Of course, you will need to keep up your OCD treatment as well, just maybe not as much over time.

"Remission" and Setbacks

Unfortunately, it is likely, or at least possible, that your OC symptoms will return from time to time. That's okay, especially if you know to expect it. If you try not to let it bother you too much, get some additional help and support if you need them, put your cognitive skills into play, and let Mr. OCD know that you were expecting him and that you no longer care to stay friends, you should be able to weather the storm. If you need to see your therapist or doctor again, that's okay, too. Remember, OCD is a disorder of the brain. It really is a neurobiological condition. It's not your fault. You can't control the fact that you have it, but you definitely can control the way you choose to deal with it.

L, Essential

Sadly, nothing can truly protect you from harm, and most people differ about which activities are generally safe. Horseback riding, hanggliding, skiing, swimming, flying on a plane—plenty of people would consider those pleasurable recreational activities. However, others would view them as terrifying and fraught with danger.

If you had, heaven forbid, a relapse of the cancer that had responded successfully once to radiation and chemotherapy, you wouldn't hesitate to go right back to your doctor. You wouldn't think, I seemed to make so much progress; he's going to be disappointed. Your doctor might indeed feel some disappointment, and so might you, that your OC symptoms had returned or worsened, but having OCD or continuing to have OCD, is not your fault. (And, anyway, if the doctor feels disappointed, that's his problem.) To paraphrase Alcoholics Anonymous's famous serenity prayer: Control what you can and let go of the rest.

Do not allow OCD to run roughshod over you. Don't let up on your vigilance against it. You will almost certainly want to "take it easy" now and then, give in to your hand-washing compulsion or your need for perfection. But it will be much, much better if you don't.

Don't Be Remiss in Your Remission

You've read about potential setbacks. Now, consider the other side of the coin: remission. Sometimes, for whatever reason, your symptoms may get markedly better. This can last for a day or for many years. If you have not done CBT or used medication for your OCD, chances are it will eventually come back.

In any case, we advise you to maximize your remissions whether they happen early in the game or after you've completed a long course of treatment.

For example: If you find yourself entertaining the idea of trying something new, something that your rational mind tells you will not hurt you, but you feel that moment of anxious hesitation—that "I shouldn't, I guess"—allow yourself the pleasure of that wholesome activity. Tell Mr. OCD, "Thank you for sharing." Then tell him to scram.

Keep Symptoms in Check

In addition to doing what you can to reduce the overall stress in your life (and no, this isn't necessarily easy, even if you *do* exercise, eat well, and try to get an adequate amount of sleep), continuing to work at controlling your symptoms will be a very good idea. So, how do you do that?

One way is to refuse to give in to the demands of your OCD. (Granted, this is also not as easy as it sounds.) If you can't refuse entirely, then refuse as much as you can. If you need help—whether from a family member, friend, therapist, support group, or doctor (or any combination of these)—get it.

Family members will almost certainly be delighted to help you fight against your symptoms. (Enlisting their help will also put you on the same "team," psychologically speaking.) They have probably felt constrained by your OCD symptoms almost as much as you have.

Asking for Tough Love

Ask your parent, spouse, or whomever *not* to allow you to check the door lock more than once, for instance, or not to go back home to make sure the stove is really off. Soliciting and substituting their constant reassurance for your own checking is still engaging in OC behavior. If you have been enlisting family members or others close to you to assist in your OC routines, now is the time to stop. In that case, ask them not to help you, to remind you gently that you're facing up to your anxieties on your own now.

Coping Strategies

Use creative distraction. Check the stove, then go for a relaxing walk around your neighborhood. (You should be familiar with this technique from CBT. If you're already able to leave your home for thirty minutes after turning off the stove, now is the time to try sixty, or a whole day.)

Reward yourself for a job well done. If you can leave your front door after one lock check, go out and do something fun: a cup of coffee and an enjoyable book at your local emporium (actually, we hope you'll go for low-caffeine tea, instead!), a shopping trip, canoeing—whatever, as they say, floats your boat!

Don't Let the OCD Win

Do not neglect to keep in touch with your prescribing doctor, your therapist, or both. It's a good idea to get regular "checkups." Finally, do not underestimate the value of a good support system. If you feel as if stress or your OC symptoms, or both, may be getting worse, talk with a trusted friend, visit your online support group, tell your mom—whatever works for you.

Will It Ever Go Away?

As you've read, OCD doesn't really go away (at least, as of now, for the general population; some people with advanced or severely resistant OCD have benefited from brain surgery). But that's the bad news. Using the methods you've learned so far, you should be able to keep your OCD manageable indefinitely. So what if it isn't technically "cured"? A little of it will probably always be with you. But it will be more like a picture on the wall than the king of your house.

Hoping the Worst Is Behind You

It's unlikely that you'll go from fearful shut-in to devil-may-care gadabout (although you might: Lucinda Bassett apparently went from severe anxiety sufferer to world traveler, lecturer, and director of a respected anxiety treatment program, so you never know). The point is that, while your OCD probably won't vanish, your worst moments with it may just become unhappy memories.

If you're using, or have successfully used, CBT, medication, stress-reduction techniques, and other strategies you've read about in this book, you should enjoy enough of a reduction in your OCD symptoms that they no longer rule over you and make all the decisions in your life. Good for you!

Can Your OCD Actually Morph?

OCD, sadly, *can* change forms. You may find that, as you begin to vanquish the kind you have, a new obsession (or more than one obsession) pops up to take its place. That can be discouraging, but don't despair. The new obsessions and compulsions generally won't be as robust as their older counterparts because they haven't had time to dig in and grow strong. Think of them as tiny weeds with small root systems. Then kill 'em. Don't waste any time. Treat any new worries as you did your old ones: Seek help and don't give in to them. You don't play that anymore.

Your Family Life

If you have a spouse, significant other, or children—in fact, if you live in a household with other people—chances are your OCD plays some kind of role. Whether other members of your household have to pick up items you accidentally drop on the floor or give in to your demands that they immediately wash their clothing after coming home from something "unclean," or cringe at the thought of upsetting your orderly kitchen, they are affected. Some family members will be kind, others not quite so understanding. (In fact, you may even see outright hostility or derisiveness, unfortunately.) In all cases, they will want to see you tame your OCD for your sake, as well as their own, and the interest of family harmony. Don't hesitate to involve your family in your treatment, if you wish. It may well be helpful for all of you.

When Both Members of a Couple Have OCD

Not only does it often happen that genetically related people have OCD, it also happens sometimes that two people who have OCD end up in a relationship together. In fact, this is not as unusual a situation as you might think.

First of all, we do tend to choose partners who remind us in some ways of our parents. So it's logical that, if your father had OCD, for instance (and we know OCD is genetic), your boyfriend or husband might, too. It's also logical that someone who has OCD really understands you—at least, when it comes to that one particular aspect of your life. Then, too, it's so much easier, in a lot of ways, to live with a person whose needs are in some ways very similar to your own (even if you don't share the same kind of OCD). Less has to be explained, in many cases.

OCD Times Two

You might not have meant to end up with someone who, like you, has OCD. In fact, you may be surprised, after having lived together for a while, when your partner or spouse is diagnosed; only in retrospect will you notice the similarities in certain aspects of your behaviors. That might present a good opportunity for you to support each other through treatment (especially as you already understand each other so well). Be aware, however, that if one partner undergoes successful treatment for OCD while the other avoids it, the prognosis for the relationship may not be so good. Seeing a partner move toward a healthier place in her life could prove intolerable for someone still mired in the old. Such situations sometimes require serious deliberation, often with the help of a competent therapist.

On the Other Side

Living with a person who also has OCD can present its own special challenges. You may, for a change, find yourself exasperated with your partner's obsessive-compulsive behavior—and she with yours! Unhappily (or maybe this is a good thing, really), just as in genetically related groups, partners who have OCD often have different types from one another. While you can certainly sympathize, even empathize, try to avoid becoming an enabler of your partner's OCD, or asking for the same.

Sexuality and OCD

Having OCD, in all probability, will not exactly enhance your love or sex life. If you have contamination phobias, of course, the pitfalls are obvious. Even if you don't, obsessions and compulsions, as you've probably learned the hard way, are not conducive to good relationships, romantic or otherwise. They tend to tax a partner's patience, for one thing, and prevent one member from participating in activities the other enjoys (indeed, OC symptoms may well prevent you from participating in activities *you* enjoy) and generally place a number of limits on a couple. The question is, what can you do about this?

Obviously, the first thing you'll want to do is get treatment, whether with medication, cognitive therapy, or one of the other methods we've discussed. However, while it's true that the more you do a thing, the less afraid of it you become, that's not necessarily the case when it comes to sex.

Fear of Illness

To a person who fears contracting a serious illness through sex, repetition, even with the same partner, will not always diminish the worry. Your mind may continue to sabotage the relationship by whispering into your ear (or your head, at any rate): *So we're a couple. I don't know where she is 24/7. Can I trust her? Even so, what was she doing before we met?* And on and on. And on.

Essential

Several authorities recommend the use of a "behavioral contract," sometimes called a "family contract." This means that the OCD sufferer and his family agree on a set of ground rules: no reassurance, no participating in the person's "rituals," and so on.

So, here's the deal: Just as you would if you didn't have OCD, you need to talk. In fact, you probably need to talk more than you would otherwise. You may want to explain, for instance, your need to jump right up and shower afterward, if that is the case. You probably shouldn't let something like that come as a surprise to a new partner. In a fledgling romance, people are apt to feel self-conscious enough as it is. Try to have this talk early, rather than at the last moment; this will allow you to avoid having the strictures of your OCD intrude any more than necessary on your new relationship.

Of course, you'll want to talk about sexual history: disclosing yours and asking your would-be partner to do the same for you. That's just good sense, whether you have OCD or not. Certainly, if you're concerned about contagious illness, you'd be within your rights to ask your potential partner to have a blood test. (Of course, the same could be asked of you. If so, are you prepared to submit to one, yourself?) We think you should know the person fairly well before entering into a sexual relationship. And we believe in practicing safe sex. But we also understand that total reassurance might not be possible for you.

As for whether to believe what you're told, that's for you to decide. Chances are, your danger sensors are so out-of-whack at this point that you don't really trust yourself to make the right decisions. If that's so for you, perhaps you could ask a friend you trust whether she gets a good feeling about your potential partner's general honesty and character. You can also ask your therapist, or a family member. Then, ask yourself, and listen hard for the answer. You want to be careful, to protect yourself and others—and you should. But you also want to have fun, enjoy life's pleasures, maybe form a long-term relationship and even have a child, or children.

Sexual Anxiety and OCD

Sexual preoccupations are not uncommon in people who have OCD. Some people who have OCD are filled with worry that they might be gay. On the other hand, some people really are gay. Of these, some are not comfortable with that. In general, the kind of intense worry about possible homosexual impulses that accompanies OCD is more an irrational obsession than any routine developmental questioning of one's sexual orientation.

How can you tell whether you're gay or just panicked about the possibility that you might be? There isn't a physical test. You won't fluoresce under bright light or anything. But there are some guidelines psychologists use. The first thing you might want to ask yourself, however, is this: What if I *am* more attracted to people of my own sex than the other one?

Another thing to keep in mind: Most educated people today believe that sexuality occurs on a continuum. In other words, no one, really, is completely gay or completely straight. Most people fall somewhere along the spectrum. However, if the possibility that you might be homosexual is worrisome to you, then it's a legitimate problem, just as any worry would be.

 Fact

> Obsessional anxiety about whether one is gay actually has a name. It is known, in some psychological circles, as "Homosexuality OCD," or simply "H-OCD." It is not that uncommon. In fact, many people who have OCD suffer from *some* kind of unwanted sexual obsession or preoccupation.

How Do You Know?

While you can't necessarily know everything you want to know, just when you want to know it and with absolute certainty, there are a few guidelines you can use. You would also be well advised to talk with a therapist if you have concerns, not with the intention of trying to "cure" you if you *are* gay (such so-called "conversion therapy" has been discredited), but because this is the kind of information that most people would like to know about themselves.

In the meantime, here's the $64 dollar question: Do you want to date, or be intimate with, people of your own sex? If the answer is:

- *And how!* Then, chances are, you don't have to worry. You might be gay and if so, that's probably all right with you.
- *No. I don't have a particular problem with homosexuality; it simply doesn't appeal to me personally*, then chances are, you're not.

Confusion and worry can come in when your answer falls in between these extremes—and, for a lot of people, it will. If you have

OCD and are constantly plagued by intrusive and unwanted sexual obsessions, things may be considerably trickier.

For some, attraction to members of their own sex will cause distress and anxiety. These folks may, indeed, be gay, but have a hard time accepting that because of social norms, upbringing, negative societal stereotypes, fear of discrimination, and so on.

Then there are those who don't feel attracted to persons of their own sex particularly, but find their minds repeatedly invaded with homosexual thoughts and impulses that disturb them.

Adding to the confusion is this: Virtually everyone—homosexual and heterosexual (and in between)—probably experiences bizarre sexual thoughts (again, both homosexual and heterosexual in nature) for no obvious reason. We don't know why this happens; we just know that it does.

 ## Question

Are there many kinds of sexual obsession?
Yes. Many people with OCD experience horrible visions about committing sexually inappropriate or violent acts, such as rape. Often, they're terrified that they might act on their fears. They almost never do. (Of course, such crimes are committed, but rarely by people who worry obsessively that they'll commit them.)

The difference between a person who has OCD and a person who doesn't is that the thoughts won't bother the person who does not have OCD. They'll show up, the person will think, *Well, that was weird*, and go about her day. The person who has OCD or H-OCD, on the other hand, will obsess and obsess: *What does it mean? Could I be gay? And, if not, why do I keep having these thoughts?*

Next time, try allowing the thought to drift into your head and then quietly drift away. Or explore it. ("Hiya, thought. I want to do what with whom? Well, I don't think so, but all right; for the moment, instead of trying my hardest to push you away, I'll just go with it. Go ahead, thought. Do your worst.")

 Fact

> *Seinfeld's* fictional George Costanza seems to have suffered from H-OCD, in at least one of the show's well-remembered episodes, and "homosexual panic" figured heavily in the plot of Albert Innaurato's 1976 hit Broadway comedy *Gemini*.

Becoming Comfortable with Yourself

The truth is, if you feel genuinely attracted to members of your own sex, but this idea bothers you for the reasons mentioned elsewhere in this section, it's probably not an OCD issue. You still might benefit from some therapy, though, to help you feel more comfortable with yourself. (Like OCD, homosexuality is now believed to originate in the brain, not in one's early life experiences and certainly not in the choices one makes.)

If you're attracted to members of the opposite sex, but just can't seem to stop these intrusive, persistent homosexual worries, chances are it's an OCD issue and will respond well to treatment.

Your Secret Weapon

Up to this point, you haven't read about one of the most powerful weapons in the arsenal of OCD fighters. (It's not bad against other life problems, either.) It's a simple thing—one you can't buy or make, although you can encourage its development. It's something no one can give you, but others can foster in you. It is a sense of humor.

If you don't have a sense of humor, get one! (Happily, most people who have OCD do seem to enjoy well-developed abilities to see the funnier aspects and absurdities of their condition. Which doesn't mean that it isn't, at the same time, terrible.) No one will tell you that

OCD is fun. But it can be funny. Even at its most horrible, it can be funny.

As a group, people who have OCD tend to be bright and creative. Many possess excellent senses of humor. This is important, particularly that last part. Think of your sense of humor as your "secret weapon" against despair, hopelessness and OCD itself.

An OCD Sufferer Walks into a Bar . . .

There are several jokes about OCD. Here's one about CBT:

It seems that Mrs. Moskowitz had a paralyzing fear of kreplach, the little meat dumplings that are practically staples of Jewish cooking. ("Kreplach," by the way, is pronounced not to rhyme with "hatch," but with a gutteral Germanic gargle-like sound, as in "ach!")

In any case, this presented more of a problem than you might think: Mrs. Moskowitz was Jewish and had a large family. Naturally, at virtually every family get-together, someone—a newcomer or a forgetful relative—would arrive bearing a pot of chicken soup with kreplach, and poor Mrs. Moskowitz would forget to ask whether the pot contained any of the offending delicacy; she would lift the pot lid, peer inside, then drop the lid back down with a clang. Her face would turn ashen, and she'd feel a chill come over her entire body. "Aiee! Kreplach!" she'd scream.

Well, Mrs. Moskowitz's children decided it was time for them to get their mother some help. They found a specialist and set up an appointment, then surprised her with the news.

 Alert

> The thing you have to watch out for, of course, when you and your significant other both have OCD is enabling. This can be hard to avoid. Ideally, you will both get therapy and, if appropriate, medication. If you can also attend couples therapy to work on your shared problem, all the better.

Mrs. Moskowitz was just as eager as they were to bring a resolution to this terrible problem. So she eagerly kept her first appointment. She explained her situation to the doctor, who listened with sympathy and obvious understanding.

"Mrs. Moskowitz," he said, "You've shown great courage by coming here and expressing the intention to tackle your kreplach phobia. It happens that I am a specialist when it comes to treating this kind of disorder. What we need is to get you acclimated to the food. So here's what we're going to do:

When you come in for your next appointment, I want you to use the side door. It leads right to my own kitchen. We are going to make kreplach together."

Mrs. Moskowitz turned a little pale but agreed to come back next time and work on overcoming her fear. The big day arrived. Mrs. Moskowitz, not wanting to disappoint her children or herself, took a deep breath and rang the doctor's doorbell. He welcomed her into a spacious, spotless kitchen.

 Fact

> On Comedy Central's "Crank Yankers," (on which actors, portrayed by puppets, made prank phone calls) Kevin Nealon performed the role of "OCD Ken," a quirky, middle-aged accountant. Interestingly, Nealon also appeared alongside Tony Shalhoub in a *Monk* episode. He played a patient in a mental hospital to Shalhoub's OCD sufferer.

Hanging on a chrome hook was an apron. A copy of a tattered but clean cookbook of favorite eastern European recipes lay open on the counter. The doctor had even gone so far as to purchase all the needed ingredients. On the table were a steel mixing bowl and various utensils, as well as onions, a brand-new bag of flour, a package of kosher hamburger, half a dozen eggs, and so on: everything Mrs. Moskowitz and her doctor would need to prepare the tasty dumplings.

"The first thing we're going to do," the doctor told her, "is to read through the recipe. What would you think of that?"

Mrs. Moskowitz dutifully read the recipe and felt only the mildest discomfort, hardly anything at all, really. Next, at the doctor's direction, she measured out the flour and poured it into the mixing bowl. The doctor was pleased enough to remark on how well his new patient seemed to be handling the stress of the exercise. She was doing well, indeed!

She managed to roll out the dough, cut little circles into it, brown the meat, chop the onions, make a mixture and place a small amount in the center of every dough circle. . . . At last, the tray of dumplings was ready to go into the pot of boiling, salted water.

Mrs. Moskowitz removed her apron and sat down at the kitchen table as the kreplach boiled.

"Mrs. Moskowitz," the doctor said, "I'm pleased with your progress. All we need do is wait for the kreplach to finish cooking. In fact, it should be ready just about now. Would you do the honors?"

The patient walked across the floor to the stove, lifted the lid off the simmering pot, peered inside, dropped the lid back into place and hollered, "Aiee!! Kreplach!"

Although this joke incorrectly portrays CBT as ineffective, it does illustrate (rather amusingly, we think), the irrational nature of OCD.

The sheer number of jokes involving psychiatrists, psychologists, and analysts (and even, as you've just seen, a cognitive behavioral therapist), not to mention M.D.s, should give you an idea about how great the need is to laugh at our challenges.

Another OCD Sufferer

An old story goes that a man is driving in an unfamiliar neighborhood when he gets a flat tire. He pulls over to the side of the road and finds himself in front of a wrought-iron gate enclosing beautiful, bucolic grounds. He gets out of the car and removes the lug nuts from the flat. As he moves toward the trunk, which holds the spare, he accidentally kicks the lug nuts—as bad luck would have it—right down a sewer grate. He curses his misfortune. A man on the other side of the gate hears the other man hollering, and calls out to him: "Hey! Mister!" The guy turns and looks. "Yes?" he asks. Just then, he notices that, carved above the door of the most prominent building on the grounds is the name of a mental hospital.

Fact

In their 1960s "2,000-Year-Old Man" comedy improvisations, Carl Reiner and Mel Brooks created a psychiatrist character who cures his patient of her paper-tearing compulsion by simply telling her that she's a lovely girl and shouldn't tear paper.

The man behind the gate continues, "Mister! I saw what happened. But you don't have to get upset. There's a simple solution. All you have to do is take one lug nut off of each of the remaining tires. That way, they'll each have three, and that will be enough to get you to a service station or auto supply store, where you can buy four more."

The other man's jaw drops. "That's brilliant!" he exclaims. "I would never have thought of that on my own." Then, he thinks for a moment and adds, "Uh. . . I hope you won't mind my asking, but, just what is a fella like you doing in a place like this?"

His new friend responds, "Mister. I'm here 'cause I'm crazy, not 'cause I'm stupid."

In spite of the now-politically incorrect portrayal of mental illness, this also points out that you can be completely rational (not to mention, very bright) in some ways, but decidedly irrational in others.

What All This Means to You

As OCD seems to affect bright, creative people, you may as well turn some of your mental energies and talent away from obsessive worries and toward the humor in everyday life, particularly yours. Humor, generally, is good for your mental health, your physical health, and (assuming it's not cruel or sarcastic) your relationships. Try to fit as much of it as you can into your life.

CHAPTER 12

Your Work Life

CONTRARY TO POPULAR PERCEPTION, people who have OCD are not specifically protected by the Americans with Disabilities Act (ADA) of 1990. In fact, nobody is! Decisions about whether an employer is guilty of discrimination are handled on a case-by-case basis. However, the Equal Employment Opportunity Commission (EEOC), the governmental body that oversees issues related to the ADA, has specific stated guidelines about what constitutes discrimination (and what constitutes a disability). The Act states that it is not lawful for an employer to discriminate (that is, to fire a qualified employee or refuse to hire a qualified one) solely because she has a disability.

"Scary" Job Duties

Virtually every job you hold over the course of your working life will require you to do things you don't like. This is true for just about everyone. However, for a person who has OCD, even seemingly mundane aspects of work life can become terrifying. Your job might require you to drive, shake hands with customers or clients, or take them to lunch. If your worries involve food, you may find breakfast or lunch meetings unbearable. You might have many worries related to travel. Your job might require you to fly, or to take a train or car. You might have to handle cash or use public restrooms. Any of those things or situations might cause difficulty.

A handicap, as defined by the ADA, is a physical or mental impairment that substantially limits a major life activity. "Major life activity" in this case could mean concentrating, taking proper care of oneself, and so on. Generally speaking, the language is meant to describe the kinds of things that most other people could do without difficulty.

 Alert

> Do not assume that you are automatically protected by the ADA. If you don't tell your employer that you have OCD until after you've been fired, you will not have a case against her. Your best bet will almost certainly be to try to work together toward solutions before problems begin.

There are other specific criteria that the EEOC would look at were you to file a discrimination complaint against an employer or former employer. These include the length of time you have had the condition, how severely and in what ways it limits your performance, and whether it is currently being managed by things like medication. But we hope it doesn't come to that. In most cases, effective treatment can reduce how much of a disability OCD has to be.

"Reasonable Accommodation"

Under the ADA, certain basic rights are protected. One is your right to keep your job if you are otherwise qualified. In other words, you can't lose your job just because your disability makes life inconvenient for your boss. However, your boss is also protected. By law (in fact, by the same law), an employer cannot be made to make accommodations that would be too expensive, for example. (This is known as "undue hardship.") That way, your boss doesn't face the possibility of going bankrupt (and therefore, out of business) spending the money to build you your own private bathroom and kitchenette. That's where "reasonable accommodation" come in.

What this term means is that, assuming that you meet the ADA criteria for disability, *reasonable accommodation* would enable you to perform the job while allowing for the limitations created by your OCD. Here are a few examples:

 Fact

Many other countries have laws similar to the ADA. In the United Kingdom, for example, the Disability Discrimination Act of 1995 covers mental and physical disabilities in the workplace. That act, too, requires employers to make "reasonable adjustments."

- Your start time is 9 A.M., but, because of your checking behaviors, you seldom arrive at your place of work before 9:30. Depending on the type of job, you and your boss might decide that 9:30 becomes your new start time, and you make up the lost half hour at the end of the day. (However, once you've agreed to the new schedule, you must stick to it. If you arrive after 9:30, under this arrangement, you would be considered late and could be subject to disciplinary action, just like any other employee.)
- If you are required to fly to the company's annual meeting and your anxiety prevents you from getting on a plane, reasonable accommodation might consist of teleconferencing or traveling to the event by car or by train. If you are a salesperson and are afraid to fly, you might have your territory switched with that of another sales rep, so that you could drive to your clients.
- If you work at the kind of job that requires you to shake hands with customers or clients, your boss might agree to a friendly Howie Mandel-style "knuckle-knock" instead so that you don't appear inhospitable. (The gesture might even catch on among fellow employees, and ultimately distinguish your company from others like it!)

Requesting Reasonable Accommodation

Requesting reasonable accommodation can be a delicate matter. You may not want to announce, the moment you're hired, that you have OCD and have special needs that must be met. To be sure, we understand.

However, if you need accommodation and don't request it, in all probability, you won't be able to make a case against your former employer or defend against your job termination if it should come to that. (OCD is a "hidden disability." That is, your employer might not know you had it unless you told him, so he couldn't be blamed for firing you for constant lateness, say, if he didn't know the reason for it.) So the time to request reasonable accommodation is before you lose your job because your symptoms have made it impossible for you to do your work acceptably. Please note: This does *not* mean you should discuss it before you receive a job offer.

Ľ. Essential

In a few specific circumstances, an employer might be exempt from ADA regulations. The EEOC has a lot of information available for both employees (and would-be employees) and employers. Search EEOC. gov for information about the Americans with Disabilities Act of 1990, and for other employment-related information.

We know: you may not like this idea. Many people who have OCD, knowing the stereotypes and lack of knowledge that surround it, try to keep their behaviors hidden. So we suggest that you see how things go for a bit. If you should start to run into problems—for example, your boss reprimands you for refusing to accept a client's outstretched hand, you're continually late for work—this would be the time to say, "I want to do a good job, but I have obsessive-compulsive disorder and can't shake hands with strangers. Can we work out something else?"

Remember, too, that accommodation, although it may make you stand out in a different way than you would hope, might also make it possible for you to do your job more effectively. In other words, it can be good for both you and your employer.

If Reasonable Accommodation Cannot Be Found

A would-be employer is under no obligation to hire you, so if you mention your OCD before you're offered the job, and the employer doesn't think she'll be able to accommodate you, she can simply decide you're not qualified for the position, and choose another candidate. If you reveal it once you're hired, your employer will have to try to make reasonable accommodation.

However, suppose that's just not possible? Say you are afraid to drive to work and your boss contends that the job cannot be done adequately from home?

 Fact

> While not specifically disallowed by law, it would be extremely hard for any employer to have a no-OCD hiring policy because it would be his responsibility to prove that it would be impossible for virtually anyone with any kind or degree of OCD to do the job. (The Army is one exception.)

In that case, your employer would be expected to offer you a different job at the same level (that is, not a promotion, just something different). She would not be obligated or expected, however, to fire someone else in order to do so, or to create a new position for you.

Sad to say, there may not be a solution. If a different position is not an option, and no other resolution can be found, it could be decided that you are no longer qualified to perform your job. You don't have to get fired, however. You could be laid off due to disability. Again, we hope it doesn't come to that. We hope that you and your employer will try to work together, in case that elusive solution can be found. If you do think you've been discriminated against, or prejudged, because you have OCD, you may have grounds for a discrimination case or complaint.

If You Can't Work

In relatively rare cases, OC symptoms might become so severe that it is no longer really possible to work. If you weren't diagnosed prior to that point, or if treatment has failed (or if, perhaps, you have not been able to begin treatment), you might find yourself limited in the amount and type of work you can do. As you probably know, treatment is your best option.

Essential

The Job Accommodation Network (JAN) is part of the President's Committee on the Employment of People with Disabilities and the United States Department of Labor. The JAN information line is: 1-800-526-7234. (In West Virginia, call 1-800-526-4698.)

You might be a good candidate for an in-patient OCD treatment program. (Several are listed in Appendix B.) We hope you will investigate this possibility. Such programs are often the best courses of action for people whose symptoms are advanced. You will have a safe, supportive place in which to get better and begin your transition back into the world of employment and everything else. In the meantime, we urge you to get the support you need—from online groups, therapy, your family, and any other healthful source—and to work on stopping any behaviors you may have that are causing you obvious harm. We also urge you to beware of work-at-home "opportunities." If depression is a problem, please look at Chapter 10, or get in touch with your mental health provider, or emergency services.

Special Circumstances

While your prospective employer (with a few exceptions) is not allowed by law to ask about your medical conditions or history prior to offering you a job, you may be asked once an offer is made. In some cases, such as if your employer can demonstrate that a person who has your particular kind of OCD cannot do the job even if reasonable accommodation is made, the offer can legally be withdrawn. But the employer would have to be able to prove his statement if you were to file suit.

 Alert

Do not lie to an employer or prospective employer. You may be tempted to do so if you feel cornered, but resist, as you will probably lose any protections you might have enjoyed otherwise.

If you are asked a question on a pre-employment test that suggests to you that the potential employer is trying to find out whether you have OCD or a similar condition, or if you are asked such a question during an interview, you may file a complaint with the EEOC. However, there are questions, such as whether travel might be a problem, that an employer may legally ask.

Public Service Jobs

Currently, we know of no specific provision regarding police recruits who have OCD. While each police department in the country can establish its own employment policy, most departments make hiring decisions on a case-by-case basis, and usually take into account such factors as medication. Of course, the biggest criterion is whether the applicant can meet the essential requirements of the job.

This appears to be true of most fire and EMT (emergency medical technician) departments, as well. Most, if not all, U.S. fire departments administer complete psychological evaluations, and many will request information about psychiatric history. However, it does not seem as if OCD per se will exclude an applicant from service.

The U.S. Army

If you want to serve in the Army, you're out of luck—at least as of this writing. The United States Army does not currently allow a person who has, or has had, OCD to serve. Once again, however, we hope you won't feel discouraged if it is your dream to join the military. A lot has changed in the armed services in recent years. Further changes may come as the general population becomes more educated about things like OCD, and individuals challenge their statuses. Such things have happened in the military before.

 Question

> **Can you become an astronaut if you have OCD?**
> In theory, yes; however, there are medical requirements. (You cannot if you've had vision-correction surgery.) NASA physicians must determine that you're free of medical problems that would impede your participation in space flight, or that would be worsened by it.

A few other jobs do require psychiatric evaluations, and OCD is still considered, in many quarters, to be a psychological illness. This will probably change, as well. Please do not assume, by the way, that you cannot pass a psychological exam just because you have OCD.

Finding a Job

When you look for a job, you should look for something that meshes with your interests, talents, and experience, rather than for something that's close to your home or that, in some other way, will allow you to avoid your feared situation or situations. Your best bet, if you still have strong OCD issues, will be to continue to work with your cognitive behavioral therapist (or whatever other therapy might work for you) and to take medication (if you currently do so) while you work at a job you enjoy (at least to some degree).

The Benefits of the Job

While you shouldn't necessarily look for jobs that do the least amount of damage to your "comfort zone," it is wise to look at companies that offer employee assistance programs (EAPs) and health insurance, particularly mental health services, as CBT would fall under that heading.

If you're offered a job that looks ideal, except for one thing—say, you're required to travel by plane to an annual conference—perhaps, once the offer has been made, you can ask about accommodation. If it is a situation like flying, it can almost be said that you're in luck: many people have a fear of flying. Your boss might, too. In any case, she might be willing to offer a compromise. Perhaps you can tele-conference or travel by train. Creative thinking will probably benefit both of you.

Making Your Own Arrangements

Of course, as you no doubt know, you can probably find your own way around certain difficulties without involving an employer: preparing a thermos of coffee for yourself if you don't want to share the office coffeepot, toting your own snacks for lunch meetings, leaving your home extra early in the mornings so that you can get to work on time, and so on. Most coworkers will probably be engrossed enough in their own lives that they might not take notice of behaviors like these, unless those behaviors really stand out. If you're unlucky enough to have nosy coworkers, you might want to rehearse a breezy half-truth. ("Oh, I've gotten so used to my own coffee over the years that nothing else really tastes right to me.") You might look a little eccentric, but so what? Anyone who doesn't have some kind of idio-syncrasy probably isn't very interesting.

Thinking Up Ideas

Some problems may at first seem hard to solve. While it's nearly impossible to come up with usable ideas for every potential OC situation, here is some general advice for solving problems: Think about the problem often, and ask yourself, How can I solve this? Assume that there *is* a solution. If that doesn't work, or takes too long, ask a friend or peer who has a similar problem. You might even put specific questions to an online or in-person support group.

A Memo to Employers

If one or more of your employees has OCD, you are, first of all, to be commended for wanting more information. Presumably, you want to do right by all of your employees, and this is a great thing.

 Question

Is "workaholism" a kind of OCD?
Many researchers believe it is. It certainly has a lot in common with OCD, as the sufferer usually does not enjoy his compulsion to work, but, against the advice of friends, family members, health professionals, and even coworkers, will continue to do so. (In Japan, there is even a word—*karoshi*—for death from overwork.)

Employees who have OCD can present certain challenges to employers, as you may know. For one thing, a person who seems "perfectly normal" in virtually every way might suddenly shock you with the information that he can't touch money or drive other employees to off-site events. Or he might exhibit some other seemingly strange behavior.

On the other hand, on occasion, OCD might actually work in an employer's favor, as when a perfectionistic worker is driven to try her absolute hardest for the company.

Hyperorganizational behaviors are another possible asset to a company, though they can act as a double-edged sword if the person is also easily upset when others disturb his space. If the employee's job involves public safety, or if lives depend on her performance, you will probably be a lot better off with an OC employee than with a sociopathic one (or possibly, just about any other kind)! But, as you may also know, a person who has OCD can also present puzzles and even problems.

What Is He So Scared Of?

A person who has OCD might have issues related to the work environment, such as a fear of shared restrooms, handling cash, eating in front of other people, or of flying, giving presentations, driving over highways or bridges, taking elevators, working on a high floor, shaking hands with clients or customers, and more.

Almost anything you can imagine has probably panicked someone who has OCD.

Then again, OCD might create undesirable *situations*: an employee who is constantly late to work (because she's spending so much time showering or checking locks and appliances before leaving for work in the morning, or turning back along the way because she fears she may have accidentally hit an unlucky pedestrian), someone who needs constant reassurance that he has completed a task, or done so to your satisfaction, and so on.

 Fact

A Missouri realtor found that keeping a small monkey by her side wherever she went significantly reduced her anxiety. Her doctors were pleased, but neighbors complained to the health department, which agreed that the animal posed a threat to public health. (As of this writing, the case has not been resolved.)

OCD is a neurological condition. It is not, for what this may be worth, an emotional problem. However, this can be hard to remember. After all, a person who has OCD doesn't need a ramp or a helper dog. He might seem perfectly "normal" in every respect but one. It may even seem as if he merely wants to gain attention or be "different."

Trust us, this is almost never the case. The great majority of people who have OCD feel ashamed and try not to call attention to their differences. In some cases, an employee might reveal his condition only as a last resort against being fired.

L. Essential

For some people, OCD will surely constitute a disability. For others, life, especially work life, will be hard, but not impossible. For still others, OCD per se won't be a problem on the job (and may even, as we've discussed, be something of an advantage).

Of course, if your company has an EAP, it would be wise to make that known. Your human resources person should also be able to give you a little guidance.

If you would like to request a release form from your employee, so that his treatment provider can talk with your company's physician or EAP to help decide what accommodations might be reasonable, you would be within your legal rights to do so.

Oh, Come On! Afraid of What?

If you have OCD and are an employer, then you already know firsthand the challenges your situation can present. If you do not, you may be tempted to think that your employee is faking, or that he would jolly well be able to do the things you ask of him if he were motivated enough by the thought of financial, or other, reward, or by the fear of losing his job. This may be true to a degree—but it is true of you, also. Wouldn't you jump into a sewer if it meant escape from a vicious armed criminal who had it in for you? But you wouldn't jump in otherwise, right? Sufficient motivation might make anyone do anything. Hard to understand though it may be, for many people who have OCD, even simple tasks can be fraught with terror.

It's hard to say, of course, whether your employee actually has OCD. It's always possible to manipulate information to one's advantage. But OCD is a real and terrifying neurological condition that often causes genuine suffering. No one who really has it is faking anything. (As a matter of fact, most people who have OCD do everything they can to hide their symptoms from as many people as possible, for as long as possible.)

Essential

An employee's disclosure of a disability or request for reasonable accommodation is confidential, regardless of whether it contains diagnosis or treatment information. Any medical information about an employee or employees should be kept in a separate medical file accessible only to a very few specific persons, not in the employee's personnel file.

For the Employee Who Has OCD

As you read in other chapters, having OCD doesn't have to affect your life in an entirely negative way. Not only can your difficulties help make you a more compassionate person than you might be otherwise, but also, some OCD tendencies—perfectionism, doubt, organization, worry—could actually help you to do a better job than you might otherwise. This does not mean, of course, that you want your OCD to stick around or, heaven forbid, get worse. It only means that if you can use some of your particular traits to advantage in certain situations, you might as well. Jobs in which your OCD might be an asset include housecleaning, any job that requires organization, and medicine. (After all, washing your hands really does prevent infection from spreading.)

Don't forget that, in certain circumstances, there are ways to turn a seeming negative into a positive. Advertisers have known this for years: the strong-smelling household cleaner that works "so good" or the mouthwash you hate, but use. And, of course, you may remember then-presidential-candidate Ronald Reagan, who didn't want his age to keep him out of the White House, famously refusing to "exploit" his opponent's "youth and inexperience"! In this same way, you might just make your seeming "disadvantage" work for you. Maybe your boss happens to be in luck because he's hired a person who's "OCD about" details or what-have-you. OCD works for the fictional "Monk" (at least in his professional life). Maybe, in some ways at least, it can work for you.

CHAPTER 13

Counteracting Stress
with Diet and Exercise

ONE OF THE MOST important ways to fight OCD is to keep your overall stress level down. This way, when life's large and small pressures
intrude—and they will—you will be able to start from a calmer place
to begin with. In other words, if you're in a giant panic at the outset,
adding stress will hardly help. In fact, it will undoubtedly tie you up
in knots. If you start from a position of greater calm, you will be better equipped to handle the situations life throws at you.

The Power of Exercise

Exercise is one great way to alleviate stress. There are many kinds
of exercise and relaxation practices you can try. No one is necessarily better than any other. If you already have a favorite activity,
by all means, keep up with it. If you'd like to try adding something
new, the possibilities are nearly limitless. There are many forms of
dance, for instance, or martial arts, and many communities offer
adult education classes in these disciplines. You may also be able to
find a dance or martial arts studio, or a gym, in your neighborhood
or nearby. Local schools often make their facilities available to the
general public for nominal fees, as well.

Some activities, such as the ones just mentioned, usually require
lessons. In some cases, an instructional DVD from the library can
get you started (as long as you follow through on your intention to
watch it and practice what you learn). Others, such as in-line skating,

require equipment. (You might want to try renting equipment first, until you know you like the sport or activity.)

Alert

Before you begin any kind of exercise program, make sure to talk with your doctor, to be certain you're in the right physical shape for the proposed activity (or, in fact, any kind of exercise). Most people are, but not everyone is. That's why it's important to check.

Even though both lessons and equipment normally require an initial cash outlay, you will probably find either or both rewarding. One added benefit of group lessons: You might also make new friends. And friendships are among the best blues beaters there are!

Other Exercises You Might Like

Even if physical activity has never been your thing, you might be surprised to find that some kinds of exercise can be fun. It's best to find a type you enjoy so that you'll be more likely to stick with it.

Aside from the sports that are typically associated with exercise, you might like to try rowing, canoeing, sailing, and other kinds of boating. Not only will those things keep you fit when practiced on a regular basis, but also, they'll get you out onto the water. Water, though anxiety-provoking for some, can be very calming for others. Just getting a change of scene can often help to reduce anxiety, as well. There's also horseback riding. Again, for some people, just the idea of riding a horse will produce apprehension. However, for others, it's a true stress reducer.

Riding on trails, in particular, offers changes in scenery, and can help make one feel more attuned to nature. Horseback riding also develops muscle strength and can provide a challenging workout. As in any other sport, concentrating on learning it can help refocus your attention away from your anxiety. For many people, spending time with animals can be therapeutic. If you have not ridden before, or have not done so often, beginner lessons or trails can help you to ease into it.

Some people enjoy swimming, another excellent stress buster; there is a meditative quality to counting laps. Walking, especially every day (or at least three to five days a week) for a minimum of thirty minutes, is an exceptional exercise. For one thing, humans are physically designed to walk. It's one of the most beneficial exercises you can do. For another, walking can be a great way to "get out of yourself" for a time and see familiar or different places at a slower pace than you would passing by in a car.

L. Essential

If you get in your exercise first thing in the morning, before work and other obligations intrude on your day, you won't have to worry about finding the time to do it. Plus, you'll have more energy throughout your day.

You can find any number of creative ways to get in your exercise: rock climbing, bicycling, skiing, in-line or ice skating, tai chi ch'uan (often called simply "tai chi"), and so on. Choose one or more that you can practice regularly. You might even have fun!

Finding the Time

Many people would like to get more exercise, but have difficulty finding the time to do so. If you work in an office, chances are you must arrive early and stay for a minimum of eight hours. (In fact, like many office workers, you might end up staying much longer than that on most days.) You may also have a job that requires you to sit at a desk for most of the day. And once you get home, you're probably hungry and exhausted. It may be all you can do to grab some food and get ready for the next day of work. If you have children or a spouse, they, of course, will require care and attention, too. Weekends may be devoted to necessary errands or to ferrying the kids to their various activities (which you might sometimes just watch—again, a sedentary pursuit for you).

Easy Ways to Fit In Exercise

If you find that work and family take up virtually all of your time, you might want to consider using weekends for fun athletic activities that all of you can enjoy together. Instead of (or in addition to) taking the kids to regular soccer practice, for instance, you might want to try cross-country skiing (or swimming, perhaps, if you live in too warm a climate for skiing) for the entire family. Even a day of apple picking together will use muscles that may not normally get a workout. Besides, it could also end up being "fun for the whole family," and just might create lasting memories. You get the idea: Find an activity that you like and can do with your kids, spouse, or friends. Then keep at it (or try a different activity).

Working Out at Work

As you probably already know, there are many ways in which you can get small amounts of exercise throughout your workday. One of the most effective is to take a lunch-hour walk. If you have coworkers who also want to lose weight or stay in shape, taking lunchtime walks together can be a great way to motivate one another and forge friendships.

Don't neglect to eat at lunchtime, too, however. Skipping meals will only make you eat more later and is generally not good for you. Eating lots of fruits and vegetables and small amounts of protein throughout the day, and staying well hydrated, are much more beneficial physically.

Then there are the little "tricks" office workers often use: parking far away from the entrance, if you drive to work, for instance, so that you have to walk a few extra steps. (Of course, you should definitely observe the rules of safety, too. Don't leave your car very far away from the main entrance, especially if you will be arriving or leaving in the dark.) Walking over to coworkers' cubicles to deliver information, instead of sending e-mails. Even getting up every now and then to stretch or do a few quick bounces on your toes will be better for you than just sitting for hours and hours at a time. (It will also help you to avoid repetitive stress injuries and eyestrain from staring at, and typing on, the computer without pause. At the extreme end, inactivity can lead to deep vein thrombosis, or DVT, a dangerous condition resulting from sitting for very long periods without changing position.)

Working Around Work

Other clever ways to get in your exercise include taking half an hour before work in the morning to run or walk, or to do floor exercises (such as push-ups, weightlifting, etc.). Some people even find imaginative ways to exercise while at work. If you normally work at a desk in an office, for instance, you might find that making calls and reading while walking on a treadmill keeps you fit and slim. Many offices offer all kinds of health benefits; gym memberships or on-site health facilities are the most common. If you're not sure what, if anything, your company might offer, ask your human resources person or check your company handbook.

On the other hand, you may not work in an office full-time. You might be in class all day. Of course, if you *are* in school, you probably have a variety of physical education classes to choose from. Try to take advantage of your school's P.E. offerings rather than doing the mere minimum required for credit. In addition to typical sports, many schools offer students an abundance of creative choices for staying in shape. Fencing and self-defense are two good examples. Both offer excellent workouts. Fencing fosters discipline. Self-defense has the added benefit of empowerment, and may prove useful in the future (although we hope, of course, that you will not need to use it). Chances are your school offers even more P.E. activity choices than the ones we've mentioned.

If You're Too Depressed to Exercise

Then again, you might have a hard time leaving your home; perhaps, because of your anxieties, you spend most of your time there. Or a depression problem may keep you feeling listless and barely able to move except when absolutely necessary. So what do you do? Well, first of all, if you're so depressed that moving from one room of your home to the next takes virtually all the energy you have, you need to get treatment. Please make an appointment to talk with your therapist or prescribing doctor right away. If you do not yet have one or both of these, please see Chapter 10.

General Relaxation Exercises

Essentially, there are two kinds of relaxation exercises you can practice: mental and physical. Physical relaxation includes things like deep breathing. Yoga is also a physical exercise (mostly). Mental exercises include meditation and visualization. Progressive muscle relaxation is a physical and mental exercise.

 Fact

In the 1970s, Dr. Herbert Benson wrote a book called *The Relaxation Response* about the many benefits of working with the body's ability to calm itself in terms of heart rate, blood pressure, breathing, and so on. Helping Western workaholics relax was not a new concept, but it wasn't common either. There are now many books and CDs on relaxation techniques.

At its most basic, progressive muscle relaxation consists of lying comfortably flat on your back on your bed or a mat on the floor, closing your eyes, and clenching and relaxing the various muscle groups of the body in turn, usually starting at the head and working your way down to the feet, or vice versa, breathing slowly and deeply as you proceed.

Learning to Breathe

Relaxed breathing is another well-known relaxation exercise. You might find the idea of "breathing lessons" a little amusing, but adherents of relaxed breathing—often called "abdominal" breathing—say that it can be a helpful discipline to learn.

Many of us by adulthood have learned to "hold in our stomachs," take shallow quick breaths, or otherwise interfere with the slow, deep breathing we did as children. (Watch an infant or child sleep, and you'll notice that with each intake of breath, the belly rises noticeably, falling on the exhalation. There are entire books, or sections of books, about this, as well.) Deep breathing consists of taking repeated slow, full breaths, and then slowly, completely exhaling. Your eyes may be open or closed. As your lungs fully inflate, it is the diaphragm (a large muscle at the base of your lungs) descending that is responsible for your stomach pushing out (as indeed it should).

Some people find it helpful, while learning, to place a hand on the stomach or chest in order to feel the breath coming evenly and deeply into and from the lungs.

When you feel anxious, you tend to take shallow breaths. Or you might hyperventilate (breathe far too quickly, blowing off too much carbon dioxide) and feel faint. (This is why you may have been directed to breathe into a paper bag in that case, as breathing in some exhaled carbon dioxide will alleviate that lightheaded feeling.) Focusing on taking deep full breaths for a period of time can help you to feel calm; as a regular practice, relaxation breathing can become a helpful friend against OCD and anxiety in general. In fact, it is difficult to maintain a feeling of anxiety while breathing slowly and deeply. The physiological responses associated with deep relaxation are said to be incompatible with those of heightened anxiety— that is, when you are very relaxed, it's impossible to feel anxious.

A Word about Relaxation: Relax!

Like most skills, many of these require practice before you can expect to master them. Even though things like breathing, posing, imagining, and relaxing your muscles might not seem as if they would demand a lot of effort, they do employ concentration and, in some cases, different ways of looking at things. Be patient with yourself and the exercise. Try to remember the last skill you mastered. While you may have "taken to it" right away or even had a natural knack or affinity for it, chances are there were (and probably still are) moments of frustration along the way. Take some time to experiment with different CDs, tapes, or classes until you find the relaxation method that appeals to you; it'll be worth your effort.

The Stress Busters: Yoga, Meditation, and Visualization

In today's hectic world, certain forms of exercise and relaxation, like yoga, meditation, and visualization, have become extremely popular. People go to yoga classes on their lunch hours, take group meditation breaks, and do a number of other things to relieve the everyday stress of working. If you have OC tendencies, or full-scale OCD, taking up one of these practices could do wonders for your state of being.

 Alert

> It is probably best to learn yoga as part of a class so you'll know you are doing the exercises correctly. Yoga, while generally valuable, has been known to cause back and other injuries on occasion when not practiced correctly.

Yoga

One discipline that's great for general relaxation and well-being is yoga. As you've read elsewhere in these pages, yoga is a discipline that has been helping people relax (and, in the bargain, become more flexible) for centuries. As you will discover when you begin to search, there are many different forms of yoga. You might want to explore more than one before you decide which kind you might like to practice.

L. Essential

Meditation is not always recommended for people who have anxiety or other mental disorders because spending time in deep, quiet thought can occasionally give rise to painful memories or obsessions, or other hurtful ideas. If you find that meditation unsettles, instead of calming you, just stop.

Yoga uses breathing (generally deep breathing), stretching, and various poses to induce relaxation and calm. Many of its adherents claim other benefits from the practice, as well. In addition to classes (most likely offered at your local "Y" or adult education center), there are many good books that explain, with illustrations, how to practice yoga and give information on its history and other ideas related to nutrition and meditation. There are a few instructional TV programs (most of which air in the early-morning hours) and a number of DVDs that teach yoga, as well.

Meditation

Meditation is another ancient practice known to help reduce anxiety. Like yoga, meditation sometimes makes use of various postures and deep breathing. Essentially, it is about focused awareness, usually on things that get overlooked in modern, busy lives: the body, breathing, and the sounds and sights around us.

At its simplest, meditation might consist of closing your eyes, breathing deeply and focusing on your body, your breathing or, especially in *transcendental meditation* (one branch of the discipline), a *mantra*, a word that has no meaning. (Modern meditators, however, sometimes choose words that do have positive meanings.)

There are many good books and audio materials that can help you get started. Depending on where you live, you might also be able to find meditation classes. Some retreats offer these, as well. Generally speaking, daily meditation, like most other disciplines, is best practiced in small increments (maybe twenty to thirty minutes at a time) when you first begin.

Visualization

You may also find visualization useful for general calm, as well as for helping you to attain some of the things you want. (These can be anything from quitting smoking to getting more dates to taming your OC fears and behaviors.) Visualization is usually not taught in classes, but there are several good books and audio materials that can get you started and help you practice. (Please see Appendix A for some suggestions.) Your therapist may also be able to help you learn visualization.

Essentially, visualization is like creative daydreaming. *Guided imagery* makes use of suggestions for elements to add to your visualizations. These can include coming up with your own real or imagined indoor or outdoor place of quiet and tranquility, or seeing yourself enjoying a plane ride or a walk in your local park, free from fear or anxiety.

Receptive visualization means using whatever images come to mind, as in the case of envisioning your spiritual "guide" (a common visualization exercise) or seeking the solution to a problem.

The Importance of Sleep

Another extremely important part of well-being is getting the sleep you need. Insomnia can lead to depression and irritability, as well as poor concentration and other mental and physical problems. The average adult needs at least eight hours of good quality sleep a night, but gets far less. ("Good quality" sleep is not disrupted frequently or marked by restlessness, upsetting dreams, and so on.)

Causes of Insomnia

If your insomnia is temporary—that is, caused by a stressful life event or anticipation of a situation like a major exam or a job interview—it is probably nothing to worry about. However, for chronic insomnia, you might want to work on sleep techniques. ("Chronic insomnia" means you often find yourself unable to fall asleep easily, or you wake up during the night, then lie awake for hours, and this lasts longer than, say, two weeks.)

Sometimes, pain or other physical problems such as heartburn, reflux (GERD), or restless leg syndrome, can interfere with getting a full night's sleep. Medications can be effective against arthritis, post-surgical and other kinds of pain, as well as restless leg syndrome. They can also be used to treat acid reflux, as can various lifestyle changes (also mentioned elsewhere in this book). Depression, bipolar disorder, and other conditions can cause sleep disturbances, as well.

What to Do about It

Even though there can be many causes of insomnia, let's assume for the moment that you are being kept awake by anxious thoughts. In addition to other sleep techniques listed in this book, you might try some of the following. (There are also now several very good books on getting a better night's sleep. You'll find some of these listed in Appendix A.)

Among the tried-and-true are:

- Taking a warm bath or shower before bed.
- Drinking a little warm milk or herbal (non-caffeinated) tea before bed, or eating half of a turkey sandwich (but beware of heartburn, which can keep you awake). Cashews are also said to cause drowsiness.
- Getting a massage.
- Making sure your bed is comfortable to sleep in. (The mattress should not be too hard, soft, lumpy, or saggy.)
- Making sure the temperature in your room is neither too high nor too low (although keeping your room cool and sleeping under blankets may help, as well).
- Listening to relaxing music to help you fall asleep.

If you can't sleep after lying in bed for fifteen minutes or so, get up, but don't stay up for too long or get involved in activities likely to keep you awake. After half an hour of watching TV, reading, or doing something boringly repetitive, or useful but not mentally taxing (such as light housecleaning), get back into bed and try again.

Many experts recommend setting the same bedtime every night and avoiding the temptation to nap during the day. Some suggest getting up an hour or so earlier than usual in the morning to help you fall asleep more quickly at night. Others advise maintaining the same wake-up time, even on weekends, to help your body establish a predictable routine. Try this for a while, and you may find that you are able to fall asleep more easily.

Essential

> While exercise is beneficial for sleep and overall health, do not exercise less than three hours before bedtime. Doing so can prevent you from falling asleep easily. (Avoid exercise around mealtime, as well, as this can aggravate heartburn and similar conditions.)

Your bedroom should be as dark as possible (assuming you can tolerate the dark). That means no illuminated bedside clocks or nightlights. Sex generally relaxes the body, so that, too, may be a helpful sleep inducer. (And, if not, it probably won't be a complete waste of time.) Oddly perhaps, some patients find that just thinking about sex, but not doing anything about it, creates enough of a feeling of relaxation to send them to sleep.

You may have heard the suggestion that reading or watching TV may be too stimulating, however dull the subject matter. While this seems to be the case for some people, for others just the opposite is true. The best thing you can do is try some of these suggestions and see what works for you.

Don't Sleep In

Although it may be tempting to catch up on lost weekday sleep during the weekend, some experts advise against this, suggesting instead that you develop a regular pattern, starting with the same bedtime every night. (However, some say it's okay to go to bed an hour later on weekends, as long as you don't sleep later.) Many knowledgeable advisers suggest a bedtime routine, as humans are "creatures of habit." Combining a few of these pieces of advice—for instance, a light snack, followed by a warm bath and a pleasant book—can create a comforting routine, quite conducive to restful slumber.

If All Else Fails

You might want to talk with your doctor about a short-term medication to help you fall asleep and remain asleep through the night. (Most sleep aids are not recommended for extended periods.) There are also over-the-counter products such as melatonin and others. Keep in mind, however, that such products, while they may have many devotees, are not regulated by the FDA.

If you are currently on medication, it might pay to look into a change. Some of the medicines used to treat OCD can cause drowsiness. Taken before bedtime, they might just pull "double duty," improving your OCD symptoms, while, at the same time, helping you to get a better sleep.

A Look at Your Diet

Poor diet seems to go hand-in-hand with stress and anxiety. If you eat badly (a frequent consequence of stress), you'll eventually end up feeling bad. Generally speaking, if you eat well, you'll feel well. Remember the old saying, "You are what you eat"? It really is true: A healthful diet can go a long way toward relieving anxiety and other bad feelings, while helping to promote mental, as well as physical, health.

A Note to Carb Cravers

Some researchers now believe that the carbohydrate cravings so many people experience when depressed or under stress are actually the body's attempt to increase serotonin production in the brain. However, they disagree about how often and to what extent one should give in to these cravings.

 Fact

> Sugars and simple carbohydrates (which are quickly metabolized as sugar) increase the brain's serotonin production, creating temporary feelings of well-being. Unfortunately, the sugar high is often followed by a crash, as blood sugar then plummets. Other substances that increase serotonin include alcohol and various drugs. Some consider addiction, whether to food or alcohol, a craving for serotonin, the brain's natural "feel good" chemical.

Carbohydrates such as bread and pasta can induce feelings of drowsiness, calm, and well-being. Eating too many of those kinds of foods without getting sufficient exercise can prove harmful. Carbohydrates cause blood sugar to rise, and high blood sugar over long periods can lead to diabetes. However, some nutritionists say it is inactivity rather than "good carbohydrates" (such as whole grains) that can give rise to health problems. Your best bet will undoubtedly be to eat sensible amounts of most types of foods—and, of course, to make sure to get enough exercise, as well.

If you find that you often give in to cravings for sweet foods (or things like bread or pasta) when stressed, depressed, or anxious, you might want to speak with a nutritionist, if possible. Or check out some of the readily available information on coping with carbohydrate cravings. (It might also be wise to save the bread or pasta for your evening meal or snack, when sleepiness might work in your favor, rather than in the morning, when you probably need to be alert.)

Question

Do other animals overeat when stressed?
Yes. Stress-related eating and similar behaviors (such as gnawing) have been noted in other animal species. Laboratory rats have also been known to overeat when presented with an abundance of tasty food choices.

And, of course, choosing "good carbs" such as sweet potatoes, brown rice, and whole grain bread will undoubtedly serve your body (and, ultimately, all of you) better than choosing a lot of ice cream, candy, or cookies.

The Complex, Made Simple

Simple carbohydrates mean those that are digested most easily ("simple" because they don't have to be broken down into glucose: they already *are* sugars) and include honey, molasses, and table sugar. Complex carbohydrates include pastas, cereals, and breads. (Fruit and vegetables contain both simple and complex carbohydrates.) All foods are proteins, fats, or carbohydrates (or alcohol). You have no doubt heard by now that your best food choices come from the complex carbohydrates, such as fruits, vegetables, and whole grains, and low-fat proteins. Eating a combination of these can provide you with sustained energy and balanced mood.

The Serotonin Connection

To the brain, insufficient levels of serotonin may be perceived as life threatening, which is why people who don't have sufficient serotonin levels in their systems often feel so much anxiety or dread. The craving for carbohydrates in such people is thought of more and more often as an addiction: The craver uses certain foods to produce feelings of well-being and will need ever greater amounts of the sugars found in them to achieve the same results.

Healthful, Mood-Boosting Foods

Potassium, found in bananas and other foods, can help boost mood. (A little peanut butter with sliced banana on whole wheat bread might make a good breakfast or healthful snack.)

So can salmon, which is also good for the skin and cognitive function. Avocadoes, Brazil nuts, and chamomile tea are also said to improve mood.

 ## Fact

> A 2002 survey suggested that countries that used the most refined sugar per capita (consumption information was gathered from a 1996 study) were the very same countries that also had the highest rates of depression among their citizens. A correlation has not been proven, but it's an interesting possibility.

Before you use sweet, starchy, or creamy foods to "self-medicate" on a regular basis, you should learn about nutrition, so that you can make wise choices. (Appendix A lists a few books on this subject.)

Although anxiety can make it hard to exercise, make wise food choices, and try new things, we hope you will try to make at least one healthful change. It just might pay off.

Chapter 14

OCD and Your Physical Health

OCD AFFECTS MORE THAN your mental health; it can create, or accompany, physical health problems as well. Luckily, most of these are only nuisances. However, the stress that accompanies anxiety can put you at greater-than-average risk for physical health problems of many kinds, such as high blood pressure, heart disease, insomnia (itself detrimental to good health), cognitive and memory problems, and more. And, as you may know, your OC behaviors, depending on what they are, can also place you in danger of more serious problems. This chapter presents some of the more common physical health concerns for people who have OCD.

Nuisance Conditions

There are a few conditions that can result, in one way or another, from your OC behaviors. Luckily, those covered in this section are generally more annoying than physically debilitating—but they're important to know about nonetheless. These include eczema, mitral valve prolapse (MVP), and globus hystericus.

Eczema

If you frequently wash your hands (or, for that matter, your whole body or any part of it), especially in hot water and with lots of drying soap or with alcohol or alcohol-containing wipes, you may be at risk for (or currently have) eczema, a relatively harmless, though potentially annoying, skin condition.

Eczema may be set off by any number of environmental triggers, including dry skin and excess washing and rubbing. There are many different types of eczema. Some cause itching; others, skin discoloration, and so on. Eczema also can migrate from one spot on the body to another, for no real reason. It is considered chronic and may come and go, often for long periods of time.

If it's possible for you to reduce the amount of time you spend washing, that will be a plus. If you find that you can't, you might try switching to a milder soap and using lukewarm water instead of very hot. At the very least, use lots of moisturizer throughout the day and when going to bed. (Gloves or socks can help keep it from rubbing off your hands or feet and making a mess.) It helps to keep lotion by the sink, and to apply it as soon as possible after bathing or washing. Try to pat rather than rub the skin when you dry it.

If you watch TV, keeping your moisturizer by your chair or sofa will allow you to use it easily while your hands are at rest (unless you want to eat popcorn). Your doctor may also give you a topical cream to rub in.

Avoid scratching the skin or wearing abrasive fabrics. Finally, if dry skin is a problem, you may want to consider showering or bathing every other day instead of every day.

 Fact

Overuse of antibacterial soaps has been linked to lowered disease resistance. In the great majority of cases, regular old soap should be just fine. Some health advisers even recommend nothing more than water for most situations.

Eczema tends to run in families. Keep in mind that it is not contagious, nor is it dangerous. It can just be mildly (or, in some cases, more than mildly) unpleasant. If your skin becomes infected, however, your doctor may want to give you a topical or oral antibiotic.

Severe eczema can sometimes be treated in other ways, such as through phototherapy, or treatment with light.

When going out into the cold, you would also be well advised to protect all exposed skin as much as you can by wearing gloves, a scarf, a hat, and warm, thick socks.

Mitral Valve Prolapse (MVP)

One of the more frightening (though also generally harmless) conditions that sometimes affects people who have OCD is mitral valve prolapse, which can cause heart palpitations, chest pain, fatigue, shortness of breath, or all of these.

 Alert

> If you do have a heart condition, make sure to let your doctor know that you also have an anxiety disorder. If you're not sure about the relative health of your heart, that's another good reason to make an appointment for a routine doctor visit.

Palpitations are simply heartbeats that you notice. They may or may not be especially strong or fast, but some people find them worrisome. Often, these palpitations are not the result of stressful physical activity, but happen on their own, seemingly "out of nowhere." Because they closely mimic anxiety or cardiac symptoms, people who have OCD may find them troubling.

Mitral valve prolapse is a slight irregularity of one of the valves in the heart, but again, it is generally not serious, or even harmful.

People who have MVP often have anxiety disorders. MVP seems to cause anxiety in susceptible individuals, most probably because its symptoms are exactly the same as those caused by anxiety: palpitations, shortness of breath and, in some cases, chest pain. Anxiety does not cause MVP.

⌇ Essential

> You cannot develop or catch mitral valve prolapse. Either you have it or you don't. If you do have it, keep in mind that it is not considered a serious condition (although any health concern should be checked out by your physician).

Although MVP symptoms can be disquieting, they are rarely cause for alarm. If you have never experienced heart palpitations before, ask your doctor about them. If it turns out that what you have is MVP, you may be able to stop the fluttering by pressing hard on the underside of your neck and rubbing, just inside the jaw line. (Take care, however, to massage only one side. Rubbing both at once can result in unconsciousness!) In any case, you can learn cognitive techniques to help yourself at such moments by consciously stopping to re-evaluate your response to any symptom. Reminding yourself that MVP is harmless, as are its associated symptoms, should eventually help you to reduce your worry.

The Society for Mitral Valve Prolapse Syndrome recommends avoiding humidity, saunas, undue stress, lifting heavy weights, and consuming alcohol, caffeine, and sugar. Make sure to get exercise. Start slowly, and work up to thirty minutes a day.

Panic disorder, phobias, social anxiety disorder, and depression all have been linked to MVP, as have fatigue and many other conditions.

Globus Hystericus

Sometimes, for no obvious reason, you may feel as if your throat is closing or is suddenly very "tight." It may feel like the proverbial "lump in the throat." This could be caused by globus hystericus (also known as globus pharynges or pharyngitis), another harmless, though potentially upsetting, condition that may be related to acid reflux (GERD), which is discussed in the next section. Because globus hystericus sometimes happens when you are at rest and not feeling stressed at all, it may alarm you. But it will usually go away by itself within minutes. There should be no reason for panic if you experience this symptom. (However, if you believe your symptoms are, or may be, caused by an allergic reaction, do seek medical assistance quickly.)

Gastro-Esophageal Reflux Disease (GERD) and Heartburn

GERD is essentially indigestion—really bad indigestion—often accompanied by pain in the chest area. GERD is caused when some stomach contents flow back into the throat, possibly because of lower-than-normal pressure of the lower esophageal sphincter, the muscle at the junction of your esophagus and stomach. It can cause irritation or swelling of the esophagus. If you suffer from a lot of anxiety on a daily or near-daily basis, you may find yourself with worse-than-average heartburn. Some health professionals believe this is because people who have anxiety disorders tend to swallow a lot of air. In any case, heartburn often goes along with stress.

 Alert

If you have mitral valve prolapse, you may be at a slightly higher-than-average risk of developing endocarditis, which is still very rare. It's not something to be alarmed about, but your dentist and doctor should be informed. Novocain may also trigger panic attacks in persons who have MVP.

There are several prescription medications just for GERD. The condition, though not very serious in itself, can lead to damage of the esophagus and even cancer, in rare cases. There are tests that can be done to determine whether you have GERD. Often, a prescription can be taken for a short time, maybe even just a couple of weeks, until the esophagus heals.

Reducing or Preventing GERD

One trick to preventing, or mitigating, GERD or heartburn is to make sure to eat slowly and chew thoroughly—but this is much easier said than done. Changing one's eating habits generally requires a lot of attention to be paid, and it is often hard to concentrate fully on routine activities, at least for very long. However, it's still a good idea to try.

Not only can you make an effort to take smaller bites and chew your food more thoroughly, you might also try putting down your utensils and resting between bites. Also, sip rather than gulp, beverages and try to slow down in general when you eat or drink (unless obsessive slowness is a problem for you). Not having distractions, such as work or TV, might also help you to concentrate on just eating. (Some experts, however, suggest television or conversation as a way to help you slow down while eating.)

Foods That Can Irritate

In addition, you can avoid foods known to aggravate this condition. These include peppermint, chocolate, alcohol, caffeine, citrus (such as oranges and grapefruit), chili peppers, raw onion, and tomato juice. Other foods thought to aggravate GERD and heartburn include ground beef, chicken nuggets, grains, and many dairy products, as well as fatty or greasy foods.

Eating smaller amounts throughout the day may help, as may sleeping on a wedge to keep stomach acids from backing up while you're lying down. You may want to keep a journal, making note of which foods seem to aggravate the condition. It is also not a good idea to exercise right after eating. Over-the-counter medications should be taken with caution, if at all, as they are not intended for long-term use.

IBS (Irritable Bowel Syndrome)

Although research to date has not firmly established a relationship between stress and irritable bowel syndrome, or IBS, the condition often affects people who also suffer from anxiety, depression or both, and stress *does* seem to aggravate it.

Symptoms of IBS can include bloating as well as frequent, often-urgent diarrhea, constipation, or alternating episodes of both. Related problems are also sometimes seen.

Eating certain foods (in many cases, milk and other dairy products) can cause symptoms. Sometimes, celiac disease, an inability to digest gluten (a component of many bread products and other foods), is found to be the cause of IBS symptoms. Other conditions can sometimes be responsible, as well.

What to Do

Of course, staying in touch with your doctor and reading up on IBS and related conditions is a good idea. You may also want to keep a food diary or at least mental notes, about which foods, if any, seem to aggravate the problem. Some of the newer medications have shown effectiveness against it. Several of these can help with related conditions, as well.

If you can learn stress management, visualization, or cognitive behavioral techniques to help minimize your symptoms, you should be able to enjoy life more and worry about dealing with the extreme nuisance of IBS less.

Sleep Disorders and Other Stress-Related Conditions

Many people who experience excess anxiety have difficulty falling asleep or sleeping through the night. If this is more than an occasional problem for you, you may want to speak with your doctor. If you are not taking other medications, you might want to consider taking something to help you sleep. Over-the-counter sleep medications, however, are not recommended for long-term use.

There are also many non-medicinal techniques you can practice. We talked about several of these in Chapter 5 when we discussed medications (because certain medications can cause hyper-wakefulness).

By now, it's well documented that stress can also cause or aggravate headaches, backaches, neck and shoulder pain, and stomach upset. Of course, stress can also lead to emotional symptoms. Not only will stress almost certainly exacerbate your OCD, it can also cause irritability, concentration difficulty, jumpiness, and a bunch of other negative emotions and thoughts. Stress also can affect reproduction, respiration, and your body's immune system.

More Serious Health Concerns

OCD can give rise to more dangerous conditions, as well. If you're washing with chemical solvents, for instance, you'll need to stop immediately. Please enter into therapy, or see your physician or psychiatrist, as soon as you can. As you no doubt know, your behavior is hurting you *now*. You may think you'll just have to address it later. But don't wait.

You May Be Seriously Harming Yourself

Some OCD patients go so far as to drink bleach or swallow rubbing alcohol. If this is so for you, please get help right away. You do not have to continue to suffer and to damage your health and well-being.

We know that getting started can be scary, but we urge you to do so anyway. If you need to bring a friend or family member for support, or hold your first session over the phone, do so. Whatever it takes. Getting well should be your first priority and, though this may seem hard to believe, it is quite possible to begin to make significant progress quickly.

Nutrition Problems

Some people who have OCD fear certain foods or food-borne illness. Of course, it is true that even generally wholesome foods are sometimes associated with tragic illness. Nonetheless, you may be letting yourself in for some serious health developments if you eat far too little, or if you choose only foods in one particular group. If you're eating mostly carbohydrates, such as bread, pasta, rice, and other starchy or sugary fare, you may be putting yourself at risk for diabetes, especially if you have a family history of the disease.

While most of these foods are healthful in moderation, and many people with anxiety disorders crave them for their calming proper-ties, it is unwise to subsist almost exclusively on them.

Dehydration is also possible if you avoid drinking plain water. Dehydration can result in dizziness and premature skin aging, as well as more serious health conditions.

Of course, malnutrition or poor nutrition is also a possibility. And living with constant, or near constant, hunger is not pleasant, as you may know. Insufficient nutrition can cause impaired cognitive func-tion, loss of bone density, and other ailments, many of which cannot be reversed.

In addition to a therapist, medical doctor, psychiatrist, or psycho-pharmacologist, you might want to consider consulting a nutrition-ist. Some health maintenance organizations will cover your visit. A nutritionist may be able to help you to discover alternate foods you can eat while you recover from your fears, and can also explain the consequences of too little (or too much) of certain nutrients. If you can take vitamins or nutritional supplements, you're well advised to do so. However, you should not take mega-doses, as these may be unsafe. It's best to stick with a basic multivitamin, unless your doctor tells you otherwise.

Eating disorders are also a concern. Some researchers classify anorexia and bulimia among the OCD spectrum disorders, and it's not hard to understand why. Both involve obsession, accompanied by behavior that's harmful and often feels as if it's beyond the control of the sufferer. If you have, or think you have, one or both of these, it is vital that you get treatment immediately to keep it from getting any worse. Bulimia in particular (an illness characterized by "purging") can lead to oral, dental, and esophageal problems, and malnutrition can also put you at risk for a host of serious health problems.

Fear of Doctors and Dentists

It is probably beneficial for you to have at least an occasional checkup with your doctor or dentist. And, of course, if you have any symptoms of illness, it could be very dangerous to put off doctor visits or avoid them entirely.

 Alert

If you are experiencing *any* troubling physical symptom, it is imperative that you seek medical help immediately. Bring a friend or family member to the doctor's office with you, if that will help. Promise yourself a wholesome reward for completing your visit. Do whatever you need to, to get there.

Your best bet for overall good health will be a preventive strategy, not just in terms of disease, but also when it comes to choosing your health provider. It's best to meet your doctor, and also your dentist, at least once, if possible, before the need for their services actually arises. For one thing, this will help you to assess the doctor's personal style and whether it's right for you. For another, your doctor can perform certain baseline tests. If she knows how your systems work when they are healthy, she can do a better job of helping you to heal when you're sick. Plus, generally speaking, it's not a bad idea to go for a checkup every year or two, either. It may help you to stay healthy, arrest any incipient illnesses and relieve whatever anxieties you may have about your health. If you're fearful about doctors, dentists, or their offices, it will be good practice for you, as well.

If you're working with a behavioral therapist, you might make a doctor or dentist visit a priority in your recovery. Together, you can work on achieving that.

Substance Abuse and Other Harmful Behaviors

Other OC behaviors can also damage your health, sometimes in subtle ways.

As we discussed when we talked about the dangers of "self-medicating," many people who have OCD and other anxiety disorders end up using alcohol or other illegal drugs, perhaps in greater numbers than the general population. You probably already know that this is a bad idea. Self-medicating may seem to alleviate some of your anxieties in the short term, but it will not prove useful beyond that. In addition to preventing or hindering you from getting the right treatment, it can also cause untold other problems, from dependency to dangerous behaviors to potentially serious health damage. If you find that you have difficulty stopping your alcohol or drug use, seek out an organization such as Alcoholics Anonymous (AA), Cocaine Anonymous, or other appropriate group, or look for a qualified therapist immediately. Or do both.

Getting the Right Health Care

It may be important for your primary care physician to know about your OCD. There are several good reasons for this: It could be affecting your health, as in any of the situations described earlier in this chapter. Or, it may cause you to seek more than a "normal" amount of reassurance from your doctor. Telling him now that you have an anxiety disorder may save you from having him conclude later than you've singled out his office or his habits as unclean. (On the other hand, it may be possible that your doctor will become dismissive of any concern you bring to his attention once he knows you have OCD. This is not necessarily likely, but, if it should happen, it might be wise to change physicians. You deserve to be taken seriously, OCD or no.)

 Question

> **Has a link been established between OCD and physical illness?**
> As far as we know, such a correlation has not been proved. However,
> many experts believe that stress and physical illness go hand in hand,
> and OCD definitely involves a lot of stress!

If you express a greater-than-average amount of concern about your doctor's hand washing or office cleanliness, or if you're bothered by things in her examining room, such as the garbage pail, the biohazards container, or needles, it might be wise to let her know not to take your anxiety personally. (Again, if she should decide not to wash her hands because it's only obsessive-compulsive you making the suggestion, you might want to consider changing doctors.)

If you need any special accommodations, it will probably be a good idea for you to mention this early in the relationship.

The Right Doctor for You

Some doctors just naturally have a more sympathetic manner than others. This probably cannot be taught in medical school, or anywhere else. If you do not have a doctor you like or feel comfortable with, ask friends for recommendations. You may be limited by your health plan, as many of us are. Still, you can "audition" different doctors on the plan until you find one who exudes the tranquility, cleanliness, sympathy, or other factors you seek. (Please note, however, that some medical offices charge more for a "meet and greet" than for a regular visit; you may need to make an appointment for a checkup to avoid paying the higher cost.)

A Note about Health Care Providers

Often, doctors are extremely pressed for time and stressed by the demands of their profession. Long hours, emergency calls, and a health care system that often demands they see patients for only short amounts of time may conspire to make the doctor the less patient-friendly choice. Whom, then, should you see?

Essential

> If you already like the doctor you have, but feel uncomfortable about her sanitation or other practices, it should be perfectly fine to tell her so. (Once per visit ought to be sufficient, however.) It is, in fact, essential for doctors to wash their hands before and after examining each patient. There's nothing wrong with reminding your physician about this (again, once per visit).

One choice is a nurse practitioner. Nurse practitioners, in general, know a great deal about health and medicine, and often are able to spend much more time with patients. They can also prescribe some medications. For these and other reasons, it is not unusual for a patient to find the nurse practitioner a more sympathetic presence than a doctor. (This is not to say, of course, that you won't feel differently about your doctor.) In any case, you might want to "try out" a number of doctors and nurse practitioners before deciding on the right care for you.

Other Things to Keep in Mind

You will also want to factor into your choice such things as how far your health care provider's practice is from your home or work or whether his office is located in a hospital, office park, or other structure. If you have anxieties about parking, for instance, you will want to find out what the parking situation is there. Another thing that may be helpful to keep in mind: Some doctors practice out of more than one office. One office may be located in a huge urban hospital with a multi-tiered garage, for instance, while the same doctor's *other* office is in a low-rise suburban building with a large lot just outside. If you like the doctor but not the office, ask whether he works out of another office as well.

Fact

Fear of doctors is called *Iatrophobia* and is surprisingly common. There even are commercial programs available, using CBT-type techniques or hypnosis, that promise to cure it. Some people fear needles or germs in general, making them fearful of doctor's offices specifically.

It also may be important to you to know a little bit about the doctor's professional philosophy. If you are afraid of medication, for example, how does your new or prospective doctor feel about Eastern medical practices or other alternative or integrative medical options?

Managing Your Environment and Stress Level

There are other people with whom you need to interact on a regular basis. These include barbers and hair stylists, mechanics, letter carriers, delivery people, and so on. Sometimes you will have a choice about which service provider you would like. Other times, as in the case of a letter carrier or delivery person, you will not.

Although the consequences of choosing the wrong barber are not as serious as those of choosing the wrong doctor, you will still want to take care to choose providers who are sympathetic to your needs (unless, of course, you can work through your anxieties, which would be ideal).

If your anxieties or behaviors require explanation, you might want to think about what, how, and how much, you would like to share.

Learning to manage stress, whether everyday tension or true crises, is essential to good health for everyone. There are many ways to do this. You've read about visualization, meditation, eating well, and volunteering. Here are some other techniques to help you lower the overall stress in your life:

- Develop a support network of people you trust and value: friends, your family, and others who may be important to you.
- Take time out for yourself each day, whether to read a book, share a conversation with a friend, work in your garden, or just sit quietly with a cup of tea and watch the world go by outside your window.
- Get at least a moderate amount of exercise at least four days a week, for a minimum of thirty minutes, to help boost well-being and keep you mentally and physically sound.
- Spend less time in the company of "panicky" people to avoid unnecessary stress.
- Limit the amount of time you spend watching, listening to, or reading news reports, which tend to focus on terrible events that affect relatively small numbers of persons.

If you are religious or spiritual, prayer may help to relieve anxiety and confer a sense of calm (but beware scrupulosity). If you enjoy spending time with animals, you might consider getting a pet or volunteering at your local animal shelter.

CHAPTER 15

OCD: What Is It Good For?

YOU'VE PROBABLY ALREADY FIGURED out that OCD, while it is mostly a major pain, can occasionally be good for some things, too. If, for instance, you work at a job in which attention to detail is crucial (reporting or copyediting, say) or in which a strong sense of personal responsibility is important (food service or public health), you might find that obsessive concern or focus works well for you and for the employers or public you serve. What you will want to do, of course, is to keep the best and lose the rest. The question is, how?

An Old-Fashioned Idea?

At one time, the word "channeling" referred not to spirits supposedly talking to us through other people, but to finding ways in which to use negative tendencies in healthy, more productive ways. The idea was that if a man, for instance, tended toward exhibitionistic behavior, he might be able to satisfy that need by acting onstage (presumably, clothed). The idea of putting your negative energy into more socially acceptable endeavors might also work to some degree in the case of OCD.

An example: You're obsessed about electrical appliances and constantly check your TV, toaster, and electric skillet to see that they're in working order. Let's say you channel that obsession into an interest in computers; you learn to repair them and get to know their operating systems and how they work. By channeling your interest in a positive direction, you've learned new skills that may prove useful to you and others. You may even gain a potential livelihood. Other areas in which obsessive tendencies, unless taken too far, could be a boon to you include exercise and, particularly at work, organization.

If you are a perfectionist, you are not necessarily to be pitied. The trick is, making it work for you, and possibly others. (Attention to detail: great. Obsessing over every *single* detail: not so great.) If you can channel that perfectionistic streak away from activities that serve no genuine purpose and into things that can make a living for you, enhance your professional reputation, or serve your community or the world, you will indeed have made it work for you.

L. Essential

People who are referred to as "perfectionists" may be channeling their obsessive tendencies in productive ways. And very often, the world is better off because of them. A large number of composers, artists, and other well-known creative people have been known as relentless perfectionists. Vive la différence!

Another concept pertinent to this discussion is "secondary gain." This means that, even though an illness or situation might be legitimately terrible, or all but unbearable, there may be some positive thing (or things) you get out of it. A silver lining, if you will. This secondary gain can be one reason that the situation or behavior continues.

For example, a terrible marriage may still offer financial benefits, or your disagreeable spouse might still be a wonderful parent to the children. A job you hate might provide you, even so, with needed health insurance or friendships, not to mention income.

Often, we think of secondary gain in terms of illness: A stomach problem that causes extreme discomfort and keeps you from getting the nutrition you need might at least also prevent you from gaining an unhealthful amount of weight. (We do not recommend letting such a condition go untreated. This is hypothetical.) Or a back injury that keeps you from enjoying virtually all of the activities you did before might bring out your spouse's nurturing qualities. Again, the perceived gain may be quite small, compared with the loss, but it can serve to reinforce the situation nonetheless.

Is OCD Holding You Back?

For some people, OCD might actually offer a few advantages. Perhaps you feel special or smart because you're aware of possible dangers when it seems as if others are not. You might feel just a little bit smug when you learn about disasters that you practically predicted. Or you may believe that your fear serves an important purpose: most likely, keeping you or others safe from the many genuine dangers in the world.

What should you do about this? Just be aware of it. Ask yourself from time to time whether you might be holding onto fears and obsessive behaviors at least in part because you think they benefit you in some way, however small. If you think about it rationally (as distinct from *rationalizing* your obsessive behaviors), you might realize that you have more to gain by letting go of them than by holding onto them.

Can OCD Actually Be Helpful?

Yes. Chances are, you see the world a little differently from most other people. You may hone in on fine points that others would pass over. This kind of preoccupation with detail made *Seinfeld* a coast-to-coast hit.

Or you might be slavishly devoted to your art, refusing to settle for anything that isn't pure magic. Perfectionism has served many artistic talents very well. The worlds of theater, music, and art are that much richer because of it. Perhaps you see potential danger where others walk blithely, hands in their pockets, carelessly whistling tunes. You might become a consumer safety advocate and indirectly save many thousands of lives. Or your OCD may serve you in other ways.

If you're a spiritual person, you may believe that you have OCD for a reason. If you're not, you may simply think *Well, this is what I've got. Now what can I do with it?*

Good for Nothing?

Most of the people whose names we remember from one generation to the next are those who saw things and did things just a little bit differently from "everybody else." Louisa Alcott's family thought it was right and proper for women to follow whatever pursuits they chose. This was very much out of step with their times. Many famous women, such as Dr. Margaret Sanger, Susan B. Anthony, and Gloria Steinem, among countless others, refused to do what was expected of them and went on to live illustrious lives and to benefit others.

Nor was Louis Carroll content to write only about mathematics, nor Michelangelo or Monet willing to listen to their fathers' career advice. (Michelangelo took a beating for his decision to pursue art. No child of Lodovico Buonarotti was going to have to work with his hands!)

 Fact

> Although not "blessed" with OCD, animal scientist Temple Grandin, who has autism, has written many important books having to do with autism and animals, proving that there's no need for all of us to be the same. She says her autism fosters her insights into animals' experience, allowing her to create innovations in animal care.

The message is not that OCD is something to be treasured. Far from it. You still need to battle it like you would any illness. However, being a little different from the rest isn't always such a bad deal. It may hold one or two advantages. And in any case, it's who you are.

What If You're Right?

You may have heard the unhappy story of Dr. Ignaz Semmelweis. Dr. Semmelweis was a surgeon in nineteenth-century Europe and is most often credited with the discovery that hand washing and sterilizing surgical instruments prior to contact with patients could greatly reduce the incidence of puerperal (childbirth) fever and other contagious illnesses that killed so many hospital patients (and others) in his day. Unfortunately, the doctor's peers and superiors, for the most part, weren't ready to hear what he had to say. Instead of being rewarded for this life-saving discovery, he received mostly criticism (although he did enjoy a modest amount of professional success in his lifetime) and died a miserable, premature death.

If you're old enough to remember the Watergate era, you have probably heard of Martha Mitchell, the late wife of John Mitchell, the U.S. attorney general under President Nixon. Mrs. Mitchell became famous, as the scandal unfolded, for telephoning reporters in the middle of the night with wild claims. She soon developed a reputation for instability. Rumors were leaked about her mental health and alcohol usage. But Martha Mitchell, of course, for all her apparent peculiarities, was right. Dirty doings really were going on at Democratic National Committee headquarters. Nixon later told TV interviewer David Frost that, without Martha Mitchell, "There'd have been no Watergate."

 Fact

> "The Martha Mitchell effect" is a case in which a psychiatrist mistakes a sane but fantastical claim for delusion. The late author Robert Anton Wilson is said to have coined the phrase "the Semmelweis reflex" to refer to any idea that is rejected without even cursory exploration.

So. . . could you be right about some of the things or situations you fear? Sadly, yes. That is, some of the outcomes you worry about may be possible. Dogs do, on occasion, maul humans, planes do crash, bridges do collapse, and so on. The question to ask yourself, really, is not, *How likely is that?* or *How often does it happen?* so much as, *How much of an effect do I want my awareness of this to have on my life?* (On the other hand, those first two questions are, by no means, the wrong ones. In fact, your cognitive behavioral therapist might pose them to help you learn to reassess risk.)

Few, if any, things are absolutely safe. Some are patently *un*safe. Most will fall in between.

If you know of an airline with a reputation for accidents, of course, it's perfectly sensible to refuse to fly on it. If you see that unsafe conditions exist in your town, or somewhere much larger, it's noble to call the right attention to them.

L, Essential

If you have OCD, chances are, you're not a quitter. You may shy away—or run away—from things that frighten you, but you probably also possess a great deal of perseverance. That can serve you well, in both personal and professional situations.

It's okay sometimes to worry about things you can change. If nobody did, you can be sure that nothing of any consequence would ever be achieved. There would be no safety commissions or procedures. Life would be more hazardous than it is. But . . . (you knew that was coming, right?) it is, as we say, a matter of degrees. You don't want your life to be one big worry, either.

When Bad Things Happen

Unfortunately, sooner or later the thing or things you worry about may happen. Not to you, necessarily, but to someone. And then, you might think, *See? I was right to worry about this.* Were you? Maybe. But let us ask you this: Did the worry benefit you? True, it kept you safe from your feared outcome, but it also ran your life, at least to some extent, right? Think of it as a body cast for a broken ankle: It did the job, but was all that constriction really necessary?

Simple Wisdom

We can't tell you, of course, how much worry is too much and how much is just right. (In fact, we don't know of anyone who *can* tell you that.) But we think that, if you practice CBT and perhaps take medication, after a while, you will probably find what works for you: a point at which you're still not a daredevil, but you're not a "fraidy cat," either. In other words, you will probably find something you can live with. Balance.

Making It Work at Work

Of course, as we've discussed, your OCD can have tremendous bearing on at your job. But it can also be a good thing. If you are super-organized, you will probably prove your value to the company quickly. The same is also true if you pay careful attention to your work. If you can't rest knowing that your efforts aren't "right," you may feel stressed. You may even be kind of a pain to your superiors, employees, or coworkers, but we'll bet you do good work.

Getting What You Need

You've read about reasonable accommodation. Work is not the only situation in which you might need something a little special or different. There are endless possibilities, whether you have OCD or not. You might find that you need to ask your barber for a cleaner towel (or none at all). You might find yourself tormented by the loud music at a restaurant. If so, you can politely ask the staff to turn it down. After all, you're the customer. Don't be afraid to ask for what you need (provided, of course, that your request falls within the boundaries of what would be considered reasonable). Doing so will carry more than one benefit: Not only might you get whatever it is that you've requested, but also, you will probably feel empowered instead of helpless, miserable, alone, and stressed. If you help others to help you, you will undoubtedly enjoy happier relationships with them—and they, with you.

Maintaining a Positive Outlook

Unfortunately, it is very easy to believe, from all the negative influences around us, that much of life really is unhappy, dangerous, and unpleasant. To counteract this, of course, you will need to get some other input, things that tell you life is good and worthwhile and not as hazardous as all that. There are lots of ways you can do this:

- Stop reading, watching, or listening to the news. If something happens that you need to know about, you can be sure the news will reach you soon enough.
- Surround yourself as much as possible with cheerful and contented friends.
- Practice activities you enjoy, such as playing the guitar or learning to do so, writing songs or poems, or whatever you like to spend time doing.
- Reach out to others by volunteering, giving to charity, or showing kindness to a person or persons in need (again, making sure to exercise reasonable caution).
- Travel for enjoyment. Make a list of places you would like to visit.

You can also probably come up with your own ideas for fostering well-being and banishing negativity from your life.

Where Does "Sensible" End and "Obsessive" Begin?

There isn't necessarily a right answer to this question. Health organizations such as the Centers for Disease Control and Prevention in Atlanta, Georgia, advise cruise ship vacationers to wash their hands thoroughly after touching elevator buttons, stair railings, and other "high traffic" objects. But the organization also points out that, despite many well-publicized news reports, fewer than one percent of sea travelers fall ill from noroviruses.

 Fact

> The norovirus, the stomach bug often associated with cruise ships, is also found on land and is actually believed to be the second-most common illness, after the cold. It generally doesn't last long (twenty-four to forty-eight hours) and is usually not harmful to healthy persons, although it is unpleasant. With reasonable caution, it can be avoided.

You don't want to get sick, of course—especially away from home, and on something that can rock!—but you don't want to miss out on all the fun in life, either. That's where balance comes in. Sadly, we can't tell you exactly how and where to find it. But we can advise you to look for it. And we sincerely wish you lots of good luck. (We also believe you will find it!)

A Few General Guidelines

It is perfectly appropriate to eat with clean hands, to wash your hands after touching elevator or traffic light buttons, and so on. It's more than sensible to wash your hands after you use the bathroom, and after wiping or blowing your nose (or wiping a child's nose), or caring for someone who's sick.

It's fine to take vitamin C before flying. (Anecdotal, if not factual, evidence, seems to give credence to this.) You may also want to bring your own pillow or pillowcase on flights; it's said that most airlines do not pay close attention to things like changing them.

Not to Worry

Generally speaking, you should not need to wash repeatedly. One good wash with soap (for hands, this should take less than a minute, even less than half a minute) should do fine. Unless your immune system has been weakened or you are very ill physically, you should not need to avoid elevator buttons, railings, cruise ships, airplanes, and so on.

It's probably harmless enough to rinse off and dry the tops of bottles or cans before you open them, but it is not appropriate to wash your groceries with soap before you put them away after buying them. It is, however, good sense to wash your hands after handling an animal or before putting in contact lenses.

You Can Just Be Particular

It's okay to ask for cleaner silverware in a restaurant if you're not happy with what you see, but it's not okay to bring your own (unless you happen to find yourself in a country in which it is routine for restaurant patrons to do so). Washing vegetables in running water and perhaps a little vegetable wash, prior to cooking or eating them, is fine (and is, in fact, recommended). It is a good idea to keep kitchen countertops clean (within reason).

Polishing a coin collection is okay, but it's not okay to scrub your collection of loose change. You get the idea. You can be a cautious or sensible person without taking orders from your OCD.

Feeding Your Artistic Impulses

If you are a creative person (and you probably are), your best bet may be to allow that creativity into more areas of your life. Assuming that you have to make a living, you may find yourself, as many people do, in the position of setting aside the hope, at least for a time, of using your gifts as your primary source of income. But we urge you not to let those dreams go forever. Even if you can't find a way to use your talents to make a living at this moment, you can still use them. Use them for your own enjoyment and that of your friends and family. Use them to keep in practice so that, when you finally do have a choice, you'll be ready.

Fact

> Several authors have written humorous accounts about their lives with OCD. (A few of these are listed in Appendix A.) Other artists have also put their quirky tendencies to good use. If you can see the humor in your situation, it should become easier to deal with.

Yes, daily jobs can suck a lot of the vitality and imagination from our lives. But there are weekends, vacations, hiatuses. There's the time before and after work. Even if you can't devote all of your time to your musical or other talents, you can still practice and record around your work schedule. You can take an acting class one or two nights a week, and so on. You will probably feel better for making that time count.

Exploring New Things

If you aren't particularly creative, you may still want to try a new interest or take a class. Or you might want to keep a journal, or draw, or sing. Your writing doesn't have to be star-quality, nor your art beautiful, nor your voice golden. But pursuing creative activities can help you to feel more alive and connected, and less stressed, and to channel obsessive tendencies somewhere positive.

Your Place in the World

Everybody has a place in the world. The trick may simply be finding it. Each of us, in order to enjoy any kind of a sense of well-being, must feel as if we belong: that we are not unneeded or here by some cosmic mistake. Finding your particular place in the world can take time. You might feel as if your OCD puts you "outside," and that "everyone else" enjoys things you don't. (That part may be true, but then again, other people probably also have problems that you don't.) Sadly, no one can tell you how to find your place. Just rest assured that you have one.

CHAPTER 16

Venturing Forth, Despite the Fear

IT'S A FACT: WITH OCD comes fear. Therapy, medication, or any number of other treatments can help, but you'll probably always have to contend with some anxiety some of the time. *Feel the Fear and Do it Anyway* by Dr. Susan Jeffers is a good book, and its title alone is worth remembering for its meaningful message. Venturing into new situations will often be scary, but you need to do it anyway. Great effort can bring great reward.

If at First You Don't Succeed

The Victorian-era rhyme for children written by T. H. Palmer went, "'Tis a lesson you should heed./ Try, try again;/ If at first you don't succeed,/ try, try again;/ Then your courage should appear,/ For, if you will persevere,/ You will conquer, Never fear;/ Try, try again."

 Alert

> If you're still having a hard time with your OCD symptoms, or are experiencing more depression than you had before, your medication could be at least partly to blame. See your prescribing doctor about a change in dosage or prescription, and don't wait.

'Tis a lesson we *all* should heed. Subduing a problem, or learning any new skill, takes practice and patience, both with yourself and with the process. You will almost certainly experience your share of false starts and even reverses. Just remember, if and when this happens, to "get up off the mat," as they say, and try, try again. With enough effort, you *will* succeed. (And do remember that it's also possible that the method you're using—cognitive behavioral therapy, medication, neurofeedback, or another treatment—isn't right for you; in that case, you may want to look for a different practitioner, or try something else entirely.)

Never Fear?

It's said that we are born with only two fears: falling and loud noises. (However, such a hypothesis would be all but impossible to prove.) Still, virtually everyone harbors some kind of fear. The numbers of "fearless flying" and public speaking classes attests to the fact that you are not the only person in the world who is afraid of things. Indeed, you'd have a hard time finding anyone who wasn't afraid of at least something. Your particular fears may be unusual, but there are few, if any, humans who experience no fears whatsoever.

A Little Trick

When going into a difficult situation, it may help to pretend that you are on a dangerous mission or that you have an audience. Don't forget your "secret weapon": your sense of humor. Entering into a potentially frightening situation would definitely be the time to deploy it! Read about "Improbable Mission" in Chapter 18, and imagine a commentator describing your actions and progress, step by step, and fans cheering you on.

The Buddy System

If you can find a friend who also has OCD (perhaps through a local support group or OC Foundation affiliate), you might be able to work out a mutually beneficial arrangement; for example, you agree to accompany her as she tries out new situations, if she will do the same for you. It could be fun: for instance, your friend goes to see a play with you, and you go on a drive with her. You could alternate (an activity of her choice one month, an activity of your choice the next), and make regular plans together. Practicing CBT doesn't have to be a chore. In fact, it will probably be a lot easier if you can make it more of a game. And it will probably be less frightening if you also have a friend along who can help, or at least lend support. Most difficult tasks become easier when they're shared.

Feel the Fear

What author Dr. Jeffers explains in *Feel the Fear and Do it Anyway* is that people often feel scared, but that isn't necessarily a reason not to do things. (In fact, as you may already have discovered, giving in to your worries only gives them the upper hand.) Naturally, you shouldn't do anything patently dangerous or foolish. But the other things—those you're prevented from doing only by your fears—are the things that should be done anyway. Allow yourself to feel the anxiety, the author counsels. Then plunge ahead!

Of course, if you are afraid of something truly dangerous, such as contracting a fatal illness, jumping off a bridge, or eating poison, please do not get the idea of ridding yourself of the fear for all time by running toward the flame. That would not be therapeutic. If a reputable cognitive behavioral therapist wouldn't recommend it, we don't, either. You may feel frustrated, but there are many better ways to achieve the same end without putting yourself in harm's way.

It's best to have some competent guidance from a cognitive behavioral therapist when you want to stand up to your fears. Failing that, a self-directed program, such as the one found in the *OCD Workbook*, may be able to help you get started. Reading about CBT and ERP (exposure and response prevention) may also help you on your way, particularly if you can find a psychologist who is willing to learn those techniques and help you practice them.

A Journey of a Thousand Miles

Lao Tzu is often credited with the proverb, "A journey of a thousand miles must begin with a single step." If you haven't yet begun your journey, we urge you to get started. Find a cognitive behavioral therapist in your area, go to the library, get online: read, educate yourself, connect. Then get out there and start your fight against OCD.

Ŀ Essential

It may help to think of your OCD as a brat: It might make demands, but that doesn't mean you have to give in to them. You wouldn't reward bad behavior in a child (we hope). Don't reward Mr. OCD, either!

CBT techniques can be hard at first, but very few people who've completed CBT will tell you that it wasn't worth it. Medication can also be frightening, indeed, to contemplate. But, for many OCD sufferers, that has proven helpful, as well. The decision to start—however you want to do it—will be the most important part of your journey. Almost as soon as you do start, you should begin to see positive results. (Remember, however, that medication can take a few weeks or months before it begins to work. It might take a while before you're able to take big steps with CBT, too. But keep at it. Your effort almost certainly will be rewarded.)

Remember, too, that if any one of the OCD fighters mentioned in this book doesn't work for you, you can simply try another, or check out some of the special hints elsewhere in this chapter.

Beware

It sometimes happens that, when you're ready to break free of the fear, it fights back hard. If this should happen to you, try to think of it as the last pathetic gasp of the tired old dictator as he struggles to hold onto his power. Remember that, when the fear fights back, that doesn't mean it's winning. It means you are. Continue to work with your therapist, if you have one, and make sure to enlist the help of your support "team."

The Rewards of Progress

Remember, also, to make sure to reward your successes. If you decide to stand up to your fear of public places, for instance, you might just as well go to a movie you've been wanting to see as to a board meeting. If you want to try flying, you might opt for a short trip to a place you've always wanted to visit, rather than wait for a family obligation. Feel free to reward yourself for progress you make doing "necessary" things, as well. (But use care when choosing food rewards. Keep in mind that too much sugar can definitely be a bad thing.)

 Fact

According to Forbes.com, our most common fears include animals (such as spiders, rats and snakes), water, heights, bridges, tunnels, enclosed spaces, crowds, public speaking, and storms. Many of these are said to be rooted in our primitive ancestry. (Common childhood fears include monsters, darkness, getting lost or kidnapped, or harm befalling a parent.)

Get Your Team on Board

You've read about the importance of a good support system. By surrounding yourself with supportive friends, family, a competent therapist and other care providers, and perhaps an online community of other people who also have OCD, you will be taking the first steps toward building a community formed with the purpose of nurturing *you*. Don't neglect to enlist your team's help. Having that support can be vital.

Remember, though, that not everyone will understand your situation. When getting your team on board, make sure to choose people who know and empathize with your needs, or are likely to do so. A casual workmate, for example, may not be your best choice. Close friends, significant others, family members, trusted care providers, an online community, and your mentor, if you're lucky enough to have one, should make valuable additions.

With any luck, you will be able to put together a supportive group. However, in our imperfect world, things don't always go according to plan. It may happen that someone you turn to for support might be busy with her own problems, or frustrated with and tired of yours. When and if this happens, know that there are other resources. Online OCD support groups will probably put you in touch almost instantly with others who will be pleased to hear about your challenges and offer advice, encouragement and help. Don't forget the other members of your "team," either, including your therapist or doctor.

What Brave People Know

Heroes, it's said, aren't fearless. After all, any idiot can do a courageous thing if he feels no fright. Real bravery lies in doing exactly what we fear: *feeling* that fear and doing it anyway.

 Alert

You may continue to experience obsessive thoughts, even if you make significant progress against your compulsive behaviors. Your best bet is not to struggle to get rid of these thoughts but to allow them to come. When they see that you're not interested in fighting, they'll probably just go away.

In your lifetime, you will probably be called upon to do many brave things. Maybe not the kinds of things you could expect to be awarded medals for, but the kinds of things that most of us, sooner or later, will have to do: face illnesses and the deaths of people we care about, accompany family members to the hospital, deal with problems at work or with our children, undergo medical tests or treatments, bear injustices, grow old. Your particular challenges may be typical, atypical or both, but you will have them. And you will have to deal with them somehow. You might as well do so bravely.

Another Secret: Anyone Can Be Brave

You may tell yourself: I'm not brave enough to face my fears. But the truth is that anyone can be brave in a given situation. In fact, many, if not most, people who show amazing courage say they never would have expected that they could have done it—until the moment came. Go ahead. Give it a try. You might just surprise yourself with what, and how much, you can accomplish.

Fake It Till You Make It

Don't forget your primary weapons against fear: "acting as if," and allowing yourself to anticipate the worst (in other words, to feel the fear). Even if going into the fear and deciding to take whatever comes doesn't work for you, "acting as if" you aren't afraid probably will.

Keeping Up the Good Work

Like any skill you learn, managing OCD requires perseverance. And practice. Don't feel afraid to visit your cognitive behavioral therapist for a "tune up" now and then, or to go back into therapy for a time. Definitely continue to see your prescribing doctor to stay on top of any changes you might need to your medication. Cognitive techniques may change. Medicine almost certainly will. Staying informed by keeping in touch with your providers can only help.

And remember, of course, the following tried-and-true advice. You may want to think of it as "Nurse" (NERS):

- good Nutrition
- regular Exercise
- adequate Rest
- a strong Support system

Don't neglect "Views" (VEWS), either:

- **V**olunteer, or do good for others in another way
- **E**xpress your creativity
- **W**ork (preferably at something you feel good about or enjoy at least a little)
- **S**urround yourself with happy stuff at least some of the time.

Resources

Also, remember to keep up with new developments by reading books, magazine and newspaper articles, and online information. (Just be certain, if you're not sure about whether to believe something that doesn't sound right to you, that you can confirm its accuracy by seeing whether the information appears anywhere other than that one site, book or journal. There's still some very uninformed "information" out there.)

 Question

Did Watergate figure G. Gordon Liddy practice ERP?
Kind of. Liddy claimed that, in his youth, he cured himself of a fear of lightning by climbing a tree during an electrical storm, and a fear of rats by cooking and eating one. (No cognitive behavioral therapist will expect this from you. Gross!)

What Not to Believe

We hope you'll keep in mind that, while some inaccurate information may be fairly harmless, you may hear ideas about OCD that have long been discredited. These include the notion that OCD is an emotional disorder or neurosis. As we've said, it has now been established through the use of brain scans and other methods, that OCD is a neurobiological disorder.

Some experts believe that OCD may also have a psychological element (so, while your particular psyche may lean toward worry about whether you've locked the door, another person's might lead him to fear germs). That may well be true. But the "neurosis" theory isn't.

 Fact

> The fear of anything new is called "neophobia." Fear of everything is "pan-," "pano-," or "pantophobia." (However, it would be very hard to be afraid of everything, as some fears would conflict with others. Not to mention the fact that daily life would be challenging, to say the least.)

You may hear people tell you not to let your fear run your life. While this is good advice, it is usually much easier said than done, especially when it is said by people who do not themselves have OCD, or even very much anxiety. (It's a lot like telling a smoker that he should just quit. No kidding!) It is not a matter of simply pulling yourself together or standing up to your fear (at least, for most of us). Although, of course, if you can do it, then, by all means: Go for it.

Others may try to tell you that religion will "cure" your anxieties. It might, but we wouldn't count on it. OCD is not a moral failing, nor is it caused by a lack of willpower. It is also not caused by missteps in your upbringing. It is simply a hereditary brain disorder that makes people act strangely sometimes.

You may also hear about dietary remedies for OCD. While it is believed that a balanced diet, low in sugar and caffeine, can benefit your overall mood and health, there isn't yet a reliable nutritional "cure."

Fighting Ignorance

The best way to combat ignorance, of course, is to stay informed yourself. As people get to know you, you may have opportunities to educate them subtly if you wish to. That might include politely challenging their negative perceptions or simply being a "good example": a person who has OCD and handles it without making a big deal about it.

L. Essential

In his first inaugural address in 1933, President Franklin Delano Roosevelt said, "The only thing we have to fear is fear itself." (Quite a while earlier, Henry David Thoreau said, "Nothing is so much to be feared as fear.") Roosevelt's speech, actually written by others, referred to the Depression, but is not bad advice in general.

The more information you have, the better equipped you will be to handle your own fears and OC behaviors, and the better able you'll be to help educate others, should the need arise. Don't be surprised if other people have lots of questions.

CHAPTER 17

OCD in Kids and Seniors

OCD IS A DISORDER that tends to run in families. However, as often as not, family members will have different kinds of OCD from one another. Mom may hoard, Dad may worry obsessively about health and germs, and Billy may have organizational and hyper-responsibility behaviors. Or Billy may be only mildly affected; indeed, he may be completely *un*affected, in much the same way that he may have blue eyes, although Mom's and Dad's are brown. As important as it is to know how OCD affects kids, it's equally important to know how it affects older persons. This chapter includes all you need to know.

Determining Factors

You probably wouldn't want your children to have OCD any more than you'd want them to endure any affliction. On the other hand, would it really be so bad? While OCD can cause unbearable anxiety, and obviously no reasonable person would want her child to suffer from unbearable anxiety, it is also true that OCD is more manageable now than it ever has been.

No one can tell you, of course, whether you ought to have children, or even whether those children would have OCD. It is quite possible that if you have it, then your children will have it too. If your spouse or partner also has it, such a scenario would be probable— but not assured. And, in any case, everyone, with the possible exception of the most cavalier sociopath, must experience some anxiety in life. That's just the way it is. If you're concerned about your chances of passing on the disorder, though, definitely consult a genetics counselor.

What Are the Chances?

According to the OC Foundation, genes play only a part (albeit a significant one) in determining whether a child will have OCD. In pairs of identical twins, they say, when one has OCD, there is an 87 percent—not 100 percent—chance that the other will also have it.

Most experts believe that genetics are one determining factor (and there is certainly enough anecdotal evidence to bear this out). Some believe that the other determining factors are physical, such as environmental toxins or viral infections. "Strep" (streptococcal infection) is often blamed, especially for worsening childhood OCD symptoms that already exist in a milder form.

Attack of the PANDAS?

Earlier in the book, you read about the term PANDAS, which stands for pediatric autoimmune neuropsychiatric disorders associated with streptococcal infections. In some cases, symptoms seem to come and go with the presence of certain illnesses, giving more credibility to the theory that OCD is a disorder of the brain.

Others believe that the remaining factors contributing to the development of OCD are emotional—a traumatic event, or an upbringing marked by an inflexible insistence on order or rules. Some researchers believe that some types of OCD are inherited, while others are not. But, so far, no one can say with absolute certainty just what causes OCD in every case.

Childhood OCD Versus Adult OCD

Many of the OC symptoms children experience are exactly the same as those that their adult counterparts face. Contamination and disease fears are very common, as are requirements for symmetry and order, counting, and responsibility concerns (fear of spreading disease or harming others with thoughts or actual deeds). However, there are other symptoms seen almost exclusively in children. These include:

- Extreme phobias related to school.
- Selective (sometimes called "elective") mutism: that is, refusal to speak in certain situations.
- Excessive worry and preoccupation about being watched.
- Particular sensitivity to noise, odors, or other minutiae.

Children who have OCD are also known sometimes to experience extreme separation anxiety and to exhibit greater than normal fears about things like monsters and scary television programs; they may demonstrate behavior close to obsession when it comes to certain people, things, collections, and so on. Like their older counterparts, they may become "unglued" easily if their routines or precise ways of doing things are interrupted, or if they are prevented from exercising their avoidance behaviors.

Unlike adults with OCD, children who have the disorder often can't explain their reasons for doing the things they insist on doing and, depending on age, don't always possess the sophistication needed to hide their compulsive actions.

Rages in OC Children

It's been noted that children who have OCD experience "rages" more often than their older counterparts. This may happen in response to fear, especially when the child is prevented from performing his anxiety-relieving compulsion. Also, children who have OCD tend to suffer from a higher rate of mood disorders than the general population of children. (The same is also true for adults who have OCD.)

A Numbers Game

It's estimated that one out of every 100 to 200 children (or, 1 to 2 percent of children and adolescents) has OCD. As is the case with many other conditions, it's not always easy to tell. For one thing, many children, whether they have OCD or not, seem to experience obsessions: a bedtime ritual that must be performed exactly the same way each time, an insistence that two or more foods on the same plate must not touch, or a fascination with a hobby, interest, or collection, for instance. For another, some behaviors, such as a teenage girl's excessive preoccupation with grooming, diet, or a teen idol, might seem like (and, in fact, be) normal developmental stages. Further, many children today demonstrate much more anxiety than in previous generations. Children's worries over things like school shootings, war, and other issues in the news probably says more about our times than about childhood OCD.

Treatment for Childhood OCD

Except in the case of very young children, childhood OCD can be treated successfully in the same ways as adult OCD: with cognitive behavior therapy, medication, neurofeedback, or other methods. CBT can be quite effective in the hands of a therapist skilled in its use and practiced at working with children. It can, in fact, prove more successful more quickly with children than adults, because, again, kids don't necessarily believe that they have reasons for their behaviors, meaning there's one whole component that doesn't need to be addressed.

Cognitive Therapy

The cognitive part of CBT can be useful for children (and adults) or adolescents who are tormented by thoughts of harming themselves or others. As with adult OCD, the therapist may ask the child or adolescent to write down or discuss in detail his feared scenario, then evaluate how likely it really is that he will act on his thoughts.

A child (like an adult) might be taught to remind himself that "it's only a thought; a thought can't hurt anyone."

For very young children, "play therapy," which uses toys and games as communication tools, can be useful in conjunction with (but not as a substitute for) cognitive therapy.

Parental Help

A parent can help her child overcome OC fears and behaviors by working with the child's therapist or, in cases in which therapy is not available or effective, using a workbook or other self-directed program. There are now also books containing techniques that parents can use with younger children.

Getting teachers and other school officials on board may also prove helpful. If your child's teachers or administrators do not know much about OCD, you will want to help them get the information they'll need so that they can deal with it successfully. (That knowledge will likely come in handy with future students, as well.) The OC Foundation, books or a local or online parent or family support group can likely point you in the right direction when it comes to information, especially about working with school systems.

What about Medication?

Medication, particularly by itself, is not necessarily the treatment of choice for OCD in children and adolescents. (That would be CBT, alone or in concert with medication.) That said, it can be helpful for treatment of childhood OCD (again, especially when used with CBT). Actually, medication treats some of the *symptoms* of OCD, but it can't treat the condition itself.

More and more often, therapists and even physicians are developing greater expertise in recognizing and treating OCD symptoms in children and adults. But of course, this is not always the case. You may not enjoy access to an excellent therapist or doctor. If this describes your situation, you might want to try searching your local directory under "mental health services." You can also check the OC Foundation's Web site (*www.OCFoundation.org*). Other good resources exist online and elsewhere. Some of these are listed in Appendix A.

Question

Can OCD medication be delivered through a transdermal patch?
Yes. There's now an antidepressant patch that may be used for OCD in some cases; however, it's new, so there are no long-term studies yet. A patch can be an excellent choice for children, who may resist taking medication. Please note, however, that patches carry many of the same risks as oral medications and must never be cut to size, except on the advice of your doctor.

Only a fraction of the number of medications approved for treating adult OCD have been approved for treating OCD symptoms in children. No medication that treats depression or anxiety is approved for children younger than eight years old (although they have been used in certain cases). Also, as children grow, the same medication may lose or change its effectiveness.

Medications Approved to Treat OCD in Children and Adolescents

While no medication treats the condition called OCD, several do treat its symptoms: anxiety, depression, and others. As with medication for adults, it may take weeks before any behavioral differences are noted. In the meantime, your child should be monitored closely in case of an adverse reaction. CBT should also be started, if at all possible.

New Treatment for Strep-Induced OCD

In cases in which OC symptoms worsen after a strep infection (further suggesting that OCD is a disorder of the brain, rather than of psychology), researchers at the National Institute of Mental Health tried using two procedures called plasma exchange and intravenous immunoglobulin, with positive preliminary results.

These procedures are used to treat other illnesses as well. In plasma exchange, some blood is taken from the body, cleansed of certain substances, and then returned. In the second procedure, the patient receives a shot of antibodies. The chief advantage of this treatment is that it is believed to alleviate symptoms markedly and reduce the necessity for long-term medication. However, this experiment was performed on a very small number of subjects. More research will be needed before we know whether this will prove to be an effective way to treat childhood OCD that has been aggravated by strep infection.

Essential

Although some researchers believe that OCD can worsen significantly following a strep infection, it should also be noted that strep infections are extremely common among children and rarely lead to OCD or other disorders. In other words, don't worry unduly because your child has a strep infection.

Potential Side Effects

Just as adult patients may experience side effects from medication, so, too, can children. Children may experience the same side effects, such as nausea, fatigue, and dry mouth, but also others, such as hyperactivity or aggression. There are still others, and your doctor or pharmacist should give you a list of potential side effects, and go over with you what to expect or look out for.

As in all cases involving medication, it is important to keep a close eye on your child, not only when she begins the course of medication, but throughout treatment. Keep the proverbial "lines of communication" open between you and your child, and you and your child's physician, too.

Danger Signs

Although serious side effects are rare, there are a few to watch out for. Serotonin syndrome (caused by an overabundance of serotonin, most often when medicines are combined) can induce shivering, profuse perspiration, confusion, and restlessness. It is extremely uncommon and often mild, but it can be fatal; so, it is imperative to inform all doctors of any medicines your child takes and, of course, to get medical attention for your child right away if it is suspected.

 Fact

> Compounding pharmacies make their own medications. If you need a hypoallergenic or dye-free version of a prescription, for instance, or a liquid or syrup form of a pill, you might try to locate a compounding pharmacy to solve this problem.

Other serious side effects include seizures and various motor and motion disorders.

Again, it's important to ask your doctor to provide you with a complete list of serious potential side effects. Keep in mind that they're rare, but not unheard of.

Troubles in School

It's impossible to know exactly how your child's OCD symptoms will affect his behavior, performance and overall experience in school. However, it's likely that school will present at least some challenges. For example, classrooms can generate numerous distractions for children who have counting compulsions.

Shared bathrooms may give rise to terrible anxiety on the part of a child who suffers from contamination fears. A young person who has perfection obsessions may hand in tests and papers late, because he's still not "finished" with them, or because he may feel driven by impossible standards.

OCD can produce seemingly bizarre symptoms such as fear of school lunches or even of other children. (Please keep in mind that, to your child, these worries are as real as any you might experience, yourself.) Your child may suffer from debilitating social phobias or find ambient noises intolerable. (On the plus side, observant elementary school teachers have been known to pick up on early signs of OCD in children in their classrooms, leading to sensitive consultations with parents, and early diagnosis and treatment.)

On the other hand, your child may be subject to touching compulsions, perhaps finding it impossible to refrain from touching or even kissing other students (obviously, a more common problem in younger children). How you and your child's school choose to handle these behaviors will depend to a large degree on attitudes, knowledge, creativity, and other factors.

It would probably be wise to discuss your child's situation with his teacher (or other administrators, if appropriate). Sometimes, simple modifications can go a long way toward helping your child to feel less anxious and to perform well at school.

Essential

Your child may find that other children pick on him because of his OC behaviors. If this happens, please make sure to talk with his teacher or school administrators. It should be clear to them, and to the children creating the problem, that bullying is not acceptable and will not be allowed. Most schools, in fact, now have zero-tolerance policies about bullying.

Creative solutions for bathroom fears might include allowing the child the use of a faculty facility. Or, if noise is a problem, permitting tests to be taken in an area away from the classroom. Lunch and beverages from home might take care of food phobias, at least to a degree. If your child is displaying inappropriate or aggressive behavior toward other students, of course, you will need to work on getting that under control. Parent support groups and organizations may be able to offer helpful ideas for situations like these.

If your child has washing compulsions but is limited in the number of times she may get up to leave the classroom, hand sanitizer might do the trick. (Do see that she also has topical moisturizer to take to school, though, especially if dry skin becomes a problem.) The teacher might need to repeatedly let a child with perfection compulsions know that he is not expected to turn in absolutely mistake-free work each time. Or she might allow him to type assignments on a computer, even though the other children turn in reports written by hand.

 ## Fact

Children sometimes outgrow obsessions (about 20 to 25 percent do; another 49 percent or so will see enormous symptom reduction over time). A child or anyone else who truly has OCD is not faking symptoms for sympathy or attention. Her worries or obsessions are, most likely, a kind of torture. She deserves support and treatment.

You get the idea: A little imaginative problem solving, with a hand from your child's "team," while you work on getting help for his OCD symptoms, can make school a more productive and less anxious place for him.

How to Talk to Your Kids about OCD

OCD—yours or your child's—can be talked about truthfully in a matter-of-fact way. You might want to choose words along the lines of: "OCD is a disorder of the brain that can make people have upsetting thoughts or fears about unlikely things. Having OCD doesn't mean you are crazy. It may mean that you feel nervous more often than other people do, or that you do things that might look strange. With some work, it can be managed so that you can do your work and live your life without too much bother." Emphasize that you love and care about your child, and will do whatever you can to help and be supportive.

Most children's attention spans are on the short side. You probably won't need to say more than this, but do make yourself available to answer any questions your child might have. You don't have to know all of the answers right away.

It's okay to say you will try to find out, and to follow up by doing so. Other people, such as your child's therapist, may be able to answer questions that you can't—and, in so doing, educate you and your child both. There are also many excellent books and online resources about childhood OCD.

Talking to the Teacher (or Principal)

You will undoubtedly want to discuss your child's situation with his teacher and perhaps one or two administrators, as well. Most schools today are well aware of many of the challenges faced by modern children. While OCD is relatively rare, it is certainly not unheard of. Aside from this, *many* children today have so-called "special" needs. Maybe most of them do!

 Alert

Although you may be on the lookout for side effects when your child begins a course of medication, do not forget later on that medication may be the cause of heretofore unexplained physical symptoms or behaviors. Discuss any concerns, whenever they crop up, with your child's doctor.

How equipped and aware your child's school is should determine what you'll discuss. Assuming the teacher and principal don't know much at all about OCD, here are some things you might want to keep in mind for your discussion:

- Foremost, you will want them to understand that your child's seemingly strange behavior is caused by an overabundance of worry or doubt, or sensitivity to things like noise or light.

(Those particular sensitivities are more often seen in younger children.) It is not indicative of a behavior problem, or caused by a lack of discipline. Your child doesn't want to be a prisoner of ritual or anxiety, but is.

- Perhaps you can identify the most troublesome aspect of classroom life for your child and his teacher and work on a solution together. For example, if your child is particularly sensitive to sound and can't concentrate during tests because of ambient noises, a test-taking spot in the library or conference room might be arranged for him.

- If your child has perfection compulsions, it may be wise to let the teacher know. While effort should, of course, be rewarded, it might be better for the teacher to let your child know that her work is not expected to be perfect. One wise first-grade teacher lets all the kids know early on that mistakes are absolutely necessary—and publicly revels in her own!—as they become teachable moments from which everyone can learn.

- Communication will probably serve all sides well. Be sure your child's teacher lets you know, from time to time, how things are going, and of any problems that might arise. Similarly, if you're working with a therapist on cognitive behavior techniques, you will probably want to enlist the teacher's help as well; it will be useful to be as specific as possible, so the teacher can be "on the same page" as you and your child's therapist.

L. Essential

OCD may, and probably will, cause your child distress. But it is not life threatening, just unpleasant and a little unusual. Along with your child's therapist and school "team," you can help your child to see OCD as a manageable nuisance or a simple, perhaps even truly special, difference.

The public school system, by the way, is obligated by law to provide what is called "free and appropriate education" to all of its students. In other words, a public school or teacher may not lawfully discriminate against your, or any, child because she has OCD. Or for any other reason.

In some cases, OCD may qualify a child for special education services (which may be a good idea if your child's symptoms are getting in the way of his getting an education). This usually requires an evaluation by committee, and its decision can be appealed, if you wish. The school may need to provide reasonable special accommodation, although it also can make a case for refusing to do so (and will, just as often as not, because of budget restrictions). More information about working with school systems is available in books and online. (Additional resources are listed in Appendix A.)

A Few Resources for Parents

Having an OC child can be difficult, especially if you yourself have not been through OCD and know little about it. Depending on where you live and what resources are available to you, you may encounter a frustrating lack of knowledge and compassion toward both you and your child. (Of course, your experience could be happily opposite, or somewhere in between.)

If you can, seek out doctors and others who know about OCD and are familiar with its symptoms and treatment. If that isn't possible, you may be able to learn a lot about it on your own, and then educate some of the medical and school professionals already in your child's life.

The OC Foundation Web site (*www.OCFoundation.org*) may be able to help you find therapists and other help in your area. If not, you might be able to find a local OCD support group. That may lead to more information about specialists in childhood OCD.

Today, there are many online support resources available for parents. One can be found at *http://health.groups.yahoo.com/group/ocdandparenting*. The OC Foundation can be a helpful starting point for information about the disorder and the many practical concerns surrounding it. About.com can be helpful, as well, and has a teen OCD support group. Look around at *http://specialchildren.about.com.* There are many online parent support organizations, aside from these. Type "OCD" and "children" or "parenting" into your computer's search engine. Many excellent books, written for parents or children, also address childhood OCD. (One or two of these are listed in Appendix A.)

 Fact

OCD is a neurological condition. While it's believed possible that some predisposed individuals may develop it as a result of trauma or a childhood marked by extreme regulation and rigid order, it is not "caused" by those things. If possible, educate—or if necessary, avoid—doctors and school administrators who seem as if they're blaming you for your child's OCD.

Your child's "disability" might not be entirely bad. It might help her to become expert, for instance, in certain subjects that interest her. Or it could be that a perfection compulsion helps her to come up with excellent presentations and projects (as long as you, your child and her teachers understand the enormous pressure that goes with that degree of drive). Many gifted people are known to be perfectionistic.

OCD and Older Persons

Many people who suffer from OCD are not children, but older persons. A fair number of these folks developed symptoms at a time when few, if any, doctors recognized OCD. Consequently, their behaviors, typically, have become quite entrenched over time. Then again, OCD symptoms sometimes appear much later in life for some than they do for others, often as the result of illness. Many seniors also experience depression or varying degrees of isolation. All of this and more can make life very difficult for older persons who are living with OCD.

If You Are a Senior

You may have endured anxiety for many years, without knowing exactly what was wrong. It's also possible that your symptoms developed later, after an illness. If your symptoms, or those of an adult you care about, appeared suddenly, a complete neurological and physical exam would be wise. Obviously, if there is an underlying disease, you'll want to treat it immediately, if possible.

On the other hand, OC symptoms often are known to diminish as the patient grows older. CBT, medication, or both, can prove just as helpful for seniors as for younger persons. Talk with your doctor if you believe your symptoms might be OCD.

If You Live with or Care for a Senior

It may be difficult to live with or care for a senior who has OCD. You might have a long history together. Perhaps this person's symptoms have worsened over time. The OCD sufferer may be a close family member, perhaps a parent. That kind of situation inevitably makes for tension. If you can find a support group for family members, that might be a good place to start. (And, as always, books and the OC Foundation can set you on the path to more information, as well.)

It's important to note that the sudden onset of symptoms can sometimes result from an illness; so, if your senior's behaviors seem to have started recently, "out of the blue," a complete physical exam is recommended.

Few studies have been done on OCD in the elderly, per se. Symptoms usually are similar to those seen in younger adults. Hoarding (or increased hoarding) is sometimes seen more often in older persons; this may be a result of OCD, or it may be caused by other conditions.

Medication and Older Adults

Generally, in the case of older persons, medication for OCD symptoms is administered at first in small doses. The doctor may want to give your senior a half-dosage in the morning, followed by another one at the end of the day. That's one way to minimize potential stomach disturbance. (Another is to give the medication with food.) In some cases, medication is given in the evenings so the patient won't become overly tired or even stuporous during daytime hours.

CHAPTER 18

For Friends, Family Members, and Others

UNDOUBTEDLY, YOU KNOW THIS by now: Having a family member or friend who has OCD can be an exercise in extreme frustration. Activities you enjoyed together only a short time ago may now be constrained, unpleasant, or even impossible. Your friend may act anxious where she used to seem carefree. You might well wonder: What happened? What happened, of course, is that your friend's OCD symptoms began or worsened. She may have taken you into her confidence about her anxieties, and now, you find, they seem to run her life. Worse, they are in many ways taking over yours!

A Friend In Need . . .

You may find that you are expected to give almost constant reassurance. Or that your friend avoids doing many of the things you used to do together, making excuses or perhaps giving explanations that don't make sense to you. (Can she really be so afraid of a fire that she won't leave her house, except under the most desperate circumstances? And why has this behavior started *now*?) You might find yourself roped into actions such as checking stove knobs or door locks. If the person who has OCD is an immediate family member, you may find that you're neglecting your own needs because you are so busy doing so many things for the person with OCD. (Some people who have OCD even become almost completely disabled, unable to work or experience much of life at all.)

Perhaps you would feel differently if your spouse, child, or other family member had a *physical* disability, but you may find you have far less sympathy and patience for the repetitive or seemingly foolish things your OC family member insists on doing. That's understandable. OCD is not fun for anyone. Not for the person who has it, not for the people who care about her.

When the Problem is Hidden

On the other hand, it may be that the person you care about has successfully hidden his behavior, or at least his reasons for it, for a very long time. That sometimes happens, as well, even between spouses and other close friends or family members. You might feel ashamed to tell others that someone in your family has OCD. After all, it is still thought of even now as a mental illness, and mental illness, for all of our society's ostensible progressiveness, is still stigmatized. However, it's more than likely that the person with OCD feels more ashamed of it than you do.

 Fact

Although, for many people, not getting treatment will result in worsening OCD symptoms, for some, it will only result in not getting very much better. However, if you are at the point at which you're urging someone close to you to get help, the situation is probably serious enough to warrant it.

What To Do

If someone close to you has OCD, or you suspect that he does, the first thing you will want to do, of course, is talk. Like anyone who has a serious problem, the person who has OCD may not yet be ready to hear what you have to say. That's all right. Say it anyway. Say it kindly. Rarely will anyone jump up and exclaim, "Eureka! You're right! I have OCD and must get help at once!" The more likely scenario is that you will suggest that the person get help. And he will resist. And you will have to give up for a time and try again later. This can be exhausting and frustrating, and may make you feel angry or hopeless. Take a deep breath. Take some time out if you need it. If you want to be an especially good friend or partner, say that you will be available when your friend is ready to talk about getting help.

L. Essential

If you want to be as helpful as possible, try to remove any treatment obstacle that your friend or family member may have. If you are a parent and are able to pay for behavioral therapy, for instance, do offer. It might mean the difference between treatment and raging OCD.

A Special Note to Friends

In some cases, friends or even family members part company because the OC behaviors of one have put too much of a strain on the relationship. We hope this will not happen to you. OCD is an illness like any other. You may not like the OCD (no one does), but your friend is still the same person she was before. Besides, OCD can be isolating enough on its own.

If you can offer concrete assistance, such as rides to and from the therapist's office, and are willing to provide it, please make sure to make the suggestion. For the time being, at least, you will want to refrain from talking about what your friend or family member can do for you in return. Right now, your primary concern should be just doing what you can to help him get better.

Talking Points

The way to talk about a family member's OCD is the same way you would talk about any problem that was seriously affecting your family or relationship:

- Point out that the person seems to be going through something difficult, and that that causes you distress, as well.
- Offer to help, listen, and "be there" in any way you can.
- Tell the person that you support her, no matter what.
- Let her know that, because you care about her, you can no longer "enable" her self-destructive behaviors.

Of course, you will want to get these ideas across in as loving and non-judgmental a way as you can. If you feel angry, you might want to talk another time. If you continue to feel angry, it's probably fine to talk about *that*, as well. Just remember, it's the OCD you hate, not your old friend or partner. Remember, too: Chances are, your friend isn't any happier about his problem than you are. If you look at the OCD as something to be solved, instead of as a behavior that was chosen with the intention of driving you crazy or controlling you, you will be more helpful than if you see your friend as "holding you hostage" to his fears. The truth is, no one feels more imprisoned than your friend who has OCD.

When You Encounter Resistance

Many people wonder how to "get" a friend or family member into treatment. Unhappily, the answer is, you can't, really. That said, there are ways you can encourage a reluctant family member to at least try CBT or medication.

Certainly, staying calm, offering gentle encouragement, and employing a lot of patience is one way. It is the *classic* way. Therapists disagree about the effectiveness of the second way, which is to bring more pressure to bear. While you can't force an otherwise competent adult into treatment, nor are "intervention"-style tactics recommended, we can tell you that there's a case to be made for keeping up a steady pressure, rooted in loving concern. One caveat, however: Don't expect immediate success. This technique works in the same way as brainwashing: Your friend already knows she has a problem. Over time, with you to point out to her how it is affecting her life and the lives of those around her, she may come to realize that trying almost any kind of proven treatment may be worth it, and that she has nothing to lose.

Keep in mind also that mild paranoia can often be a symptom of OCD. Unfortunately, that means that fears about getting treatment will only be magnified. This is to be expected.

Once Again

Another reminder for you, the family member or friend: Patience is your watchword. Most likely, the person with OCD is resisting your efforts because she feels afraid. Remember to take time away from the person if you need to (and you probably will). Look for support from other friends and family members of people who have OCD (but not necessarily friends or family members you share; your goal should not be to embarrass the person). This can't be overestimated. The OC Foundation has local branches, and information on its Web site (*www.OCfoundation.org*). Other support groups can be found online and perhaps in your community. You may even be able to find groups that include, or are geared specifically toward, spouses and significant others.

What Else Can You Do?

In addition to urging your friend to get good help, you will want to support without enabling. Just what is "enabling," anyway? This term comes from the twelve-step movement, which originated with Alcoholics Anonymous (AA).

 Fact

Alcoholism was once considered a deficit of willpower, and, like OCD, was considered incurable. It is now believed that the alcoholic's craving is, in fact, an obsession, and alcoholism is now considered an illness.

AA's highly successful model encouraged people to band together to battle an addiction that seemed, at times, stronger than the individual members themselves. Some of the jargon that came out of twelve-step programs remains with us. One such term is "enabling," used to describe an unhealthy relationship wherein the "enabler" believes he is helping the sufferer but, in actual fact, is just helping him to perpetuate his self-destructive behavior. In the case of OCD, enabling would refer to giving the person reassurance, checking for him, or allowing him to spend too much time doing these things.

 Alert

One important exception to stopping your enabling behavior: If the person with OCD may be suicidal, immediate therapy, and perhaps hospitalization, is essential. If the person is not suicidal but is seriously harming himself—washing with chemical solutions, for instance— hospitalization may also be needed.

Unfortunately, enabling usually does not help the person who is being enabled. Neither does it help the one doing the enabling. In fact, what usually happens is, it ends up working against everyone concerned.

A therapist might counsel family members to tell the OCD sufferer firmly, "We're ready to leave now, and will go without you rather than wait for you to check the stove knobs and door locks again."

Refusing to "help" the person who has OCD, even if it is done kindly (and we hope it will be) may feel cruel to you. You may see that you are causing genuine anguish. None of us likes to see people we love in distress. That said, it is sometimes kinder to allow the person to suffer in the short term, in order to benefit in the long term.

An Extreme Example

Think of it as you would chemotherapy, for instance: No reasonable person wants to see a family member or friend go through chemo. It causes physical suffering. The patient becomes weak, anemic, thin from loss of appetite. It's distressing for all concerned. Yet, you would never advise someone you cared about to skip the chemo because it was certain to make her feel uncomfortable! You would almost certainly say, "This is going to be tough. But it will eventually make you better." That is what we hope you will say to your friend about refusing to enable her OC behaviors.

One Caveat

At first, it will probably be difficult. You might not necessarily recognize when or realize how often you end up getting roped into helping your OC friend. Or you may not have the emotional strength to cause your child or spouse to suffer.

Some therapists advise going "cold turkey"—that is, refusing to participate in any enabling behaviors at all. Others will recommend a more gradual approach, starting slowly by saying things like, "I will reassure you one more time, but after that, we have to let it go. I don't want to enable your behaviors. I want you to get well." We recommend this second approach, although, of course, we defer to the advice of your own or your family's therapist.

One other thing to keep in mind: Even if the OCD sufferer in your life does not get better once you stop "helping," chances are you will enjoy your own life more when you are no longer spending so much of your time essentially caring for someone else.

Your Own Obstacles

It may be that you, yourself, find that you do not really want to encourage your partner or friend to take the small risks necessary for CBT to work. Why? Because you fear that they will lead to anxiety, and this will be unpleasant not only for your family member with OCD, but for you (and possibly other family members), as well. In this case, supporting your partner may feel counterintuitive in that it is not what is in your heart to do. You may actually prefer the "enabling" because that behavior involves less interruption of the status quo. In other words, sometimes it's easier and quicker to just give in.

If this is the case for you, we urge you to examine your own behavior. If it is at all feasible, we hope you will enter into treatment with your OC spouse so that OCD doesn't end up damaging both of you even more.

Remember Secondary Gain?

Another reason you might feel reluctant, even subconsciously, to stop "helping" your OC spouse is that contributing to the behavior might help you to feel needed. You may fear that, once she no longer needs you to protect her from perceived harm and do things she finds too frightening, she will no longer need you for anything else, either. Again, this may be a reason for you to seek counseling, at least for a short time. At the very least, we hope you will examine your feelings honestly.

Time To Heal

Treatment, whether with CBT, medication or any other method, takes time. Support your family member by praising his progress, even very small steps. Remember, even if you think that driving to the next town and back is not necessarily worthy of copious acclaim, to the person who finds that task difficult, it is.

How It Feels to the Person with OCD

When you stop reassuring or checking or whatever you are currently doing for your OC spouse, child, or other family member, she may feel a great deal of distress. This is not necessarily because you seem to be withdrawing your support. It may well be because "this time" it feels different. There really is a sore on her skin that looks like a manifestation of AIDS, she really did leave the stove on because she was distracted . . . and so on. As strange as it may sound to you, each time can feel like a new crisis to a person who has OCD.

If you're familiar with the British and American improvisational-comedy TV program *Whose Line Is It, Anyway?*, you've probably seen a game called "Improbable Mission." In this take-off on the late 1960s/early 1970s classic adventure show *Mission Impossible*, participants use extraordinary means, such as imaginary jet-powered devices, to take on ridiculously simple tasks. So instead of performing daring acts to preserve national security, they lower themselves into a lady's bedroom from the rooftop, for instance, in order to wax her bikini line. The game is all in fun, but that's how it can feel to have OCD: The smallest tasks often seem to require outsized effort.

To a person who has OCD, the world can seem like a place teeming with terror. A routine activity or situation that you might not think twice about can hold an OCD sufferer in dread. Example: You accidentally drop an apple slice on your kitchen floor. You answer the phone in another room and return later to pick up and discard the apple fragment. A person who has OCD (depending on what kind) might have the same experience. But, perhaps after finishing the call, he remembers the fallen apple slice and envisions rats scampering out of the woodwork, attracted by the fragment, to invade his kitchen and entire home. He may have similar thoughts many times a day; they might even have become a kind of "background music" that he scarcely takes much notice of anymore, though you can be sure they take a considerable toll.

Roadblock to Recovery

For many OCD sufferers, the biggest obstacle to recovery is fear. And fear of fear.

Many people, both those with OCD and those without, fear the long-term consequences of medications on their health or even on their lives. Often, CBT or other therapies present anxiety-making situations for the person who has OCD. He may agonize about seeing a therapist whose office is in a hospital or in a run-down part of town, or about whether he'll be expected to shake hands at his first meeting, whether other people will find out that he's in therapy (and even why), or any number of things. Although you may feel frustrated by what seems to be excuse making, keep in mind that such worries can be very daunting for a person with an anxiety disorder. Everyday activities can look, to the OCD sufferer, as dangerous as climbing an icy mountain inhabited by half-starved grizzlies.

Doing What You Fear

If your friend already knows that CBT involves doing the very things that frighten her to pieces as it is, she might understandably feel a paralyzing terror when she thinks about this kind of therapy. (However, the good news is, it's probable that on another level, she would like nothing more than to be able, eventually, to do the things she's so afraid of now.)

In any case, change of any kind is often scary. And, as we've discussed, uncertainty can be among the most feared things.

 Fact

Depression may strengthen a person's resistance to treatment for OCD. People who are depressed often lose the ability to believe in or hope for anything good. However, it's possible for a person with both depression and OCD to get help for both conditions at the same time.

Making Your Case

One thing it's important to do when trying to persuade someone close to you to enter into treatment is to focus on the benefits to *her*. If you talk about the negative ways in which her behavior is affecting the family, such as stress, wasted time, and unpleasantness, you might not enjoy as much success as you would if you instead presented treatment as a way to help her to enjoy her life more, which it will.

It isn't necessarily that your partner or family member doesn't feel bad about the ways in which her symptoms affect you and others in her world. It's just that, chances are, she's too scared of changing for that to be enough of a motivating factor.

You might want to talk instead about activities that now are very difficult for the person—driving, eating in restaurants, going out with friends—that she could, with treatment, enjoy once again.

You may want to talk about her anxiety level. A person with OCD suffers from a tremendous amount of stress. Seeing as anxiety is rarely pleasant, you might want to emphasize that lowering her anxiety probably will make life more enjoyable for her.

Other people who have OCD might fear changing their behaviors because they believe that doing so would place them or others at risk. OCD is based on irrational fears and entrenched behaviors designed to ward off dangers. A woman who fears she might hurt her infant child might therefore understandably worry about losing her anxieties. She may believe that they are the only things keeping her baby safe. Similarly, a person with a fear of falling victim to harm might worry that if he loses his fear, he will become vulnerable. As we know, some amount of healthy and realistic fear is essential to keeping most creatures alive. Oftentimes, a person with OCD will have a very inflated idea about just how much fear is useful.

It has also been noted that people who have OCD often suffer from what is called "black-and-white thinking": "Either I'm completely safe, or I'm in desperate danger." There's no in-between for them, when in reality, most things exist somewhere in that big gray place in the middle. Cognitive techniques can be very useful in helping cultivate an appreciation for the richness of life that is to be found in those gray zones.

L. Essential

The old saying goes, "Rome wasn't built in a day." While most people won't react with joy to the suggestion that they get treatment, you're laying the groundwork by suggesting it. If you keep at it, you may be able to persuade your partner, child, sibling, parent, or friend to get help.

If the person who has OCD is a family member, you, and possibly the rest of the family, might benefit from some therapy, as well. As you've seen firsthand, living with a person who has a chronic, serious disorder can be very stressful and can evoke guilt, anger, shame, and other draining emotions.

Everyone, Save Thee and Me

Many people with OCD believe that the situations they fear are perfectly reasonable. After all, bridges really do collapse, drivers really do accidentally run over pedestrians on occasion, and people actually do become incurably ill (sometimes from contagion) and die unenviable deaths. Pointing out that the odds are in the person's favor will not necessarily get you anywhere, as you will likely be told that the odds favor everyone, yet some people still fall victim to egregious misfortune. Cognitive therapists do considerable work with patients to challenge this constrained way of thinking.

 Fact

Not surprisingly, it's said that people with OCD who have supportive families generally enjoy higher rates of success with their treatments than those whose families are overtly resentful, angry or unsympathetic (or all of those things).

In many cases, a person with OCD knows that his fears are inflated, at least to some degree. He may not want to confide in a therapist or anyone else for fear that he'll look "crazy" or foolish. You can help reassure him that therapists who treat OCD have definitely "heard it all."

When the Problem is Acute

In cases of severe OCD symptoms, you and the person who has OCD may want to consider an in-patient option for treatment. This offers several advantages: The patient gets used to doing things without help from the family; family members may get a much-needed break from the prison of their loved one's OC symptoms, and success, in many cases, can be achieved more quickly than it might be with weekly, or twice weekly, therapist visits (or medication, which may take weeks before it begins to work).

Can't They Just Stop?

As a friend or family member of an OCD sufferer, you will probably often wish that the person you care about could just "turn off" her OC behaviors. Sadly, it doesn't work this way. People who have OCD can't do that, even if they know, at least to a degree, that those behaviors do not serve a useful purpose and are annoying or upsetting to others. For most people who have OCD, the compulsion serves to reduce anxiety or, more often than not, keep that awful anxiety from starting in the first place—though, of course, this goal is thwarted in the long run. Refraining from practicing a "ritual behavior" can feel like bracing to experience a horrible pain.

Feelings of Inadequacy

In addition to frustration, you might also feel guilt that you are not patient enough with your OC friend. You may feel isolated because you don't know other families who are going through this, too. You might also feel resentful that the person's OCD seems to be "taking over." Or you may feel afraid that it is turning your once-functional friend into someone you hardly know. Any of these feelings (and others) are perfectly normal. The key is to keep your feelings in check so that you don't cause the person, or yourself, undue anguish. Seek out others you can talk to, and come up with your own coping strategies. Taking out your frustration on the person who has OCD will only make things worse.

Setting Realistic Expectations

People who receive treatment for OCD can experience almost unbelievable gains. They can enjoy activities that were once all but unthinkable. They can go back to living productively, returning to work or to other previously enjoyed activities. But they won't be cured. Nor will they turn into entirely different people. It's important for you to know this. If a person was phobic about germs before, he may be able to shake hands after receiving medication or CBT. But he probably won't go around extending his palm toward every passing stranger, either. As you've read before in this book, it's a matter of degree.

L. Essential

OCD is often kept a secret, and keeping secrets can be hard. It's stressful and it's tiring. That said, it's probably the right thing to do if the person in question has asked you not to reveal his OCD to the world, or to anyone. This may change in time.

Remember: As in any situation involving the illness of a family member, it's important for you to make sure that your own needs are met, also. Seek emotional support from others, preferably other families of OCD sufferers. Make sure that you don't neglect good nutrition and adequate rest. Let yourself feel anger or frustration sometimes. Get counseling for yourself if you need it.

A Note to Health Care Providers

If you are a health care provider, you might want to help your more-anxious patients to feel comfortable with you and your office and staff. Your patient may like you personally and trust your abilities, but if she does not feel comfortable with your office or techniques, she will likely avoid visits or choose a different provider.

What Can You Do?

There are several small but important ways in which you can help patients who have anxiety disorders to feel comfortable.

Space may be small, but do try to keep biohazard containers far from examination areas. Wash your hands, as well as you can, in front of your patient. Put on a new pair of examination gloves as soon as you enter the room (preferably after the patient has seen you give your hands a good wash).

If your patient seems nervous, ask gently what she is worried about and what you can do to help. Try not to sound impatient or to make her feel as if her concerns are silly. Chances are, the patient already feels self-conscious. You may also want to allow extra time for your visits.

The Best Medicine?

Obsessive-compulsive disorder and anxiety tend to favor intelligent people. Most sufferers know, on some level, that their fears are unfounded. Still, they require reassurance, and lots of it.

Ask in advance what kind of music your patient likes. Offer to play something funny, such as Spike Jones or Tom Lehrer. It is difficult indeed to laugh and feel nervous at the same time. Try it!

Keep everything in the office as visibly clean as possible, and instruct staff to treat the person with extra kindness. Remember that, to you, your concerns seem perfectly reasonable, too!

Always explain what you are about to do (unless your patient requests otherwise) and ask if it is all right. If the patient rejects an examination or procedure you consider important, explain your reason for requesting it, and ask how you can put him at ease. If he is not in immediate danger, you may need to delay it until his next visit. Let him know you would like to "work up to" the procedure; this will give him time to prepare psychologically. Patients value providers who are sympathetic to their needs, and often will reward them with loyalty.

CHAPTER 19

The Media and OCD

EVEN THOUGH OCD HAS never been more visible in the media, you shouldn't necessarily expect everyone you know to understand the particulars of the disorder. It seems as if there are more conditions and diseases now than ever! In the past forty years or so, many new maladies have emerged and many other conditions have been identified, particularly among children. This chapter discusses the information out there, the misconceptions people might have about OCD, and how you can deal with both.

Public Perceptions of OCD

All of a sudden, it seems, every other child has a malady not widely known before the 1960s, such as Asperger's syndrome (a disorder itself related to OCD), allergies, autism, and attention deficit disorder (sometimes with hyperactivity). Celiac disease, a syndrome arising from gluten and other dietary sensitivities, has also become more prominent, along with any number of other heretofore little-known health problems. The average person can hardly be expected to keep up with each newly identified condition. For that and other reasons, you may notice a lot of mistaken perception about OCD on the parts of friends, acquaintances, family members, and the various media.

Then, too, for many years, the only thing the general public seemed to know about OCD was that people who had it couldn't stop cleaning their homes or counting things. (These days, people also know to associate OCD with excessive hand washing.) While this is true for many OCD sufferers, to be sure, it is not true of all!

Private Lives

Friends, family, roommates, coworkers, and significant others: The more time you spend with any of these people, the more obvious your symptoms will likely become. What can you do? Any number of things.

However, how and whether you will want to try to educate others about OCD in general or your OCD in particular will depend on a number of things, such as:

- Whether they're open to hearing what you, or others, have to say
- Whether you have the right tools to give them
- How much time and effort both sides are willing to invest
- Whether you *want* to try to educate other people
- Whether they have the desire to learn more about OCD
- Any number of other factors particular to your unique situation

The first thing you'll want to decide is, whom do you want to educate? For the time being, the answer may be no one. And if that's what you choose, it's fine. You have the perfect right to remain silent about your disorder (which is, after all, *your* business). There are plenty of ways to deal with OCD without sharing your information with the world at large.

The Choice is Yours

On the other hand, you may feel as if OCD is nothing to be ashamed of, and decide to share with everyone you know, and lots of people you *don't* know. That's fine, too. Why not? You may even take it upon yourself to become a sort of informal ambassador for the condition, putting a friendly and knowledgeable face on it.

More likely, you will choose a few close associates to start with, and you'll tell them because it's important to you, or because you think your behavior needs explanation at this point. (Or because they've asked.) Once you do make the decision to talk with close friends or family members, you will want to determine how much information is good for all of you.

The Deluxe Plan

If your friends or family are particularly interested in supporting you and learning about OCD and its effects, that's good news, indeed. There are now huge numbers of books and other resources available. Several of these are listed in Appendix A. Some even are written exclusively for *families* of OCD sufferers.

To Get Started Right Away

The OC Foundation in New Haven, Connecticut can be a great place to start. Online, it is at *www.OCFoundation.org* (by phone, it's 1-203-401-2070). There, you can find information about OCD itself, teen and other support groups, news developments, and articles on topics such as hoarding.

You may also want to check out Obsessive-Compulsive Anonymous (*http://members.aol.com/west24th*), a free fellowship organization founded on the principles of Alcoholics Anonymous.

Talking about It

Your local or online library or bookstore can also provide you with almost unlimited information. If you're seeing a therapist for your OCD, she will probably be able to give you advice and information for talking about it with the important people in your life, as well. Of course, if you are already in a support group, you might find helpful tips there.

Honest, non-judgmental conversation between you and your friends, family, or potential romantic partner will probably prove the best resource of all. As long as both sides make a sincere effort not to bring old or new conflicts into the conversation, or to place blame or judgment, you may enjoy a real chance to effect a change for the better—and, in the bargain, help others to gain some understanding about you and your disorder. Remember, everyone has problems. This one just happens to be yours.

 Fact

> OCD often becomes "second nature," so that you no longer think about why you avoid certain things or situations. You may "space out" while checking door locks or stove burners so that the action doesn't really "register." Your OC symptoms may even show up in your dreams.

Education Can Be Fun

Perhaps a more enjoyable way to educate others about OCD is to steer them toward sensitive portrayals in the media (now that sensitive portrayals exist), which you can then discuss together. Cable TV's *Monk*, for example, might help friends to recognize your behavior while at the same time enjoying a gentle laugh *with* you. Of course, it is important for any viewer to understand that *Monk*, and other TV shows and movies, are fiction. For one thing, no real OCD sufferer could endure as many compulsions as the fictional Adrian Monk. (And no real detective, obsessive-compulsive or otherwise, could solve such a high number of complex homicides!)

The Personal Touch

If you are currently in therapy, you might be able to bring along an interested family member (or members) to one of your sessions, so that you can talk together with your therapist. (Alternatively, your therapist might be willing to hold a phone conversation with a family member who is particularly distressed or concerned about your behavior, or geographically distant from you.)

Try To Be Accommodating

One thing to keep in mind is flexibility. Although you may feel enthusiastic about a movie or TV show, for instance, that you believe illustrates your situation almost perfectly, your friend may prefer reading about the disorder to watching TV or renting a DVD. Accept any interest as a good thing, and offer alternatives if you can.

Another thing to remember is that, unfortunately, not everyone may want to be educated. Friends or family members might feel overwhelmed by your OCD and not wish to talk or hear about it. That may feel hurtful, but it is a possibility that you will also need to accept, at least for the time being.

If You Prefer Not to "Share"

Of course, you may not care to talk about your OCD with people you spend a lot of time around but do not necessarily feel close to, such as coworkers or roommates. (It probably will make sense, in most cases, to confide in at least one or two people who *are* close to you.) In that case, you have other options.

Among Friends

The best of these might be finding fellowship among other people who have OCD. Talking about your situation with those who share it can be a great way of developing inner strength, not to mention, feeling less alone. When you join with others who are going through the same thing, you will likely feel understood. There will be no need to explain things. Another benefit of fellowship is the practical advice you may get from people who are very interested in dealing with the same condition.

Where Do You Go?

Many larger communities offer OCD support groups. Here again, the OC Foundation can be an excellent starting point. Its Web site (*www.OCfoundation.org*) offers searchable support information, including help with finding groups in your area.

Essential

> Many OCD support groups meet in the evenings, often at churches or hospitals, sometimes at mental health facilities. If any of these factors is a problem for you, you might want to start your own group. One source of information on how to do that can be found at *http://under standing_ocd.tripod.com/ocd_supportgroups.html.*

Online support groups are not necessarily abundant, but may be worth seeking out, particularly if you can find one that offers a moderator or therapist. If your OCD symptoms or job or schedule prevent you from attending live meetings, you might want to do some searching for an online option, at least for the time being.

There may not be a relevant online group available at the time you happen to be looking. Some groups may be open only to one segment of the population, such as teenagers, to which you do not belong. Other groups may be defunct. However, there is always the possibility of a new one starting.

You Are Not Alone

Not at all! Many celebrities in the worlds of sports, music, and entertainment have, or are believed to have, OCD, along with many in the general population. OCD, it seems, has never been more prominent or better understood than it is right now.

Media Portrayals of OCD

One of television's first obsessive-compulsive characters was Felix Unger, in the 1970s series adaptation of Neil Simon's Broadway smash, *The Odd Couple.* Felix worried a lot about his health, but, more obviously, cleaned his home constantly and fussed about all kinds of "picky" household and culinary details—much to the distress of his roommate, notorious slob Oscar Madison.

While Felix's cleaning preoccupation showed one facet of OCD, many viewers probably came to believe that that was its sole characteristic. (That is, assuming that they even made the association between Felix's behavior and OCD, which was not mentioned per se.) At around that time, compulsive cleaning enjoyed a short vogue in the media. It was a start.

Several *Columbo* fans have suggested that the iconic 1970s TV detective embodied several OC tendencies, such as obsession (dwelling on his cases until they were solved) and repetition (at least insofar as wearing the same clothing and eating the same lunch every day constitutes repetition). This underscores the classic question of whether a person is obsessive-compulsive or merely quirky.

Flash Forward

Although some in the OCD community may have taken offense at Jack Nicholson's portrayal of life with OCD (particularly the apparently quick resolution to his problems) in *As Good As It Gets*, the 1996 film may have been the first mainstream movie to deal with this subject. Nicholson's character, wildly successful novelist Melvin Udall, takes extremely long showers, washes his hands with brand-new soaps and scalding water, carries his own plastic utensils to restaurants, and displays, along with many other typical OC characteristics, an aversion to being touched by strangers. (He is also bad-tempered: mean, intolerant, rude and profane, unlike most people who have OCD!)

The 2004 movie *Dirty, Filthy Love*, originally made for British television, presents a main character who has OCD as well as Tourette's syndrome.

There is even an obsessive-compulsive character—played strictly for laughs, of course—on *The Simpsons*. After many episodes, the otherwise unnamed "rich Texan," an obnoxiously wealthy tycoon, reveals that he has OCD. In that episode, the stereotypical oilman compulsively taps his foot in counts of four each time he fires his revolver (at the same time, keeping count out loud)! The show's

Latino game announcer also confesses—right in the middle of calling a bullfight—to fears about having left the stove on at home.

In 2002, USA Network's detective series *Monk* introduced an obsessive-compulsive character who suffered from so many phobias and compulsions, it is unlikely that such a person could have existed in the "real world," if only because his behaviors would have "canceled one another out." (A fear of germs *and* the compulsion to touch parking meters? Probably not.)

Monk, however, illustrated the very real suffering that so often goes along with OCD. At the same time, the program underscored the humor that many OCD sufferers manage to see in themselves.

 Fact

Another not-quite-human television character often mentioned in the context of OCD is the compulsive counter on *Sesame Street*: The Count. The Count's "birthday," October 9, was shared by the late John Lennon and is also the birthday of Tony Shalhoub, who plays an OCD sufferer on *Monk*.

Monk's therapist visits are a regular part of the show's action, and his conflict over whether to take medication formed the cornerstone of at least one memorable episode. Monk also has the understanding of the police force (now that he's proved his worth) and an assistant who helps him do things that are hard for him. Would she be considered an "enabler" in real life? Probably. (Not to mention that the department might not give her "clearance" for all that sensitive information she comes into contact with as a result.)

Another salient point worth noting about this program: Monk's disorder, while it has kept him off the San Francisco police force, does not hinder his abilities. In fact, it is his hyper-attention to detail that allows him to do his work as well as he does, even though *Monk* does not try to sugarcoat the very real difficulties faced by people who have OCD.

 Fact

> Prior to starting work on *Monk*, title actor Tony Shalhoub prepared by visiting a psychologist who specialized in OCD. Shalhoub, therefore, began with a lot of knowledge about the condition and those who have it. (He's also acknowledged that he's a little fanatical about the way dishes are loaded into his dishwasher at home.)

Getting It Right

On television's medical comedy *Scrubs*, Michael J. Fox guest starred as a brilliant pathologist with OCD. Fox's character makes his seeming disability work for him: In medical school, he directed his need for repetition into poring over his textbooks endlessly and, as a result, became the best diagnostician in his field. (In fact, he is even able to "diagnose" the food in the hospital cafeteria!) But he still has to walk over thresholds multiple times and run home during the day to use his own bathroom.

OCD in the Spotlight—Past and Present

With OCD affecting more than two percent of the general population, it should not be surprising that many well-known people have suffered from it. Eighteenth-century man of letters Dr. Samuel Johnson, whose life was chronicled by his friend, biographer James Boswell, was among the first famous persons to be recognized, after the fact, as an OCD sufferer. There is evidence to suggest that he may also have had Tourette's syndrome. Johnson was known to perform all kinds of elaborate motions for no readily apparent reason. He is also recognized as having had one of the most brilliant minds of his day. How frustrated he must have been, not understanding, or enjoying the ability to control, his own unusual behavior!

 Question

> **Does baseball superstar Nomar Garciaparra have OCD?**
> Garciaparra's repetitive rituals at the plate have earned him many mentions in connection with OCD (and some good-natured kidding on the parts of his teammates). But is he merely following superstitious tradition like so many other sports figures? It isn't always easy, or possible, to tell.

Many other well-known people likely had OCD, as well:

- If the condition had been understood properly more than a hundred years ago, *Remembrance of Things Past* author Marcel Proust and many others probably would have been diagnosed with it.
- Centuries earlier, Martin Luther, for whom the Lutheran religion is named, is believed to have suffered from OCD symptoms, too.
- Howard Hughes, who died in the 1970s after an illustrious career in both aviation and film, became a virtual prisoner of OCD, spending more and more time alone, obsessing about physical illness and germs, and allowing fewer and fewer people into his space. This was during the 1950s (although his symptoms began decades earlier), when little was known about the disorder. According to friends' reports, Hughes sorted one of his favorite foods—peas—according to size before eating. He was also known to be obsessively perfectionistic while working on his films. Some recent biographers have also suggested that late-stage syphilis may have been responsible for many of Hughes's more bizarre actions. However, he also exhibited at least one classic OC behavior: touching objects only through paper towels. And here are some contemporary names you may have heard in connection with OCD:

- Radio personality Howard Stern has written and spoken publicly quite often about his struggles with OCD. His symptoms have included repetition obsessions and magical thinking. He has also acknowledged that, in an effort to distance himself from the disorder, he tormented other OCD sufferers on his popular syndicated radio program.

- Actress Cameron Diaz has acknowledged that she cleans her home slavishly and can't bear to touch doorknobs.

- Television's *Deal Or No Deal* host Howie Mandel refuses to shake hands with his on-camera guests, preferring a "knuckle-knock" instead. He has said that he built a special germ-free enclosure on his property to retreat to during stressful times, and that he prefers to keep his head clean shaven, in part because he considers that hygienic.

- The late entertainer Tiny Tim (born Herbert Buckingham Khaury)—who was, in fact, a frequent guest on Howard Stern's radio program—was plagued with an especially bad case. At one point, and for perhaps as long as forty years, he showered and brushed his teeth as often as six times a day. In addition to the several baths or showers he took each day for no known reason, he reported that he also took short showers after every visit to the bathroom. Tiny Tim's fanatical adherence to his unchecked compulsions must have taken great amounts of energy.

- Musician Joey Ramone (born Jeffrey Hyman) of the celebrated punk rock group The Ramones was known to have had OCD. His song "Like A Drug I Never Did Before" is said to mention it by name. The Ramones song "I Wanna Be Sedated" deals with an overwhelming anxiety about flying.

- U.K. actor Patrick McGoohan, whose behavior might be considered excessively fastidious by some, reportedly turned down the role of James Bond over objections about the character's loose morals, and because he didn't want to have to kiss actresses he did not know well. According to one report, the actor once told a TV director who was expecting to film a love scene that there was only one woman he would consent to kiss: "*Mrs.* McGoohan." According to entertainment legend, writers for the 1960s cult classic television series *The Prisoner* came up with McGoohan's signature "Be seeing you" line because the star refused to shake hands with other members of the cast. However, it has also been noted that the program created a sterile and paranoid universe in which characters might have operated clandestinely for fear of observation.

- Comic Paula Poundstone says she has OCD, and openly discusses her cleaning and organizing behaviors. (She also says she has a compulsion to talk too much about herself.)

- The late musician Warren Zevon, unfortunately, took his obsessive fears to tragic extremes. Afraid of doctors, he avoided them. By the time he received a cancer diagnosis, the disease had spread too far to be halted. Zevon's song "Worrier King" reveals his anxieties plainly.

- Zevon's friend and neighbor, actor-director-musician Billy Bob Thornton, has often discussed his own OCD symptoms publicly. His obsessions are legendary and include repetition. He has often acknowledged a fear of antique furniture. His phobia about genuine silverware is so strong, he gave one of his cinema characters the same characteristic so he wouldn't have to eat with spoons of unknown origin while performing. Like Jack Nicholson's character in *As Good As It Gets*, Thornton insisted on using plastic instead.

- Soccer star David Beckham reportedly has severe OCD and has said that he has order and symmetry fixations of epic proportions, and even has a pain addiction that drives him to get more and more tattoos.

- Woody Allen's health and death obsessions are well known, as is his sense of humor about his dark preoccupations. Some would probably consider aspects of his behavior obsessive-compulsive.

Although many well-known athletes, actors, and others have been associated with OCD, many more do not wish to have this personal detail made public, and, like countless private citizens, try to hide their OC behaviors. As OCD becomes recognized as a group of symptoms particular to people who have certain chemical imbalances of the brain, greater acceptance will probably not lag far behind. Public personalities who've acknowledged that they have OCD can be said to be doing a service for others who have it: helping to further de-stigmatize the condition.

 Fact

In both *Monk* and *As Good As It Gets*, minimal mention is made of the terms "OCD" or "obsessive-compulsive." In discussing his disorder with a romantic interest, the protagonist of the movie refers to his "ailment."

Many more names, from Albert Einstein and Michelangelo to any number of rock stars, actors and TV personalities are claimed as OCD sufferers on lists all over the Internet (rather like speculation in the 1970s about which actors were gay). However, it isn't always easy to know exactly where more or less normal quirks leave off and true OCD begins.

CHAPTER 20

Making Use
of Resources

THE MODERN WORLD OFFERS abundant resources for people who have the OCD. So much more is known about OCD now than was known even twenty-five years ago. For a great many OCD sufferers, new therapies and medications have made symptoms manageable and life bearable. There is also a lot of support available out there. "Out there" can mean a local in-person support group, but it can mean online communities, as well. Developing a strong support system of any kind is one of the most helpful things you can do for yourself.

Finding Support in Your Community

As you read earlier, you might want to consider a group that you can visit regularly or occasionally. There are a few kinds of in-person group. One is the simple support group.

Typically, members get together to share information and cheer one another on. Some groups are led by therapists, some by facilitators. Others are led by the members themselves. Some groups, particularly those that are therapist-led, charge a fee. Others do not, and still a few others might charge only a nominal amount for things like room rental or juice and cookies.

Specific Information

There is also a twelve-step program modeled on Alcoholics Anonymous (AA), called Obsessive-Compulsive Anonymous. OCA maintains groups all over the country. Its main number is 1-516-739-0662.

 Fact

> The OC Foundation holds a conference every year for researchers, therapists, people who have OCD, and anyone else who would like to learn more about the disorder or get together with others who are also interested in it.

The OC Foundation produced a video and pamphlet called *G.O.A.L.* (for "Giving Obsessive-Compulsives Another Lifestyle"), which gives specific advice on setting up and running support groups. It's available for sale through the OC Foundation Web site (*www.OCfoundation.org*).

In case this is helpful to know, groups will be open only to people who have OCD, but not to their families or partners. Others will be open *only* to families of people who have OCD. And still others may have different restrictions. Some groups include all different kinds of members.

Then, of course, there is group therapy (something else entirely), in which persons with the same disorder meet with a single therapist, with an eye toward becoming mentally healthy (or, in this case, becoming free from most of their OCD symptoms). This almost always carries a cost and is considered therapy rather than support alone.

Group Options

If you haven't yet checked out the OC Foundation at *www.OCFoundation.org*, you are encouraged to do so. The site provides practical information about various aspects of OCD and about finding support organizations. There are other online resources, as well, some of which are mentioned in this chapter or in the appendices.

In addition to *www.OCFoundation.org*, which lists groups by state, you might want to look into mental health facilities in your area. These may offer on-site groups, or be able to refer you to some. If you are currently in therapy, your therapist may be able to recommend a support group. Your medical doctor might, as well. You might even enjoy some luck by typing "OCD support" or similar words into a search engine, along with the name of the largest city in your area. (Of course, as always, we urge you to use reasonable care and check out the group as thoroughly as possible before you attend or give any personal information.)

An Oft-Neglected Opportunity

If you're currently employed, don't forget to look into your company's health insurance plan or employee assistance program (EAP). Your EAP may be able to put you in touch with a counselor who can recommend specialists who work with people who have OCD. Similarly, your health insurance plan may offer mental health services. In all likelihood, live telephone help will be available if you're having trouble navigating your plan's voicemail or Web site. (A word to the wise: You may need to employ extra patience until you can get a live person who can help you.)

Starting Your Own Group

The OC Foundation Web site also contains information for forming your own group. Some reasons you might want to do this include a lack of support groups in your area, or problems with scheduling or venue. (As mentioned previously, many groups meet in hospitals—not ideal if you have contamination phobias. Then again, with sufficient motivation, you might be moved to try to set your worries aside for an hour every month or week, depending on how often the group meets.)

On Your Own

If you decide that you would like to look into creating your own in-person support group for people who have OCD or for their families (or both), you will need to decide whether you would like a therapist (or perhaps two alternating therapists) to facilitate your meetings, and whether you would like to employ a formal structure, such as a lecture each week, followed by a meeting.

Essential

A few of the more fun Web sites that deal with OCD (at least in part) include *http://USANetwork.com/series/Monk*, about the TV program *Monk* (choose "community," then "bulletin board" from the menu) and Markmaynard.com, a blog that sometimes includes entries (often very amusing ones) about the writer's OCD.

If you would like to engage a facilitator, of course, you will have to find one. Going online, asking your current therapist for recommendations, or looking in your local phone book may be more or less the only ways to go. And they may be quite successful—many such groups already exist.

Finding a therapist, or therapists, who will agree to facilitate an OCD support group on a regular basis may be difficult (but it is not impossible): Most people today have a lot less free time than they would like. You might suggest, as did one successful support-group founder who reported on the OC Foundation's Web site, that facilitating a group might be good for business: The therapist will be surrounded by potential patients. She will also have a chance to learn a lot more about OCD firsthand.

Once you have this part of the puzzle in place, your next step will be to let people know about it. Therapists you've contacted might be willing to tack small notices about your group to their office bulletin boards. If you want to have information cards printed, you can offer those.

Other venues include your local chapter of the OC Foundation and classified ads.

If you think creatively, you can probably come up with still more ways to publicize your group. Oh, and remember this old rule: Whenever you're looking for an apartment, a job, or a relationship, tell everyone you know. Apply it to your proposed group and see if that doesn't bring the results you're looking for.

 Fact

Phobialist.com contains the proper names of more than 500 phobias, indexed and alphabetized, along with information pertaining to phobia naming, and other features related to fear and anxiety (although the poster writes that his interest, primarily, is in the names, rather than in treating phobias).

Think Globally

Online support groups and lists provide a way to "talk" with fellow OCD sufferers and the people who care about them, all over the world. This can be a terrific option if your area doesn't offer much in the way of in-person groups, or if your schedule makes it difficult for you to make the meetings. It can also be ideal if you suffer from agoraphobia, contamination phobias, or social phobias and have not yet progressed to the point that in-person meetings make sense for you. Online support also offers the advantage of being available twenty-four hours a day every day of the week and giving you hundreds of people to talk with, as opposed to the small group you might find at an in-person meeting. (One caveat: as you probably know by now, people can sometimes behave more abruptly online than they would in person.)

Internet Interaction

As we've said, you'll want to exercise reasonable care when it comes to giving out personal information on the Web. In some cases, you may be asked to provide e-mail and other information. That's not necessarily a bad thing.

Read the site's privacy policy: Your information may be used for various purposes.

If this concerns you, then simply find sites that do not insist on gathering this information. Or contact the site administrator and ask why certain information is requested. In some cases, for instance, a birth date is required to cut down on the possibility of underage users. As long as you are over the age specification, however, you should be able to answer this question any way you like. If you're under the age limit, look for sites specifically for teens or children.

Essential

There are many books and Web sites for parents of children and teen-agers who have OCD. These resources can be found all over the world. Some deal specifically with OCD, others with related disorders; some with practical issues, such as school, others with more emotional concerns, such as support. (Some are listed in Appendix A.)

Some sites may allow you to "lurk"—that is, read other users' posts without contributing yourself—even if you don't register. While not necessarily ideal, reading firsthand accounts of other peoples' experiences with OCD may help you to learn, draw emotional strength, and feel less alone.

Finding Fellowship Online (and Elsewhere)

The following are a few other resources you might find useful:

- Healthyplace.com offers chat rooms, articles and other resources related to OCD and virtually all other mental health concerns.
- Stuckinadoorway.org provides forums and information. (You can lurk, but registration is required before you're allowed to post. Year of birth is needed for registration.) You may have to navigate the site before finding the place to register. You'll find FAQs at:

http://forums.stuckinadoorway.org/faq.php. You are also allowed to delete cookies.

- Yahoo.com offers an online support group: *http://health .groups.yahoo.com/group/OCD-Support/.* Understanding OCD (*http://understanding_ocd.tripod.com/ocd_links_resources .html*) features a bulletin board, and other resources and links.
- Cyber Psych Pen Pals for Anxieties (*http://cyberpsych.org/ anxdisor*) includes message boards on which posters can share their thoughts and read others. (Be aware, however, that the site, like many others, can be found easily through Google and other search engines, and that an e-mail address is requested. However, nicknames seem to work just fine.) The site also provides links to other resources.

Others you might find helpful include *http://www.ocd-world.org .uk/* (part of a mental health Web ring) and *http://top10links.com.* (This is not an OCD site per se. Go to the site's search engine, type in "OCD," and you'll be presented with a list of potential resources.) Please note: we have not investigated all of these, so exercise caution when doing so yourself.

There are many others, and new ones form from time to time. Search around and, as always, observe the general rules of Internet safety. (We'll bet you know and do that anyway!)

The Old-Fashioned Way

Don't forget the library as a source of virtually limitless resources. Your local library, or a larger one in the nearest city, probably houses a great many books on OCD. There are books for people who *have* OCD, books for the *families* of people who have OCD, books *by* people who have OCD, books that tell personal stories, books that offer information, and so on.

Libraries can also borrow books from other libraries, if they don't have what you want. Don't be afraid to ask. Your library may also have a Web site you can access from home.

You need not feel embarrassed about taking out books about OCD. Libraries have books so that people will read them. (And, as you now know, there is no reason to feel ashamed about having OCD; it's simply a neurological condition.) However, if you do feel shy about using the library, or if you still feel uncomfortable handling the library's books or computers, any brick-and-mortar or online bookstore should be able to offer many excellent choices, as well. Of course, if you feel as if you're not on the "same wavelength" as the author of one book, there's always another. And another.

 Fact

HappyNews.com posts alternatives to the usually depressing local, national, and international news offered online, in newspapers, and on TV. As its name suggests, it carries stories that are well researched and factual, upbeat in nature, and heartwarming, too.

Reading works for and about people who have OCD can be like meeting new friends: others who share your struggles and symptoms, and who understand. Like true good friends, they can offer support and guidance and help you to feel less alone. Also, knowledge truly is power. The more you learn about the OCD dictator, the less control he will have.

Don't Overlook These Resources, Either

Whether you're succeeding beautifully against your OCD, struggling hard with it, or falling somewhere in between, you will be well served to keep on getting the support you need. Two resources not to overlook are your therapist and your friends.

A therapist, of course, can help keep you on track making strides, and, unlike a friend, will be able to offer therapeutic assistance and will not expect you to listen to his problems or drive him to the airport, and so on. (At any rate, this is to be hoped. If your therapist *does* behave this way, find a new one—pronto!)

It's good to have someone you can "check in" with either regularly or from time to time, if you have more-or-less completed your therapy.

Friends also have an important place. If you have one or two friends in whom you can confide during stressful times, or with whom you can share personal success stories, that will probably go a long way, as well. And friendship is free.

If no one happens to notice your progress, feel free to announce to your spouse or best friend, "I did something difficult today, and it went just fine!" Some kind of emotional support is essential for every one of us.

Your Personal Support Network

Another important step toward well-being is to surround yourself with sympathetic and supportive people. How do you do that? By choosing them, of course!

Obviously, you can't choose everyone in your life—parents, for instance, or siblings—but you can do a lot with the choices you do have. For example,

- You may not be able to choose your coworkers, but you can choose friends from among them, and from other departments within your company.

- You can't necessarily choose your boss, but you can choose to work for a different boss.
- You may not be able to choose your parents or other family members, but you can choose the way you try to educate them about OCD.
- And you definitely can choose roommates, friends, your spouse or significant other, your beautician, mechanic, physician, dentist, and other people you will deal with on a regular basis.

Choose people who will applaud your successes or sympathize with your struggles.

FYI

One thing to keep in mind: Once your OCD is largely under control, you may actually find yourself feeling depressed. Why? One reason may be that OCD's obsessions and rituals demanded a lot of your time and attention; they will have become the focus of daily life, at least for some people. You might find that suddenly, you have more time, and it can feel like a vast void that will now have to be filled. Be sure to talk with your therapist about these feelings, so you can learn to manage them before they get out of hand.

Staying in Shape, Emotionally

If we were to give you our best advice for keeping OC symptoms to a minimum once you've begun treatment, it would be this:

- Keep busy. Nothing defeats OCD more soundly than purposeful activity.
- Exercise at least one half hour every day, at least six days a week.
- Consciously resist compulsions.
- Pay as little attention as you can to obsessions. Talk back to your inner voice and tell it that whatever you're worried about simply isn't true.

- Continue to learn as much as you can about OCD. You might find that every case sounds more or less like yours, and that might serve to diminish a lot of the old dictator's power.

How to Help Others

One of the greatest joys you may experience is being able to help others over the rough spots from which you've just extracted yourself (or from which you are in the process of successfully extracting yourself). Look around. Perhaps you hear a person with OCD being discussed by her friend; perhaps one of your friends shows anxiety about social situations or driving. You can gently point the way toward recovery. Few will be in a better position to do so than you: You have knowledge about the condition, additional resources to suggest, and the compassion of one who has been through the same thing. With any luck, your struggle has made you a better person than you might have been otherwise. Use that experience to offer help and support to others. (We do urge you not to become obnoxious, however.)

Speaking Up

Although, as we've demonstrated, we think that the ability to laugh at ourselves is essential (and we've also demonstrated that we don't always feel bound by the tenets of political correctness), there is also a lot of joking about OCD that shows a clear lack of understanding. If you hear ignorant remarks and feel comfortable doing so, you can politely educate friends and acquaintances about what OCD really is—and isn't—and what it is like to live with the disorder.

Getting Strength in Order to Give It

When it comes to helping other people who have OCD or would like to learn about it, you will probably be able to do a more effective job if you, yourself, have the support you need. Life can be difficult. Life with OCD can be *very* difficult. Everyone needs help sometimes. There's nothing wrong with seeking it out.

Support for Life

It isn't terribly important how you get support for your OCD, only that you do. By becoming part of a community, you can supplement the help you receive from your doctor or therapist (or both), and gain information, insight and fellowship. And then you, in turn, may be able to help others. It's a win all around.

Now that you've been there and you know the way, you might find that you'd like to share what you know. Some ways in which you may be able to help other people who also have OCD, or who care about someone who does, are:

- Starting a support group
- Reaching out if you suspect that a friend or a friend of a friend is affected by OCD
- Staying educated, yourself, by reading about the disorder and staying informed about new research developments
- Volunteering your services to an OCD self-help organization that already exists
- Spreading the word by writing or blogging about your experiences

Sometimes, of course, it's hard to offer help. You may feel shy or wary, or the other person may rebuff your suggestions. Our best advice: Don't worry about it. If you're shy, maybe you won't be next time. If the other person shows resistance to your suggestions, just think back to when you began to learn about OCD. You may not have been pleased to hear your diagnosis, or completely brave about taking medication or doing CBT. (Few people are!) You may simply have to give the person time. Let him know that when he's ready, all things being equal, you will be, too. In the meantime, try to feel good about yourself because, when you do, you'll be at your best. And projecting a positive image of a person who has OCD but is not ruled by it is one of the best ways you can help others who are starting out now from the place where you once were.

Resources

Books

OCD, General/Self-Help

The Boy Who Couldn't Stop Washing: The Experience and Treatment of Obsessive-Compulsive Disorder, by Judith Rapoport, M.D..

Brain Lock: Free Yourself from Obsessive-Compulsive Disorder, by Jeffrey Schwartz, M.D..

Getting Control: Overcoming Your Obsessions and Compulsions, by Lee Baer, Ph.D.

Obsessive-Compulsive Disorders: A Complete Guide to Getting Well and Staying Well, by Fred Penzel, Ph.D.

The OCD Workbook: Your Guide to Breaking Free from Obsessive-Compulsive Disorder, by Bruce Hyman, Ph.D. and Cherry Pedrick, R.N.

Tormenting Thoughts and Secret Rituals: The Hidden Epidemic of Obsessive-Compulsive Disorder, by Ian Osborn, M.D..

Personal/Humorous

Devil in the Details: Scenes from an Obsessive Girlhood, by Jennifer Traig

Everything in Its Place: My Trials and Triumphs with Obsessive Compulsive Disorder, by Marc Summers and Eric Hollander

Hidden Howie: True Stories from the Private Life of a Public Nuisance, by Howie Mandel

Home Town, by Tracy Kidder

Just Checking: Scenes from the Life of an Obsessive-Compulsive, by Emily Colas

Life Is Just What You Make It: My Story So Far, by Donny Osmond and Patricia Romanowski

Naked, by David Sedaris

Passing For Normal, by Amy Wilensky

Anxiety/Meditation

Feel the Fear And Do It Anyway: Dynamic Techniques for Turning Fear, Indecision, and Anger into Power, Action, and Love, by Susan Jeffers, Ph.D.

From Panic to Power: Proven Techniques to Calm Your Anxieties, by Lucinda Bassett

Full Catastrophe Living: Using the Wisdom of Your Body and Mind to Face Stress, Pain, and Illness, by Jon Kabat-Zinn

Meditation (Exploring a Great Spiritual Practice), by Richard Chilson

Wherever You Go, There You Are: Mindfulness Meditation in Everyday Life, by Jon Kabat-Zinn

Relaxation and Calming Techniques

The Little Book of Calm, Paul Wilson

The Little Book of Instant Calm, Paul Wilson

The Relaxation Response, Dr. Herbert Benson and Miriam Klipper

Visualization/Sleep

Creative Visualization: Use the Power of Your Imagination to Create What You Want in Your Life, by Shakti Gawain

Say Goodnight to Insomnia: The Six-Week Solution, A Drug-Free Program Developed at Harvard Medical School, by Gregg Jacobs and Herbert Benson

Visualization for Change, by Patrick Fanning

Childhood OCD

Freeing Your Child From Obsessive-Compulsive Disorder: A Powerful Practical Program for Parents of Children and Adolescents, by Tamar E. Chansky, Ph.D.

Obsessive-Compulsive Disorder: Help for Children and Adolescents, by Mitzi Waltz

For Families

Loving Someone with OCD: Help for You and Your Family, by Karen Landsman, Ph.D., Kathleen Rupertus, M.S., M.A., and Cherry Pedrick, R.N.

Obsessive-Compulsive Disorder: New Help for the Family, by Herbert Gravitz, Ph.D.

Yoga

Dr. Yoga, A Complete Program for Discovering the Head-to-Toe Health Benefits of Yoga, by Nirmala Heriza; medical consultant Dr. Sandra McLanahan, M.D.

Nutrition

The Carbohydrate Craver's Diet, by Judith Wurtman, Ph.D.

Food & Mood: The Complete Guide to Eating Well and Feeling Your Best, by Elizabeth Somer and Nancy Snyderman

The Food & Mood Cookbook: Recipes for Eating Well and Feeling your Best, by Elizabeth Somer and Jeanette Williams

Jane Brody's Nutrition Book: A Lifetime Guide to Good Eating for Better Health and Weight Control, by Jane Brody

Managing Your Mind and Mood Through Food, by Judith Wurtman, Ph.D.

Employment Negotiation/Positive Attitude

Getting to Yes: Negotiating Agreement Without Giving In, by Roger Fisher, William Ury, and Bruce Patton

How to Win Friends and Influence People, by Dale Carnegie. (We like the original 1937, out-of-print edition.)

Success Through a Positive Mental Attitude, by Napolean Hill and W. Clement Stone

Depression and Other Mood Disorders
Feeling Good: The New Mood Therapy, by David Burns, M.D.

Web Sites

Exercise, Yoga, Healthful Eating and Lifestyle
http://deniseaustin.com

Fun/Interesting
http://brainphysics.com
http://crimewaveusa.com
http://happynews.com
http://markmaynard.com
http://phobialist.com
http://usanetwork.com/series/monk

Fellowship
http://geonius.com/ocd/index.html
http://ocdcentre.com
www.planetocd.com
http://stuckinadoorway.org

Neurofeedback
http://eegspectrum.com

Kids and Family
www.aboutourkids.org/aboutour/articles/about_ocd.html
http://groups.yahoo.com/subscribe/ocdandparenting

Treatment Facilities and Programs

McLean Hospital OCD Clinic
115 Mill Street
Belmont, MA 02478
1-617-855-2000
www.mcLean.harvard.edu

The Ross Center for Anxiety and Related Disorders
5225 Wisconsin Avenue, NW, Suite 400
Washington, DC 20015
1-202-363-1010
www.rosscenter.com

Westwood Institute for Anxiety Disorders
921 Westwood Boulevard, Suite 223
Los Angeles, CA 90024
1-323-651-1199
www.hope4°cd.com

The Phobia and Anxiety Center of the Southwest
12860 Hillcrest Road, Suite 119
Dallas, TX, 75230
1-972-386-6327
www.anxietysouthwest.com

Midwest Center for Stress and Anxiety
(Self-directed audio/video program; not for OCD per se)
1-800-611-0857
www.stresscenter.com

The OCD Resource Center Of Florida
3475 Sheridan Street, Suite 310
Hollywood, FL 33021
1-954-962-6662 or

Interstate Plaza Building
1499 West Palmetto Park Road
Executive Suites
Boca Raton, FL 33486
1-954-962-6662
www.ocdhope.com

Center for Cognitive-Behavioral Psychotherapy
(Potentially lower-cost option for CBT)
137 East 36th Street, Suite 4
New York, NY 10016
1-212-686-6886
www. cognitivebehavioralcenter.com

The Obsessive Compulsive Foundation (OCF)
676 State Street
New Haven, CT 06511
1-203-401-2070
www.ocfoundation.org/ocd-intensive-treatment-programs.html

Obsessive-Compulsive Information Center
Madison Institute of Medicine
7617 Mineral Point Road, Suite 300
Madison, WI 53717
1-608-827-2470
www.miminc.org

Index

The Everything® Health Guide Series
Supportive advice. Real answers.

New this season.

Trade Paperback
ISBN: 1-59869-410-3
$14.95

Trade Paperback
ISBN: 1-59869-405-7
$14.95

Trade Paperback
ISBN: 1-59869-435-9
$14.95

Trade Paperback
ISBN: 1-59869-395-6
$14.95